Computer-Based Robust Engineering

Also Available from ASQ Quality Press:

The Certified Quality Engineer Handbook
Donald W. Benbow, Roger W. Berger, Ahmad K. Elshennawy, and H. Fred Walker, editors

The Process-Focused Organization: A Transition Strategy for Success
Robert A. Gardner

Fundamental Concepts for the Software Quality Engineer
Taz Daughtrey, editor

Integrating Reengineering with Total Quality
Joseph N. Kelada

Enterprise Process Mapping: Integrating Systems for Compliance and Business Excellence
Charles G. Cobb

Reengineering the Organization: A Step-by-Step Approach to Corporate Revitalization
Jeffrey N. Lowenthal

ISO 9001:2000: Achieving Compliance and Continuous Improvement in Software Development Companies
Vivek (Vic) Nanda

Quality Engineering Statistics
Robert A. Dovich

The Desk Reference of Statistical Quality Methods
Mark L. Crossley

To request a complimentary catalog of ASQ Quality Press publications, call 800-248-1946, or visit our Web site at http://qualitypress.asq.org.

Computer-Based Robust Engineering

Essentials for DFSS

Genichi Taguchi
Rajesh Jugulum
Shin Taguchi

ASQ Quality Press
Milwaukee, Wisconsin

American Society for Quality, Quality Press, Milwaukee 53203
© 2005 by American Society for Quality
All rights reserved. Published 2004
Printed in the United States of America

12 11 10 09 08 07 06 05 04   5 4 3 2 1

Library of Congress Cataloging-in-Publication Data

Taguchi, Genichi, 1924—
    Computer-based robust engineering : essentials for DFSS / Genichi Taguchi, Rajesh Jugulum,
    and Shin Taguchi.
        p. cm.
    Includes bibliographical references and index.
    ISBN 0-87389-622-X (hard cover; case binding : alk. paper)
    1. Taguchi methods (Quality control)   2. Design, Industrial.   3. Six sigma (Quality control
    standard)   4. Information technology.   I. Jugulum, Rajesh.   II. Taguchi, Shin.   III. Title.

TS156.T27 2004
658.4'013—dc22   2004021395
ISBN 0-87389-622-X

Publisher: William A. Tony
Acquisitions Editor: Annemieke Hytinen
Project Editor: Paul O'Mara
Production Administrator: Randall Benson

ASQ Mission: The American Society for Quality advances individual, organizational, and
community excellence worldwide through learning, quality improvement, and knowledge
exchange.

Attention Bookstores, Wholesalers, Schools, and Corporations: ASQ Quality Press books,
videotapes, audiotapes, and software are available at quantity discounts with bulk purchases for
business, educational, or instructional use. For information, please contact ASQ Quality Press at
800-248-1946, or write to ASQ Quality Press, P.O. Box 3005, Milwaukee, WI 53201-3005.

To place orders or to request a free copy of the ASQ Quality Press Publications Catalog, including
ASQ membership information, call 800-248-1946. Visit our Web site at www.asq.org or
http://qualitypress.asq.org.

Quality Press
600 N. Plankinton Avenue
Milwaukee, Wisconsin 53203
Call toll free 800-248-1946
Fax 414-272-1734
www.asq.org
http://qualitypress.asq.org
http://standardsgroup.asq.org
E-mail: authors@asq.org

♾ Printed on acid-free paper

To my parents, Sarala Bai and Gopala Char, and Rekha and Aaroh.

—Rajesh Jugulum

*"Do not look where you fell,
but instead you should examine where you slipped."*

—*Old Chinese proverb*

Contents

Preface

Contemporary engineering activities usually make use of computers and information technology. Use of robust engineering methods in the design, development, and testing of a product, process, technology, software, or information system can be cost-effective and extremely useful in enhancing overall performance. Robust engineering methods also play a crucial role in design for Six Sigma (DFSS) activities in all areas, including software and information technology.

Computer-Based Robust Engineering is a unique text because it focuses on the use of robust engineering methods in computer applications. This book will be useful to DFSS Green Belts and Black Belts, and also several other audiences:

- Engineers in various disciplines

- Robust engineering practitioners and researchers

- R&D personnel

- Simulation specialists

- Software testing personnel

- Computer programmers

- Information technology and artificial engineering specialists

- Statisticians

- Managers

- Academic community members, as an extension of quality engineering

This book will help them accomplish the following:

- Provide suitable means to achieve robustness of processes and products by simulations.

- Provide a suitable method to test software programs and minimize bugs.

- Help design good information systems for effective information management.

- Help IT specialists understand need of robust engineering in their activities.

- Provide access to several case studies that demonstrate the use of robust engineering in computer applications.

This book is divided into three sections, and each section is further divided into chapters containing theory and case studies. The first section, with four chapters, is based on *simulation-based robust engineering*. Computer simulations are rapidly replacing hardware experiments because:

- Simulation-based robust engineering can serve as a key strategy for research and development.

- Simulations help conduct functionality-based analysis.

- Simulated experiments are typically inexpensive, less time consuming, and more informative than actual experiments, and many control factors can be studied.

Once a simulation method is available, it is extremely important to optimize the concept for its robustness. While using simulation-based experiments, it is important to select suitable signals, noise factors and output response along with a suitable noise strategy. The signals always correspond to the customer usage conditions that affect the functionality of the product/process/system. Because of presence of noise factors there will be functional variation. Robust engineering aims at minimizing functional variation in all usage conditions by minimizing the impact of noise factors. In this section, procedures/methods for achieving robustness using simulation is clearly described with appropriate noise strategies, and two-step optimization, in which variability is reduced in the first step and process setting is adjusted to the desired level in the second step.

The second section focuses on *software testing and software algorithm optimization* and has two chapters. Good software should perform its intended function under all combinations of the user conditions. These user conditions are referred to as active signals. Two examples of active signals are inserting an ATM card, punching the personal identification number (PIN), and selecting the desired transaction; and typing the address of an airline ticket booking Web site and moving the mouse and using the keyboard to select flight schedules and get a price.

For given software, the user conditions are unique and the total number of combinations of these conditions can be very high (sometimes in the order of billions). Usually, the designer tests the software performance under the user conditions separately (like one factor at a time experiments). Even after such tests, the software may fail because of the presence of interactions between the active signals. The software designer must, therefore, study all the interactions and take appropriate corrective actions before the release of the software. To test the interaction effects, the software should be tested under various combinations of the signals. In this section, we will explain how the principles of robust engineering can effectively be used to test software with a minimum number of signal combinations at the lowest cost.

The third section, with two chapters, discusses *design of information systems using the Mahalanobis-Taguchi Strategy (MTS)*. We would like to emphasize that *information systems* is not just related to software activity. The use of *information systems* is necessary in variety of applications where multidimensional diagnostic systems are used. A system characterized by more than one variable is referred to as *a multidimensional system.* Examples of multidimensional systems include medical diagnosis systems, rainfall prediction systems, fire sensing systems, inspection systems, credit card approval systems, and voice or face recognition systems.

Mahalanobis-Taguchi strategy combines principles of robust engineering with Mahalanobis distance. This strategy helps in developing a measurement scale and uses appropriate measures to make accurate predictions or decisions. Unlike most of the methods, MTS is data analytic (that means MTS can be applied irrespective of the type of input variables and their distributions).

Having a measurement scale based on the characteristics of multidimensional systems greatly enhances the decision maker's ability to make judicious decisions. While developing a multidimensional measurement scale, it is essential to keep in mind the following: (1) having a base or reference point to the scale, (2) validation of the scale, (3) selection of important variables that adequately measure the degree of abnormality, and (4) future diagnosis with a measurement scale developed from the important variables. This section gives a description of MTS method along with successful case applications.

Since the topics in this book cover mainly computer-based issues in robust engineering, we think that the title of this book, *Computer-Based Robust Engineering,* is justified. As in many cases, there may be other methods related to computer-based robust engineering; the methods described in this book are based on functionality thinking to improve performance of products, processes, and systems. If these methods can serve as a means to change the mindset of engineers, information technology specialists, and managers to think in terms of robustness, it will have served a fruitful purpose.

Genichi Taguchi
Rajesh Jugulum
Shin Taguchi

Acknowledgments

The challenging and creative process of writing and preparing a book for publication cannot be successfully completed without the help of other people. We would like to extend our appreciation to several people who have contributed to the creation of this book.

First, we would like to thank the late Professor Yuin Wu for his tireless contributions to the subject of robust engineering. His sincerity, dedication, and hard work inspired many robust engineering professionals and made them successfully apply robust engineering concepts in various industries. We would like to sincerely acknowledge his sacrifices, hard work, and efforts to keep the robust engineering flag always high.

We would also like to thank Jim Wilkins, Alan Wu, Subir Chowdhury, and Hilario Oh (Larry Oh) of the American Supplier Institute (ASI), for their efforts in promoting robust engineering subject in various industries. Thanks are also due to all other members of ASI for their cooperation and support. We also thank the Japanese quality engineering society for taking a lead role in disseminating robust engineering knowledge to Japanese industry and academia. In particular, we would like to thank Professor Hiroshi Yano for his tireless efforts to promote robust engineering through this society.

We are also thankful to all contributors and respective organizations for sharing their experiences through presentations in robust engineering symposia. Their contributions are acknowledged at the beginning of the discussion of each case study.

We are very grateful to ASQ Quality Press for giving us the opportunity to publish this book. We are particularly thankful to editors Annemieke Hytinen and Paul O'Mara, production administrator Randy Benson, publisher William A. Tony, and marketing representative David Luth for their cooperation and support. We are also grateful to Angela Williams Urquhart and Amanda Hosey of Thistle Hill Publishing Services for their cooperation and support during this project. Our thanks are also due to Quality Press reviewer Mel Alexander for very helpful comments that improved the contents of the manuscript. Finally, we would like to thank Mr. S. B. Koimattur for carefully reading the manuscript and providing valuable suggestions.

Glossary of Terms and Symbols

ANOVA	Analysis of variance
M	Input signal
S_T	Total sum of squares
r	Sum of squares due to the input signal
S_β	Sum of squares due to slope
S_e	Error sum of squares
V_e	Error variance
SSE	Error sum of squares
α	Statistical level of significance
β	Estimate of the slope
C	Correlation matrix
C^{-1}	Inverse of correlation matrix
E(X)	Expected value of X
K	Number of variables
MD	Mahalanobis distance
D^2	Mahalanobis distance
Scaled MD	Scaled Mahalanobis distance
MS	Mahalanobis space or reference group
MTS	Mahalanobis Taguchi strategy
GSP	Gram-Schmidt's orthogonalization process
MTGS	Mahalanobis Taguchi Gram-Schmidt's process
OA	Orthogonal array

$L_a(b^c)$	Representation of OA
	Where L denotes Latin square design
	a = the number of experimental runs
	b = the number of levels of each factor
	c = the number of columns in the array
QLF	Quality loss function
RE	Robust engineering
S/N ratio	Signal to noise ratio
dB units	Decibel units
s.d.	Standard deviation
TM	Taguchi methods
$U_i's$	Gram-Schmidt's variables
$V(X)$	Variance of X
$X_i's$	Original variables
$Z_i's$	Standardized variables

SECTION I

Simulation-Based Robust Engineering

1

Introduction to Robust Engineering

Robustness can be defined as designing a product in such a way that the level of its performance under various customer usage conditions is same as under nominal conditions. Robust engineering methods (also known as Taguchi methods because they are the result of a research effort of a team led by Dr. Genichi Taguchi) are intended as cost-effective methods to improve the performance of a product by reducing its variability in customer usage conditions. Because they are intended to improve companies' competitive position, these methods have attracted the attention of many industries and academic communities across the globe.

Quality, in the context of robust engineering, can be classified into two types:

1. Customer-driven quality

2. Engineered quality

Customer-driven quality leads to the size of the market segment, and it includes product features such as color, size, appearance, and function. The market size becomes bigger as the customer quality gets better. Customer quality is addressed during the product planning stage, and is extremely important in creating the new market. On the other hand, engineered quality includes defects, failures, noise, vibrations, pollution, and so on. While customer quality defines the market size, engineered quality helps in winning market share within the segment.

All problems of engineered quality are caused by three types of uncontrollable factors (called noise factors):

   I. Various usage conditions
     – Environmental conditions
  II. Deterioration and wear
     – Degradation over time
 III. Individual differences
     – Manufacturing imperfections

Robust engineering (RE) methods or Taguchi methods (TM) aim at improving the engineered quality.

While designing a new product, optimization for robustness can be achieved in three stages:

1. Concept design

2. Parameter design

3. Tolerance design

Most RE applications focus on parameter design optimization and tolerance design. It is widely acknowledged that the robustness will be greater if you start the designing process by selecting a robust concept. Techniques like Pugh concept selection, the Theory of Inventive Problem Solving (TRIZ), and Axiomatic Design and P-diagram strategies developed for conceptual robustness through the Ford-MIT collaboration by Jugulum and Frey (2001) can be used to achieve robustness at the concept level.

The methods of robust engineering are developed based on the following:

1. Energy transformation principle and signal to noise ratios

2. Exploitation of interaction between control and noise factors

3. Use of orthogonal arrays

4. Two-step optimization

5. Quality loss function and online quality engineering

Taguchi (1987), Phadke (1989), and Park (1996) provided detailed discussions on the Taguchi Methods, which have been successfully applied in many engineering applications to improve the performance of the product/process. They have proven to be extremely useful and cost-effective. Following are brief illustrations of the different aspects of these methods.

1. **Energy transformation principle.** The most important aspect of Taguchi methods is to find a suitable function (called the ideal function) that governs the energy transformation in the system from input signal to output response. It is important to maximize the energy transformation by minimizing the effect of uncontrollable or noise factors. The Taguchi approach measures the functionality of the system to improve the product performance (quality). The energy transformation is measured in terms of signal to noise (S/N) ratios. A higher S/N ratio means better energy transformation and hence better functionality of the system.

2. **Exploitation of interactions between control and noise factors.** In TM, we are not interested in measuring the interaction between the control factors. We are interested in the interaction between the control and noise factors, since the objective is to make design robust against the noise factors.

3. **Use of orthogonal arrays (OAs).** OAs are used to minimize the number of runs (or combinations) needed for the experiment. Many people are of the opinion that Taguchi Methods focus only on the application of OAs and

analysis of experimental results. However, it should be noted that the application of OAs is only a part of Taguchi Methods.

4. **Two-step optimization.** After conducting the experiment, the factor-level combination for the optimal design is selected with the help of two-step optimization. The first step is to minimize the variability (maximize S/N ratios). In the second step, the sensitivity (process setting) is adjusted to the desired level. It is easier to adjust the setting after minimizing the variability.

5. **Quality loss function and online quality engineering.** This aspect is related to the tolerance design and online quality engineering. Having determined the best settings using parameter design, the tolerancing is done with the help of the quality loss function. If the performance deviates from the target, there is a loss associated with the deviation. This loss is termed "the loss to society." This loss is proportional to the square of the deviation. It is recommended that safety factors be designed using this approach. Online quality engineering (QE) is used to monitor the process performance and detect the changes in the process.

In the following section, we describe the concepts that are used in robust engineering.

1.1 Concepts of Robust Engineering

1.1.1 Parameter Diagram (P-diagram)

A parameter diagram is a block diagram, which is quite helpful in representing a product or process or a system. In Figure 1.1, the energy transformation takes place between input signal (M) and the output response (y). The goal is to maximize energy transformation by adjusting control factors (C) settings in the presence of noise factors (N).

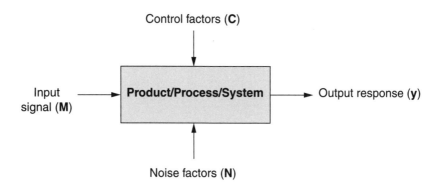

Figure 1.1 Parameter diagram or P-diagram.

1. **Signal factors (*M*).** Signal factors are set by the user/operator to attain the target performance or to express the intended output. For example, the steering angle is a signal factor for the steering mechanism of an automobile. The signal factors are selected by the engineer based on engineering knowledge. Sometimes more than one signal factors are used in combination; for example, one signal factor may be used for coarse tuning and one for fine tuning.

2. **Control factors (*C*).** Control factors are the product parameters specification whose values are the responsibility of the designer. Each control factor can take more than one value, which will be referred to as levels. It is the objective of the design activity to determine the levels of these factors that will best make the product either insensitive to or robust against noise factors. Robustness is the insensitivity to noise factors.

3. **Noise factors (*N*).** Noise factors are the uncontrollable factors. They influence the output y and their levels change from one unit of the product to another, from one environment to another, and from time to time. As mentioned before, noise factors can be one of or a combination of the following three types: (1) various usage conditions, (2) deterioration and wear, and (3) individual differences.

1.1.2 Experimental Design

Experimental design is a subject with a set of techniques and body of knowledge to help investigators conduct experiments in a better way, analyze results of experiments, and find optimal parameter combinations for the design to achieve the intended objectives. In experimental design, factors affecting the product/process performance are varied (by changing their values or levels) in a systematic fashion to estimate their effects on product/process variability, thereby finding the optimal factor combination for a robust design. There is an extensive literature on this subject. A typical experimental design cycle is shown in Figure 1.2.

Types of Experiments

There are typically two types of experiments: full factorial experiments and fractional factorial experiments. In the literature, the individual experiments are also called treatments or runs. The levels of factors are also called settings.

Full Factorial Experiments

In full factorial experiments, all combinations of factors are studied. All main effects and interaction effects can be estimated by using such experiments.

Fractional Factorial Experiments

In fractional factorial experiments, a fraction of the total number of experiments is studied. This is done to reduce cost, material, and time. Main effects and selected interactions can be estimated with such experimental results. Orthogonal array is an example of this type.

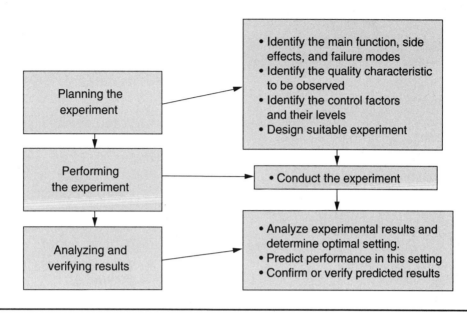

Figure 1.2   Experimental design cycle.

Orthogonal Arrays (OAs)

In robust engineering, the main role of OAs is to permit engineers to evaluate a product design with respect to robustness against noise and cost involved by changing settings of control factors. OA is an inspection device to prevent a "poor design" from going "downstream."

Usually, these arrays are denoted as L_a (b^c), where:

a = the number of experimental runs

b = the number of levels of each factor

c = the number of columns in the array

L denotes Latin square design

Arrays can have factors with many levels, although two- and three-level factors are most commonly encountered. An L_8 (2^7) array is shown in Table 1.1. This is a two-level array,

Table 1.1 L_8 (2^7) orthogonal array.

Factors	A	B	C	D	E		
Experiments	1	2	3	4	5	6	7
1	1	1	1	1	1	1	1
2	1	1	1	2	2	2	2
3	1	2	2	1	1	2	2
4	1	2	2	2	2	1	1
5	2	1	2	1	2	1	2
6	2	1	2	2	1	2	1
7	2	2	1	1	2	2	1
8	2	2	1	2	1	1	2

where all the factors are varied with two levels. In this array a maximum of seven factors can be allocated. The eight combinations with 1s and 2s correspond to different experiments to be performed. 1s and 2s correspond to different settings of factors.

1.1.3 Signal to Noise (S/N) Ratios

The term *S/N ratio* means signal to noise ratio. The S/N ratio tries to capture the magnitude of true information (i.e., signals) after making some adjustment for uncontrollable variation (i.e., noise). From Figure 1.1, we can say that a system consists of a set of activities or functions that are designed to perform a specific operation and produce an intended or desired result by minimizing functional variations due to noise factors. In engineering systems the input energy is converted into an intended output through laws of physics.

These engineered systems are designed to deliver specific results as required by customers. All engineered systems are governed by an ideal relationship between the input and the output. This relationship is referred to as *ideal function*. Robust engineering approach uses this relation and brings the system closer to the ideal state (Figure 1.3).

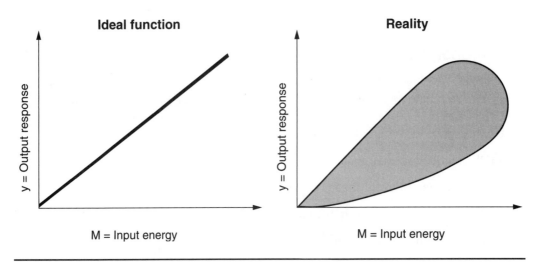

Figure 1.3   Ideal function and reality.

If all input energy is converted into output, then there will be no energy losses. As a result there would be no squeaks, rattles, noise, scrap, rework, quality control personnel, customer service agents, complaint departments, or warranty claims. Unfortunately it does not happen, because reality is much different from ideal situations.

In reality there is energy loss when input is transformed to an output. This loss occurs because of variability and noise factors. This energy loss will create unintended functions. Further, the bigger the energy loss, the bigger the problems.

The S/N ratio measures robustness as it measures energy transformation within a design. S/N ratio is expressed in decibel (dB) units and defined as:

S/N Ratio = Ratio of energy (or power) that is transformed into intended output and energy (or power) that is transformed into unintended output.

= Ratio of useful energy and harmful energy.

= Ratio of work done by signal and work done by the noise.

The higher the S/N ratio is, the more robust the system's function is.

Example: AM/FM Radio

As shown in Figure 1.4, the S/N ratio in this case is the ratio of power of the signal that is heard to power of the noise that is heard.

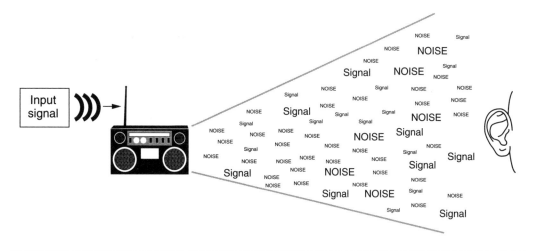

Figure 1.4   S/N ratio for AM/FM radio.

1.1.4 Classification of Design Problems

Design problems can be broadly classified into static and dynamic problems depending upon the absence or presence of signal factors, respectively. Depending on type of design problem, we use an appropriate S/N ratio.

Static Problems

Static problems are characterized by the absence of signal factors. Depending upon the desired values of the response and whether the response is continuous or discrete, we have the following classes of static problems:

1. **Smaller-the-better.** The response is continuous and positive. It's most desired value is zero. Examples include the offset voltage of a differential operational

amplifier, the pollution from a power plant, and the leakage current in integrated circuits. The objective function for this case is

$$\eta = -10 \log_{10} (\text{mean squared response})$$

For a description of the differential operational amplifier example, see Phadke (6).

2. **Nominal-the-best.** The response is continuous and it has a nonextreme target response. Examples include A) in the window photolithography process of integrated circuit fabrication we would want all contact windows to have the target dimension, 3 microns, say, and B) in making copper cables we would want the wires to have constant resistance per unit length. The S/N for this case is

$$\eta = 10 \log_{10} \frac{\mu^2}{\sigma^2}$$

Here μ and σ represent the predictable and unpredictable parts of the response.

3. **Larger-the-better.** This is the case of continuous response, where we would like the response to be as large as possible. The strength of a material is an example of this class of problems. The S/N is defined as

$$\eta = -10 \log_{10} (\text{mean square of the reciprocal response})$$

4. **Ordered categorical response.** This is the case where the response is categorized into ordered categories such as very bad, bad, acceptable, good, and very good.

   Accumulation analysis described by Taguchi (1987) is the most practical way to analyze such data.

5. **Dynamic problems.** Dynamic problems are characterized by the presence of signal factor M and the response variable y. The signal factor corresponds to different customer usage conditions. The robust design is obtained by finding factor settings such that output, y, is minimally affected by noise factors. Usually, the relation between y and M is given by the following equation.

$$y = \beta M \tag{1.1}$$

where β slope of the best-fit line between M and y. The S/N ratio in this case obtained by

$$\eta = 10 \log_{10} \frac{\beta^2}{\sigma^2}$$

$$(1.2)$$

Observe that σ^2 is the variance of *error*, which is the unpredictable and undesirable part of y; β^2 is the variance of the predictable and desirable part except for the range of M.

The readers are advised to refer to Appendix B for detailed equations of various types of S/N ratios.

1.1.5 Two-Step Optimization

Two-step optimization is a very important strategy in robust engineering. In the first step, we seek a design that maximizes the signal to noise ratio or minimizes variability. In the second step, we adjust the response to meet the requirement. The design is validated only if it meets all other requirements. The variability is a key issue in robust design. It is always difficult to reduce variability as compared to adjusting the process to meet requirements. This is why we should aim at reducing variability first.

The two-step optimization is carried out for the responses obtained in nominal-the-best design problems and dynamic design problems. In the nominal-the-best case, in the second step we will adjust the mean to meet the requirements and in dynamic case we will adjust the slope β of the equation between input signal M and output response y.

1.1.6 Strategies for Countering Noise

The following strategies can be used to counter the effect of noise factors:

1. **Ignore noise.** In most cases this results in firefighting later on. However, it can be less expensive to ignore unimportant noises rather than to control them.

2. **Control/eliminate noise.** Another method of addressing noise is to control or eliminate its effect. Examples include standardization, control charting, poka-yoke (mistake proofing), traditional quality assurance activities, and tolerance design.

3. **Compensate effect of noise.** These methods include feedback control and feed-forward (adaptive) control methods. Engineers are excellent at figuring out how to compensate in these ways. This is also a cost-quality trade-off countermeasure. Note that when one decides to add a compensation system, it

must be optimized for robustness through its function. A compensation system typically includes a measurement/sensor system and adjustment. Examples include feedback control, adaptive control (feed-forward control), engine control, matching assembly, and antilock brakes.

4. **Minimize effect of noise.** Another method is to optimize control-factor settings so the energy transformation of system is most insensitive to noises. This is the most cost-effective approach in developing a robust design. This countermeasure should be the first priority, and the better we achieve it, the lower the cost will be than when we need to use additional countermeasures, such as controlling/eliminating noise or the compensating effect of noise. An example is robust optimization (parameter design).

1.1.7 Inner Arrays and Outer Arrays

While performing experiments to identify a robust design, the control factors are assigned to an orthogonal array. The array where control factors are assigned is called the inner array. If there are noise factors with different levels, they are assigned to another orthogonal array, called the outer array. A typical experimental layout with control and noise factors is shown in Figure 1.5.

In this case, for each experiment of inner array we have 36 noise combinations with three levels of input signal. For each experiment in the inner array, based on responses, we calculate signal to noise (S/N) ratios and sensitivities (S). These quantities help us identify a robust design to meet various requirements. The total number of runs to be conducted in this case would $36 \times 36 \times 3 = 3888$. Performing so many experiments is expensive and time consuming, whether it's hardware experimentation or simulation-based experimentation. In order to overcome this situation, the noise factors can be *compounded* into one factor with only two levels. These levels correspond to two extreme conditions of noise factors. For example, consider a case where there are four noise factors, $N1$, $N2$, $N3$, and $N4$, with each at two levels. These noise factors can be assigned to an outer array, L_8 (2^7) with eight experiments. By using *compounding strategy* one can choose two extreme settings instead of all sixteen combinations of the four noise factors. Here, if K denotes total number of experiments in the inner array, the outer array approach requires 8K runs, whereas *compounding strategy* requires only 2K runs. The compounding strategy layout with two compounded noise levels corresponding to Figure 1.5 is given in Figure 1.6. For each input signal level ($M1$, $M2$, and $M3$), there are two compounded noise levels. Corresponding to each experiment in the inner array, the data are collected for each compounded noise level under each input signal. In this case for each inner array experiment there are six data points. S/N ratios and sensitivities are obtained based on these six data points.

As mentioned before, for each experiment in inner array, based on responses, we calculate signal to noise ratios and sensitivities to identify a robust design to meet various requirements.

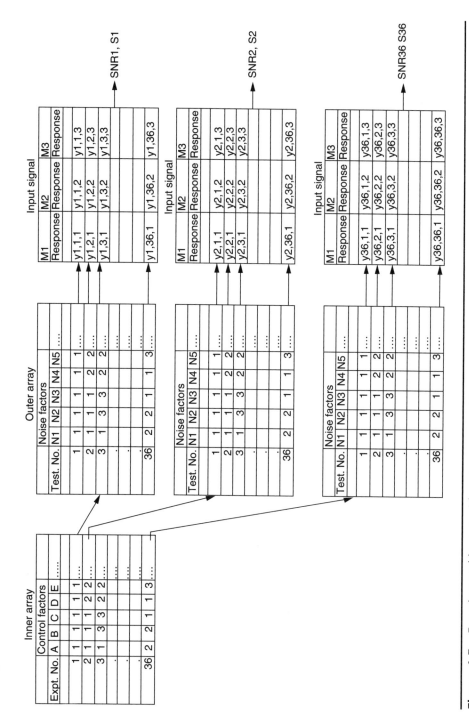

Figure 1.5 Experimental layout with outer array and inner array.

Inner array

Expt. No.	Control factors					
	A	B	C	D	E	.....
1	1	1	1	1	1	1 ...
2	1	1	1	2	2	2 ...
3	1	1	3	3	2	2 ...
.						...
.						...
.						...
36	2	2	1	1	3	3 ...

Input signal

	Outer array		Noise factors			
	M1		M2		M3	
	N1	N2	N1	N2	N1	N2
	Response	Response	Response	Response	Response	Response
	$y_{1,1,1}$	$y_{1,1,2}$	$y_{1,2,1}$	$y_{1,2,2}$	$y_{1,3,1}$	$y_{1,3,2}$	→ SNR1, S1
	$y_{2,1,1}$	$y_{2,1,2}$	$y_{2,2,1}$	$y_{2,2,2}$	$y_{2,3,1}$	$y_{2,3,2}$	→ SNR2, S2
	$y_{3,1,1}$	$y_{3,1,2}$	$y_{3,1,1}$	$y_{3,2,2}$	$y_{3,3,1}$	$y_{3,3,2}$	→ SNR3, S3
	$y_{36,1,1}$	$y_{36,1,2}$	$y_{36,1,1}$	$y_{36,2,2}$	$y_{36,3,1}$	$y_{36,3,2}$	→ SNR36 S36

Figure 1.6 Experimental layout with compounding of noise strategy.

1.2 Robust Engineering in Conjunction with DFSS as a Corporate Strategy

Many companies around the globe use robust engineering methods in conjunction with design for Six Sigma (DFSS) initiatives as part of their corporate strategy. Many engineers are being trained in these methods by exposing them to real-world applications. Use of robust engineering in the early stages of design reduces firefighting significantly by providing a robust design with higher sigma quality. This can be explained with Figure 1.7.

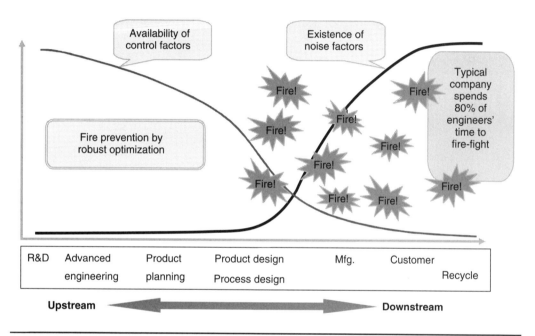

Figure 1.7   Robust engineering for fire prevention.

Typically, 80% of engineers' time is spent in firefighting. This is because in the later stages of design activity the existence of noise factors increases and availability of control factors decreases. As we know, for robust optimization we need to select the best control-factor setting in the presence of noise factors. Since the availability of control factors in the initial stages of design is higher, we have a lot of freedom to select appropriate control factors by anticipating noise factors. If we recall elements of p-diagrams, only control factors are in the engineer's control and all other elements are out of the engineer's control. This is shown in Figure 1.8.

Therefore, it is recommended to use robust engineering methods at early stages of design to achieve higher sigma levels. Use of robust engineering will also reduce time to market. By using these methods we can develop a robust technology element in a short period by using two-step optimization, as shown in Figure 1.9. In the first step, we can perform robust optimization of key technology elements, and in the second step, we can adjust the elements to family and future products. With these two steps, we can quickly assess the performance and send it to market in the shortest possible time.

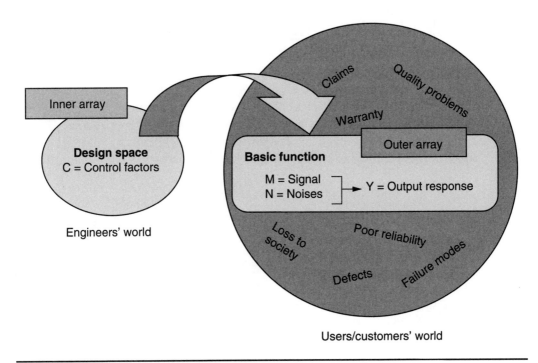

Figure 1.8   Engineers' world and customers' world.

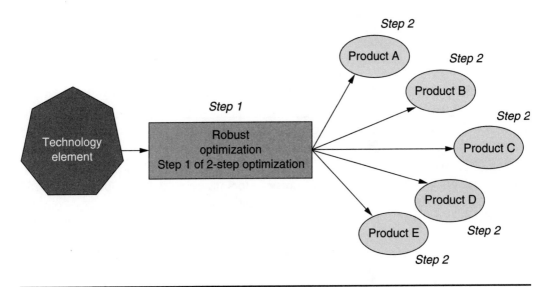

Figure 1.9   Robust optimization as a corporate strategy.

The concepts presented in this chapter are used in the subsequent chapters of this book under three sections: computer simulation experiments, software design and testing, and information management. The discussions are provided with several case applications demonstrating the power of these concepts.

2

The Development of Robust Engineering

In this chapter we will describe the development of the subject of robust engineering by tracing its origin and development of this pragmatic approach to the design of experiments from the end of World War II to the present. We will also discuss the treatment of error (noise), the place of mathematical statistics in robust engineering, and the role of the orthogonal array in industrial experimentation.

During a panel discussion of the Third Symposium on Taguchi Methods, held by the American Supplier Institute in October 1985, the late Professor William G. Hunter mentioned the following concerning professional attitudes regarding the functions of a manufactured product:

Engineers	:	Make it work
Scientists	:	Understand why it works
Mathematicians	:	Don't care

There is a great difference between science and technology. Science is to study natural phenomena. The laws of nature cannot be changed. The task of engineering is to design a product that does not exist in nature yet performs the customer's desired function. The task of an engineer is not merely to "make it work." He has to "make it work" with increased reliability. The real purpose of technology, however, should be to let unit manufacturing cost (UMC) take precedence over quality. Quality improvement is necessary only after the cost has been reduced below a certain value. Because the price of a product is several times the UMC, if the cost rises, the consumer suffers a loss several times beyond the UMC. If making a system work were all that mattered, there would be countless systems to choose from. If system element variation could be improved without regard to cost, any system could have sufficient reliability. However, there would be great differences in price.

The manufacturing cost burdens the customer with a loss that is multiplied several times in the price. If the customer suffers additional losses in electric power, fuel costs, breakdowns, reduced length of product life, noise, harmful components, adverse effects, or poor safety, these are losses that the product inflicts upon society after shipping. In the context of robust engineering, all these losses collectively are taken as the measure of quality.

The key question is, "How does one improve productivity?" The basis of productive product development is a method that achieves quality improvement under cost conditions by providing competitive advantage. Let us begin by explaining the historical development of robust engineering method.

2.1 Design of Experiments

Dr. Motosaburo Masuyama applied design of experiments to the production of penicillin in Japan near the end of World War II. The layouts used were based on the orthogonal Latin square, devised to improve the precision of comparisons between levels of a factor T. They were used at the beginning of this effort to obtain optimum combinations of numerous control factors, such as the quantities of cornstarch and phenylacetic acid, types of mold fungi, temperature, and agitation conditions that would improve the yield of penicillin. The objective was to raise the mean values of larger-the-better target characteristics, such as yield and efficiency. As long as it is concerned with only main effects, this method (i.e., testing, estimation, confidence intervals, optimum level combinations, and prediction of the process average) was quite adequate. When Dr. Genichi Taguchi was in the same capacity as Dr. Masuyama, he began assisting in designing experiments at the Morinaga Pharmaceutical Co. in 1948. The generalization of orthogonal Latin squares into orthogonal arrays started then. Dr. Taguchi also assisted in experiments with caramels carried out by the parent company of Morinaga Pharmaceuticals. This project involved working with data obtained from sensory tests, such as flavor and aroma. An objective was set to determine whether it was possible to produce caramels whose plasticity would not change when the room temperature changed. A scientist would need only to vary the room temperature and draw up a relationship equation showing how the plasticity varied. However, engineers are required to create an ideal product—a new and improved product. This was not a problem of science, of constructing a mathematically correct model, but rather a problem of creating an ideal product that did not yet exist.

Let the room temperature be denoted by N. In the caramel project, three levels were chosen: $N_1 = 0°$ C, $N_2 = 20°$ C, and $N_3 = 40°$ C. The objective was to reduce the major changes on plasticity caused by N by using controllable factors such as mixing and other factors. The strategy of the experiment was to determine interactions between the control factors and uncontrollable (or noise or error) factor, N. This method of assigning the control factors to an orthogonal array, for treating noise to identify the interactions between the control factors and the noise factor, was used for a considerable period of time.

At INAX Corporation, an experiment with tiles was carried out in 1953 and published several years later by Masao Ina in a Japanese publication. Here, control factors were assigned to orthogonal array (called the inner array), and the noise, which was the location in the oven where the tiles were baked, was assigned as an outer factor. Interactions between the two were determined.

In experiments at the Electrical Communications Laboratory (ECL), beginning in 1950, data for the percentage of change, which became the prototype for the signal to noise (S/N) ratio of today, were used. There were many experiments in which materials and parts were produced under a variety of conditions. Here, the value of the initial-period characteristic, y_0, and the value after a degradation test, y_t, were determined. Then, using the percentage of change y (as shown in Equation 2.1) as the response, the combination of levels of the control factors giving the minimum percentage of change was chosen.

$$y = \frac{y_t - y_o}{y_o} \times 100\% \tag{2.1}$$

This method was very useful in minimizing trouble, such as that caused by changes in the characteristics of carbon or of electrical relays. Its drawback lies in the fact that analyses for dispersions of the initial-period value had to be performed separately, making analysis difficult when there are, for example, values at intermediate time points. There were even instances where, regardless of the number of data, points standard deviations and ranges were used as measures to minimize the dispersion of the whole. In a case at an Indian plant, Mysore Lamps, in 1955, the range for the watt value of electric light bulbs was used as a target characteristic.

In an experiment on the uniformity of the anode film thickness at Hindustan Aeronautics Limited in India in 1955, the Chi-square method was used. The method of grouping data in experiments for uniformity and comprehensively studying their influence on the mean of the distribution and its dispersion (distribution form) was used as a method separate from interactions, standard deviation, range, and data analysis of the percentage of change.

When the Chi-square method was applied, a factor that had no effect on film thickness was found to be significant. The methods of accumulation analysis and minute analysis were developed as an alternate to the Chi-square method.

Reducing the percentage of change is reducing variability caused by noise factors that are not related to the chance causes. Because it is a practice in robust engineering to treat errors unrelated to chance (probability), analysis was made by not considering normality assumptions.

From about 1950, when design of experiments seminars were started in Japan, Dr. Taguchi started to determine the effects of factors using orthogonal arrays for cases where theoretical equations exist. Orthogonal arrays were used in order to analyze responses. The At that time, more variables were investigated than with recent methods using the S/N ratio.

At the Electrical Communications Laboratory, the problem of selecting good-quality characteristics and the problem of assigning a variety of factors had to be solved. Techniques such as the multiway split-unit design; pseudo-factor design; partially expanded design; randomly combined design; and interaction partially omitted design were developed as methods for assignment using orthogonal arrays. The importance of these methods lies not so much in the techniques themselves, but in the assurance they provide to engineers to match various technical requirements.

The distinction between control factors and noise factors, the method of expressing the purpose of the experiment for reducing variability caused by environment and deterioration, minimizing the importance of mathematical statistics, applications to theoretical equations, not emphasizing interactions between control factors, the use of S/N ratios, and the treatment of classified data are all termed robust engineering or Taguchi methods.

The Taguchi philosophy of robust engineering differs from other approaches in that it uses an efficient research method for design, which is not intended to find responses (functional relations) but to reduce deviations from ideal functions.

In technical research, however, Taguchi methods provide a way of using small-scale experiments in the laboratory so that one can find optimum designs for large-scale production and for the marketplace.

2.2 Simulation-Based Experiments

In earlier years, experiments were performed as hardware experiments. The present-day trend is toward simulation-based experiments. Computer simulations are quite important in robust engineering because:

- Simulated experiments play a significant role in reducing product development time because there is no need to conduct all hardware experiments.

- Simulation-based robust engineering can serve as a key strategy for research and development.

- Simulations help conduct functionality-based analysis.

- Simulated experiments are typically inexpensive, less time consuming, and more informative, and many control factors can be studied.

Once a simulation method is available, it is extremely important to optimize the concept for its robustness. The results of simulated experiments are analyzed by calculating S/N ratios and sensitivities. However, the optimal combination is tried using hardware experimentation to confirm the results. This book focuses only on simulation-based experiments. While using simulation-based experiments, it is important to select suitable signals, noise factors, and output response.

The example given in section 2.2.1 explains how to conduct simulation-based experiments. This example also explains the differences between Taguchi methods of robust engineering and other methods of design of experiments.

2.2.1 Example

Consider a circuit stability design as a simple example with a theoretical equation.

The output current, y in amperes of an alternating-current circuit with resistance, R, and self-inductance, L, is given by the equation (2.2) below.

$$y = \frac{V}{\sqrt{R^2 + (2\pi f L)^2}}$$

(2.2)

where:

V　:　Input alternating – current voltage (V)

R　:　Resistance (Ω)

f　:　Frequency of input alternating current (Hz)

L　:　Self-inductance (H)

and $\omega = 2\,\pi f$

The target value of output current y is 10 amps. If there is a shift of more than 4 amps during use by the consumer, the circuit no longer functions. It will be assumed in that event that the loss to society, A_0, is 15,000 yen. This is the value that obtains when functional trouble occurs in the marketplace if the output current shifts 4 amps from the target. The target value of y is 10 amps and the tolerance is 10 ± 4 amps.

The central value and the tolerance of the target characteristics are, in many instances, determined by the user requirement. If this is the case, one must include this requirement. But it is best to study the extent to which one can vary the output before real trouble occurs. If trouble actually occurs, the user will definitely change his requirement.

The tolerance, Δ_0, is to be found for the output characteristic and the mean loss, A_0, (when values go out of tolerance). There are three steps in the design of a product or process:

1. Concept design and development

2. Parameter design

3. Tolerance design

Concept development is the step in which one seeks and determines what combination of circuit and parts possesses the target function. In the example above, the circuit is already given. This means that concept design is already completed. Many inventions are made in concept development stage, and the main research effort is in this stage of the design. It is best to develop new systems not found in the literature.

In contrast, the purpose of parameter design is to determine the parameter levels (normal values and types) of a system of elements. For example, it determines whether the nominal value of resistance R in the circuit is to be 1 or 9. Parameter design plays an important role in quality (dispersion of function) improvement.

The purpose of tolerance design is to determine the tolerance around the nominal value of the parameter. Trading off between loss due to variability and cost is necessary for determining tolerances, and it is advantageous to use the quality loss function. However, tolerance design involves the problem of separately determining the tolerances for individual systems. It does not address the problem of distributing the tolerance of the target characteristic value among the system elements. With parameter design, the cause of dispersion is considered comprehensively. We will, therefore, consider the problem of design for the circuit in Equation (2.2) as an example of parameter design.

Control Factors and Noise Factors

Those variables in the equation whose central values and levels the designer can select and control are the control factors.

The input voltage is 100 volts AC in the case of a household source, and because the designer cannot alter this, it is not a control factor. Neither is the frequency, f, a control factor.

Only R and L are control factors. The designer sets the resistance value at 1Ω, 3Ω, or 9Ω. The same is true with regard to self-inductance, L. It is obvious that since the target value of the output current is given as 10 amps, once one decides the central value of the resistance R the central value of the inductance L will be determined by the equation.

In this case there are only two control factors, and the target value is already determined. But when there are three or more control factors, it is best not to consider such limiting conditions. The reason for this is that it is more advantageous to adjust the output to the target value by changing the levels of those control factors that have little influence on stability after an optimum design for stability has been determined. Factors that are favorable for adjustment are factors that can be used to change the output to the target value. One of the major characteristics of the design of experiments method is that it does not consider restricting conditions. Rather, one performs parallel analyses for the S/N ratio and for the mean, which are measures of stability and sensitivity, and adjusts the mean after variability has been reduced.

Because it is possible to consider restricting conditions relating to the control factors later, one does not have to worry about the target value or objective characteristic curve. One can simply change the control factors independently. In the present case, we choose three levels of R and L independently, as follows.

$$R_1 = 0.5 \ (\Omega) \qquad R_2 = 5.0 \ (\Omega) \qquad R_3 = 9.5 \ (\Omega)$$

$$L_1 = 0.010 \ (H) \qquad L_2 = 0.020 \ (H) \qquad L_3 = 0.030 \ (H)$$

An orthogonal array is used if the control factors are more numerous, but since there are only two here, we can use a two-way layout. An orthogonal array to which control factors have been assigned is termed an *inner orthogonal array* or *control orthogonal array*. One should use as many control factors as possible, take a wide range of levels, and assign only the main effects.

Next, let us examine noise factors. *Noise factor* is a general term for a cause that disperses the target characteristic from the ideal value. Such factors can be categorized into the following three types:

1. Dispersion of environmental conditions; this is outer noise.

2. Dispersion due to deterioration; this is inner noise.

3. Dispersion among products; this is also inner noise.

In parameter design, the three types of noise may be regarded as the same. This is because environmental differences change the characteristics of the parts, materials, and elements used for a product, and as a result, they cause the target characteristics to disperse. Deterioration of a product causes dispersion of the function. This happens because of deterioration of the parts, materials, elements, and so forth. This is the same as the change of the characteristic values of the parts, materials, and elements.

Dispersion by the environment consists of the following two factors in this example, and their levels are considered as follows:

Voltage of input source V 　 90 　 100 　 110 　 (V)

Frequency f 　 50 　 60 　 　 (Hz)

The environmental temperature and so forth also changes the value of the resistance R and the coil inductance L although only slightly. However, changes due to deterioration of the resistance and coil are greater than the effects of environmental changes. After considering changes due to dispersion of the initial-period value, deterioration, and environment, let us select the levels of resistance R and coil inductance L as follows:

First level 　 Normal value $\times 0.9$

Second level 　 Nominal value

Third level 　 Nominal value $\times 1.1$

The levels of the noise factors are as given in Table 2.1. It should be noted that a prime has been affixed to symbols for the noise factors, R and L. In this instance, it means there is no error with respect to the noise factors V, R', and L' when they are at the second level. Frequency f is 50 Hz or 60 Hz, depending on the location in Japan. If one wishes to develop a product that can be used in both eastern Japan and western Japan, it is best to design it so that the output meets the target when the frequency is at 55 Hz, midway between the two. Sometimes one uses an intermediate value that has been weighed by the population ratio.

Table 2.1 Noise factors and levels.

Noise factor levels	First level	Second level	Third level
V	90	100	110 (V)
R′	−10	0	+10 (%)
f	50	55	60 (Hz)
L′	−10	0	+10 (%)

Here, let us assume that 55 Hz is to be used. Because the output will be adjusted later to exactly 10 amps when noise factors are at their center values, that is, 100 volts and 55 Hz, it is fine to assign only the two levels at both ends.

But now, as is evident from Equation 2.2, the output becomes minimum with $V_1 R_3' f_3 L_3'$ and maximum with $V_3 R_1' f_1 L_1'$. If the direction of output changes is known when the noise factor levels are changed, all the noise factors can be compounded into a single factor. If the Compound factor is expressed as N, it has two levels. In this case:

$$N_1 = V_1 R_3' f_3 L_3' \quad \text{Minus side (minimum value)}$$

$$N_2 = V_3 R_1' f_1 L_1' \quad \text{Plus side (maximum value)}$$

When we know which noise factor levels cause the output to become large, it is a good strategy to compound them so as to obtain one factor with two levels, or one factor with three levels, including the central level. When we do this, our noise factor becomes a single compounded factor, no matter how many factors are involved. Since one can determine the tendencies of all four noise factors in this example, they have been converted essentially into a single compounded noise factor N with two levels. Thus, we need merely investigate the value of the outgoing current for these two levels.

Compounding of noise factors is even more important when there is no theoretical equation. This is because with a theoretical equation, the calculation time is short, usually no more than several seconds. In our example, even if noise factors are assigned to the columns of a separate orthogonal array, there is little improvement in the efficiency of calculation. Compounding was necessary in the past when computers were not available. However, compounding is necessary even in present-day computer experiments with large numbers of noise factors, because it saves time, money, and resources.

Parameter Design

Design calculations are performed for all combinations of the inner orthogonal array to which control factors R and L have been assigned (two-way layout, here) and the noise factor assignment (two-level noise factor here). The assignment is shown in Table 2.2.

Table 2.2   Calculations of SN ratios and sensitivities.

Experiment number	R	L	Data		S/N ratio	Sensitivity
			N_1	N_2	η	S
1	1	1	21.5	38.5	7.6	29.2
2	1	2	10.8	19.4	7.5	23.2
3	1	3	7.2	13.0	7.4	19.7
4	2	1	13.1	20.7	9.7	24.3
5	2	2	9.0	15.2	8.5	21.4
6	2	3	6.6	11.5	8.0	18.8
7	3	1	8.0	12.2	10.4	20.0
8	3	2	6.8	10.7	9.6	18.6
9	3	3	5.5	9.1	8.9	17.0

Because the design conditions for the first experiment are $R_1 = 0.5\Omega$ and $L_1 = 0.01\text{H}$ in Table 2.2, the levels of the two-level noise factor, N_1 and N_2, are as follows:

$$N_1 = V_1\, R_3'\, f_3 L_3' = 90\text{V}, 0.55\Omega, 60\text{Hz}, 0.011 \text{ H}$$

$$N_2 = V_3\, R_1'\, f_1 L_1' = 110, 0.45\Omega, 50\text{Hz}, 0.009 \text{ H}$$

R_3' and L_3 are +10% of 0.5Ω and 0.01H, becoming 0.55Ω and 0.011H; R_1' and L_1' are −10%, becoming 0.45Ω and 0.009H. Therefore, from Equation 2.2, the values of the current y for N_1 and N_2 are as follows:

$$y_1 = \frac{90}{\sqrt{0.55^2 + (2\pi x 60 x 0.011)^2}} = 21.5 \tag{2.3}$$

$$y_2 = \frac{110}{\sqrt{0.45^2 + (2\pi x 50 \times 0.009)^2}} = 38.5 \tag{2.4}$$

These are the data points for N_1 and N_2 of experiment 1. The important point is that the calculations have been performed disregarding the target value, 10 amps. This improves the efficiency of design study.

For other experiments, similarly, the value of the output current for N_1 and N_2 are calculated. They are shown in Table 2.3.

Table 2.3 Factorial effects.

	η	S
R_1	7.5	24.0
R_2	8.7	21.5
R_3	9.6	18.5

	η	S
L_1	9.2	24.5
L_2	8.5	21.1
L_3	8.1	18.5

A measure of stability (robustness) in the case of a nominal-is-best characteristic is the ratio of the mean value m to the standard deviation, σ. The square of this ratio is the S/N ratio and is denoted by η.

$$\eta = \frac{m^2}{\sigma^2} \tag{2.5}$$

The S/N ratio is the reciprocal of the square of the relative error (also termed the coefficient of variation, $\frac{\sigma}{m}$). Although the equation for the S/N ratio varies, depending on the type of quality characteristic, all S/N ratios have the same properties. When the S/N ratio becomes 10 times larger, the loss due to dispersion decreases to one-tenth. The S/N ratio is a measurement that also has economic rationality. S/N ratios (η) and sensitivities (S) are computed based on the following equations, and are expressed in decibels.

$$\eta = 10 \log \left[\frac{\frac{1}{n}(S_m - V_e)}{V_e} \right] \tag{2.6}$$

$$S = 10 \log \left[\frac{1}{n}(S_m - V_e) \right] \tag{2.7}$$

where
n = number of data points in each experiment (sample size). Here $n = 2$.

$$S_m = \frac{(y_1 + y_2 + .. + y_n)^2}{n}$$

$$V_e = \frac{\sum_{i=1}^{n}(y_i - \bar{y})^2}{n-1}$$

Therefore, in our example we can estimate η and S, which are the values of the S/N ratio and sensitivity, by these equations. For the first run the calculations are as follows:

$$S_m = \frac{(21.5 - 38.5)^2}{2} = 1800.00$$

$$V_e = \frac{(21.5 - 39.5)^2}{2} = 144.5$$

The S/N ratio and the sensitivity are:

$$\eta = 10 \log \frac{\frac{1}{2}(1800 - 144.5)}{144.5}$$

$$= 7.6 \text{ decibels}$$

$$S = 10 \log \frac{1}{2}(1800 - 144.5)$$

$$= 29.2 \text{ decibels}$$

It was in this way that the values of the S/N ratio and sensitivity in Table 2.2 were obtained. The S/N ratio is a measure for optimum design, and sensitivity is used to select one (sometimes two or more) factor(s) by which the mean value of the output will be adjusted to the target value, if necessary.

To compare the levels of control factors, we construct average response tables for the S/N ratio and sensitivity. For example, in the case of R_1, average of S/N ratio for R_1:

$$\overline{R_1} = \frac{1}{3}(7.6 + 7.5 + 7.4) = 7.5$$

Average of sensitivity for R_1:

$$\overline{R_1} = \frac{1}{3}(29.2 + 23.2 + 19.7) = 24.0$$

In Table 2.3, the average values are given for the other control factor levels.

Focusing our attention on the measure of stability, the S/N ratio, in Table 2.3, we can see that the optimum level of R is R_3 and the optimum level of L is L_1. Therefore, the optimum design is $R_3 L_1$. A confirmatory calculation is performed using $R_3 L_1$, and one finds the mean value of the output. If there is no difference between this mean value and the target value, one may leave matters as they are. But if there is a difference, one then compares the influence of the factors on the S/N ratio, and on the sensitivity, one uses a control factor whose effect on sensitivity is great compared to its effect on the S/N ratio in order to adjust the output to the target. In this case, under the optimum design $R_3 L_1$, the calculated output value is No. 7 in Table 2.2. The current are $y_1 = 8.0$ and $y_2 = 12.2$; the mean value is 10.1; and there is no difference from the target value. If the differences in the result were high (for example, if the mean value were 15 amps), it would be necessary to lower the sensitivity by its difference (in decibels) from the target value:

$$10 \log 10^2 - 10 \log 15^2 = -3.5 \text{ decibels}$$

Because the effect on *S* is greater in the case of *L* than in that of *R* (see Table 2.3), we would adjust by using *L*. Such adjustment is easy. Even if there are numerous control factors, factors that have a great influence on the sensitivity but that are independent of the S/N ratio can be readily found.

The approach of minimizing the percentage change of Equation 2.1, which was used in the past, is more or less the same as the method used here. In the case of percentage of change, it is assumed that the initial value can be adjusted to the target value. The method of searching for factors to adjust the mean of the initial value is equivalent to analysis of the sensitivity in parameter design. The concept of S/N together with sensitivity analysis considered very important for parameter design.

Control of Error

The remarkable progress in Japanese technology is attributable for the practice of aggressively changing parameters and of trying changes in a design once trouble is discovered. The improvement in quality has been given impetus by differences in design among competing companies. Japanese companies have made constructive changes, by testing design alternatives and design and production condition changes as efficiently as possible once failure is experienced. It is believed that this is the reason for the improvement that has been noted in Japanese product quality. Millions of such experiments are performed in Japan annually.

Fundamentally, the method of design of experiments seeks to identify a mathematical models based on data with considerable variability. The aim in that field has been to decide what kind of data should be collected, to decide what kind of mathematical model should be applied where real world variability exists, and to find a method to minimize error. Since there is error, models were also constructed based on the distribution of error. The Japanese contribution is that the techniques of controlling error and design of experiments were carried into the field of technical research, which, as we have seen, is different from scientific research. These techniques were used to efficiently determine responses, including experimental assignment and decomposition of variation. The techniques were pioneered in the applications to penicillin production by Dr. Masuyama. In contrast with the traditional method of using design of experiments (such as randomization of experiments and blocking in order to control error) the Japanese method began with the concept of finding stable conditions in the presence of error.

Role of Orthogonal Arrays

Orthogonal arrays have existed for a long time in forms such as the magic square. They are a class of fractional factorial designs.

One wishes to use experiments in the laboratory to find those optimal conditions and design that can be reproduced in large-scale production and in various marketplaces. The existence of interactions can compromise the reproducibility of experimental results.

If the control factors are expressed as *A, B, C, . . .* , when the optimum level of *A* differs according to the level of *B*, it means that the interaction $A \times B$ is significant. If the optimum level of *A* varies with the conditions of other control factor such as *B, C, . . .* , then the optimum level of *A* at the site of production might also differ from that found in the laboratory. Or, perhaps when the optimum level of *A* differs according to downstream conditions (conditions in the production process, market place conditions, etc.), an experiment in the laboratory is worthless. Experimentation is then necessary on site and in the marketplace.

In the laboratory, we wish to find conditions that will be optimum even downstream. There is no other way to guarantee this other than to prove that there are no significant interactions among control factors. If the optimum level of *A* stands in spite of the conditions of other control factors, the possibility is strong that it will also remain valid under downstream conditions.

In order to prove that there are no interactions, one assigns only main effects to the orthogonal array and finds the optimum conditions. One assumes that there is no interaction and estimates the process average. If there is no interaction, the estimated value of the process average and its confirmatory experiment value will match well. If the effect of interactions is large, these two values will differ greatly and it becomes necessary to take additional measures, such as redoing the experiment on site, improving the design according to marketplace information, or redesigning with different quality characteristics so that there will be no interactions.

The orthogonal array is a means of detecting the adverse effect of a quality characteristic. It is important that interactions be confounded with the main effects. If there is in an interaction, the experiment is designed to detect the extent of the interaction. When an interaction is significant, this indicates that the optimum level of a control factor will differ, depending on the levels of other control factors. This also means the optimum conditions we have found will not be useful downstream where conditions differ. This is true because if there are interactions between control factors, there will also be interactions with the manufacturing scale and interactions between laboratory and marketplace conditions. Experience shows that optimum conditions determined after finding interactions do not stand up under large-scale production conditions. Moreover, problems frequently develop in the marketplace as well.

Failures occurred with considerable frequency when researchers used orthogonal arrays to which only main effects had been assigned. But the discovery of such failures is the purpose of an experiment using an orthogonal array. This led researchers to consider the problem of selecting the quality characteristic. We discovered that when percentage of change was used as a quality characteristic or when the interactions between control factor and noise factors were determined in experimentation, failures rarely occurred. The reason there were few failures when data of stability were used is that the measure of stability is important for optimum design.

That is why the orthogonal array itself is not the solution to the problem, but, like a litmus test, it tests the additivity of quality characteristics. If one cares only for apparent success and wishes to invite trouble on-site and in the marketplace, it is all right to experiment with the characteristics values that have been in use. But if one wishes to perform a reliable experiment, one must grapple with the rationality of quality characteristics.

In order to assign only main effects to the orthogonal array to prevent lowering efficiency compared with the one-factor-at-a-time method, it has become necessary to employ various assignment techniques. These techniques, along with the use of orthogonal arrays, are not absolutely important, but we believe they are useful for rationalizing experiments with regard to additivity. It is our belief that the orthogonal array is useful in that it makes one select as many control factors as possible. There are many people who, when experimenting with one factor at a time, stop the research once the problem is solved by a certain factor. But when an orthogonal array is used, because the scale of the experiment does not change, one tends to be guided toward using as many control factors as possible to fill the columns of the array. This makes it possible to solve the problem by the least expensive method.

An orthogonal array can be constructed from a magic square, orthogonal matrix, or an orthogonal Latin square. We suggest that, even if there are interactions, only main effects should be assigned to an orthogonal array. The process average is then estimated, and one compares this process average with the values of the confirmation experiment. With this method, the reproducibility of the experimental results downstream is evaluated.

2.3 Discussion

The most important distinction between Taguchi methods and traditional design of experiments is that it is counterproductive to assign interactions, whether or not there are interactions. Orthogonal arrays should be used to help us discover experimental failures when interactions exist.

It is not important to inspect a product and find it to be good. The product would have passed even without testing. Testing has value only when rejects are discovered. If one could succeed merely by experimenting with the one-factor-at-a-time method, it means that an experiment with an orthogonal array would not be required. An experiment using an orthogonal array has value only when the estimated value of the process average and the confirmation run are compared. This is important because the results of the experiment warn us that on-site results cannot be taken to the marketplace if there are interactions.

When experimenting with factors one by one, the apparent percentage of success will rise, because it is impossible to distinguish between main effects and interactions. However, this is risky if it is unclear what happens to the validity of the optimum design in large-scale production and under unknown marketplace conditions. The advantage to using orthogonal arrays is not to increase the reliability but to evaluate the reliability. To increase reliability, it is necessary to correctly perform an evaluation of stability. Stability should be evaluated by finding a measure like S/N ratio, not response.

AT&T Bell Laboratories concluded that it has become possible to obtain reproducibility in large-scale production since the S/N ratio came into use. In order to increase reliability, the S/N ratio, which refines long-used measures such as the percentage of change, is important. Refer to Chapter 1 for a discussion of S/N ratios.

3

Simulation-Based Robust Engineering in Research and Development

3.1 Reduction of Research and Development Cycle Time

3.1.1 Role of R&D and Management

Evaluation of functionality is a research and development (R&D) activity. It increases the efficiency of R&D. This type of work in R&D differs from what engineers are doing. Engineers develop new technologies or new products. However, improving efficiency in engineering is a different kind of activity in a specialized field.

The role of R&D or engineering is to establish the strategies for the development of engineering. There are four strategies for technology development. They do not belong to specialized technologies, but they can be applied to a wide range of engineering applications for a long period of time.

Selection of the Subjects for Technology

In basic research, selection of subjects that could be useful for the development of creative products is an important activity. This can be done through focus groups, customer surveys, and customer usage conditions. These tools help us capture the "voice of the customer" via tools like quality function deployment (QFD). It is desirable that the research be started before planning a new product. The research includes the use of test pieces, which cover future products; small-scale research; study without a prototype; study without testing; and study using simulation.

Concept Creation

Create a complicated system that leads to the development of a highly reliable product. A complex system with several control factors usually ensures increased robustness.

Conduct Parameter Design

As mentioned in Chapter 2, parameter design includes the evaluation of functionality and the assurance of downstream reproducibility. Functionality is evaluated with S/N ratios, and downstream reproducibility is ensured with orthogonal arrays and tests of additivity.

Provide Required Tools

Research requires various hardware and software tools such as computers, finite element or circuit calculation methods. Orthogonal arrays can be used to evaluate different combinations.

The above four strategies relate to robust engineering. In robust engineering, it is recommended to use a complex system and to conduct parameter design in the very beginning, instead of trying to think of countermeasures after problems have occurred. The third strategy, conduct parameter design, is the core of robust engineering.

Quite often, a company needs to create products or technologies in short periods of time; otherwise it would not withstand competition. The creation of a concept or the selection of a new system is a creative work to be provided by the engineers in a specialized field by thinking outside the box and by adopting newer thought processes and paradigms. The process of of design parameters in a system is nothing but an operation. The operation should be rationalized and computers should be used for this purpose.

R&D must continually develop new products and technologies that are competitive and contribute to the survival and growth of the company.

The job of the R&D department is to develop products and technologies. It is important to improve the efficiency of a broad range of engineering activities. The approaches, which are universally applicable in the whole area of technology development, are indeed strategies of technology development. Such approaches are called *universal technology.*

Universal technology aims at the improvement of the efficiency for measurement and evaluation. Most of the time and money in R&D will be spent evaluating ideas: conducting experiments (including simulation), making prototypes, and conducting tests. These activities should focus on reproducing small-scale experimental results in the large-scale production process in such a way that product performance is consistent in all customer usage conditions.

The tactic in management is product development by including the features of customer quality and engineered quality. Those who work in engineering, especially in product design, must keep customer quality and engineered quality in mind to design a robust product. With competition, it is desirable that the quality be superior to the competitors' quality. The engineering department (the department responsible for tactics) is evaluated by product quality and engineering quality as well as by cost.

3.1.2 Product Quality and Design

A manufacturing company plans and arranges a product to provide what the users want. It would be ideal if a company could provide order-made products. Toyota Motor Company can deliver order-made cars of various kinds, including model, appearance, and navigation system, in about three weeks. It is easy to deliver ready-made sample cars immediately, but it takes a while to deliver a car selected from millions of possible selections. A goal of a good production-engineering department is to design a process that can efficiently produce single units among multiple products.

There are some cases when only the function is important, such as a unit or a subsystem that cannot be seen from outside. For such cases, all that is required is to improve the objective function.

Selection of Systems

Engineers provide a system or a concept that performs an objective function. There are many ways to perform the same function. From a robust engineering viewpoint, it is recommended that engineers start with a complex system.

For example, a transistor is an element used for amplification. But a transistor is such a simple system that it is difficult to reduce its functional variability. A commercially developed amplifying circuit is 20 times more complicated than a transistor. The design of a transistor transmitter circuit by Hewlett-Packard Company is an example.

There are two types of functionality to be improved.

1. Adjusting the output to an objective function under standard condition; this is called tuning.

2. Achieving robustness of a function so that the performance does not change under various market conditions.

In order to improve both types of functionality, we need to have many control factors, which can be freely varied vary at the design stage. The more complex and more nonlinear the output, the greater the possibility for improvement in robustness. Since a complex system has many simple systems, it is possible to make the system function close to the ideal.

A typical example of tuning to the objective function is the development of LIMDOW (light modulated direct overwrite disk) is the project jointly developed by Nikon Company and Hitachi Maxell. The invention is called the magnet-optical (MO) disk, which can read and write and is said to be the disk for the next generation. Since new data can be written without erasing the old data, the speed is twice as fast as the existing type.

However, the existing MO disks had only one magnetic layer and the new LIMDOW disks needed at least six layers and a maximum of nine. Initially, the new manufacturing process was not stable at all, and that delayed the development. There were about 10 control factors for one layer. With a nine-layer disk, there would be more than 90 control factors to be manipulated. Moreover, there would be interactions between layers. It meant that a change of the optimum conditions of a certain layer would affect the manufacturing conditions of other layers. The optimum conditions would depend on the type of characteristic to be used to evaluate the product. As a result, the development was in chaos.

Building and testing were repeated for six years without producing even a satisfactory prototype. After applying Taguchi methods, however, engineers stabilized the multilayer film-forming process within three years. In 1995, the success of mass production was not far away. The standards for MO disks using LIMDOW type has been set by ISO. Today, most of the major disk manufacturers are trying to develop similar products. The company that first succeeded in developing the disk now monopolizes the market.

System selection is the task of engineers specialized in their pertinent technology. Robust engineering suggests selecting a complex system. Because there will be more control factors—the factors engineers can freely use or discard and set them at different levels—the improvement of robustness as well as tuning can be well accomplished.

3.1.3 Functionality Evaluation and Product Design

The use of orthogonal arrays is unique in robust engineering. Other tools are important for processing information, but not particularly for robust engineering.

Orthogonal arrays are used not only to calculate the difference of factorial effects but also to *evaluate the reproducibility of functionality under downstream conditions*, which is very important in robust engineering.

Sometimes we have to design products by simulations using theoretical equations, which are incomplete. We should use test pieces or study in a small-scale experimental setup to evaluate a product's downstream functionality, such as in large-scale manufacturing or in various users' conditions. For this purpose, it is necessary to evaluate the function that includes the signals and the noises in the market.

Design engineers optimize a system by changing design parameters called control factors. Design parameters are not users' conditions but the means in a design (including systems and parameters) that can be freely selected by engineers for optimization. Even if the quality of a product were evaluated by the function, the optimum condition cannot be found when signal, noise, and measuring characteristics are wrongly selected.

The success of finding the optimum condition depends on the successful evaluation of downstream reproducibility of results under large-scale manufacturing conditions and usage conditions in the market. Reproducibility is evaluated at the development stage, when parameter design is conducted using orthogonal arrays, or after development, when functionality is evaluated by a quality assurance group using the benchmarking approach. It is desirable to use the first approach, since there is a lot of room for improvement. In the latter case, a paradigm shift is needed for quality assurance engineers to use S/N ratio.

From the robust engineering viewpoint, finding an equation that explains the objective output characteristic relates to physics, not to engineering. No matter how well the equation predicts the results, the economic aspect needs to be considered. The objective of physics is to find an equation that explains natural phenomena. It is important in science, but it has nothing to do with designing a product that is artificial. The difference between two designs of a product is always compared by cost and quality. If a company's product in a certain market segment costs less and imparts much less trouble or pollution than its competitors, the company's market share will increase. Good market productivity means not only good quality under the standard condition but also a low manufacturing cost and high engineering quality (fewer troubles and less pollution).

Improving market productivity (including product quality) is a way of generating profit for a company. Design and production are the means to improve market productivity. Such market productivity needs to be correctly predicted at the development and design stages. The study of market productivity includes the prediction of manufacturing cost and product functionality, as well as marketability. It is design evaluation. Although design evaluation can also be performed after product development, it should be made during product development stage when the design can be easily changed. The optimum design must be determined under laboratory conditions (using test pieces and small-scale or limited test conditions). We need to study if the effects of a design change can be reproduced under downstream conditions (applicable to the actual product, large-scale manufacturing, and various usage conditions within the product life).

In order to study the design for downstream reproducibility, the characteristic for evaluation must be changed, besides changing signal and noise factors. We must recognize that various market conditions are either signal or noise. We must select the characteristic to be measured and select the levels of signal and noise factors so that appropriate S/N ratio can be calculated. The reason of assigning only the main effects of control factors to orthogonal arrays is to check the additivity of control factors on the S/N ratio. It is not the study of the relationship between the control factors and the output.

3.2 Two-Step Design, Standard S/N Ratio, and Orthogonal Expansion for Tuning

3.2.1 Robustness and Tuning

The design quality of a product and manufacturing process determine the position of the manufacturing company. In service industries such as communications, transportation, or finance, the design quality of the system that provides services determines the position of the company. There are two steps in a product design process:

1. Synthesis

2. Analysis

In robust engineering, synthesis is further divided as follows:

1. Selection of a concept

2. Determination of the coefficients of system parameters (design constants)

Item 1 is the stage where creativity is required. A new method can be protected by intellectual property rights. Item 2 is the area of robust engineering, which relates to the speed of developmental process. Depending on chosen design constants and parameters, the reliability of the product's function under various usage conditions changes. To reduce the deviation from the ideal function of a product under various usage conditions, robustness must be improved by selecting an optimal combination. As mentioned earlier, this is called parameter design. After the robustness of a function is improved, the trade-off between cost and quality is made to improve productivity. This is done by using the loss function.

It is important to select a new system or a new concept, but it will not be clear if the system will be competitive in the market without conducting parameter design. It is important to complete parameter design efficiently within a short time. Development must be made concurrently in a large system with feedback systems. The total system is divided into modules such as subsystems, units, component parts, elements, or materials. It is important to improve the efficiency of the total design.

We can use simulation methods to find the solution closest to the objective function. But this step, which is called *tuning* (the second step of two-step optimization) must be done after improving robustness by maximizing the S/N ratio.

In simulation experiments, it is not necessary to provide the noise factors that relate to environmental conditions and deterioration. Instead, the parameters are varied around their nominal levels. If the experiments take longer, noise factors usually are compounded in two levels. Of course, the trend of each factor must be studied before using compounding. For this purpose, the initial design conditions (often set as the second level of control factors) are used as the basis.

After robustness is improved, tuning is done to fit to the target curve. In many cases, it is sufficient to use only the coefficient of a linear term, β_1, and a quadratic term, β_2. An example is shown in the next section.

The strategies recommended here include the use of the S/N ratio for functional evaluation and the ways of treating noises. These strategies have totally changed design study using simulation. The strategies are as follows:

Strategy 1. Since it is not easy to know the deterioration under usage environments, noise conditions are chosen from design parameter levels and then compounded. It is adequate to consider only two levels for noise conditions. Robustness is improved using these two levels of the compounded noise factor.

Strategy 2. The optimal control factor setting (with a higher S/N ratio) should produce consistent results at any signal factor level. A preliminary analysis using the finite element method to study a few points in the whole range or to study the initial few points, may be considered for improvement.

Strategy 3. Tuning (to match the function with the target function) is performed under the standard condition using one or two control or signal factors. For this purpose, orthogonal expansion is performed to calculate the coefficients of linear term β_1 and quadratic term β_2. The candidates (factors) will then be selected for tuning.

3.2.2 Two-Step Design Process

In robust engineering, all customer conditions are considered either signal or noise factors. Signal factors are either active or passive. The active signal is the one that a customer can actively apply in order to vary the output. A passive signal measures the true value changes, such as measuring equipment or receivers. In the development of hardware, either the true values or transmitting signals can be varied for study.

The most important point in two-step design is that we should not use the cause and effect relationship between control factors and the output. In a circuit study conducted in the Bell Laboratories, testing was done under the standard condition to design the circuit until objective function was obtained. The function was then tested under 16 usage conditions.

It is not appropriate to use an engineering model or correlation to adjust the differences caused by usage conditions because there are innumerable usage conditions. Tuning is to be done only under the standard condition. The countermeasure for a usage condition (noise) must be taken using the interactions between control and noise factors.

Testing Methods and Data Analysis

In the design of hardware, let the signal factor be denoted by M and its output that is considered as the ideal function be $f(M)$. In the two-step design, control factors (and/or indicative factors) are assigned to an orthogonal array. For each experimental run, the outputs are obtained at the following conditions:

N_0 : standard condition (without noise)

N_1 : compounded negative side condition

N_2 : compounded positive side condition

Let the value of $f(M)$ at each of the k levels signal factor $(M_1, M_2, \ldots, M_k)$ at N_0 be $f(M_1), f(M_2), \ldots, f(M_k)$.

Table 3.1   Data for S/N ratio analysis.

N_0	M_1 M_2 .... M_k	Linear equation
N_1	y_{11} y_{12} .... y_{1k}	L_1
N_2	y_{21} y_{22} .... y_{2k}	L_2

Step 1. To reduce variability, the S/N ratio is calculated, without sensitivity. For the optimum condition, output data under N_0, N_1, and N_2 are collected.

Step 2. For the optimum condition, the outputs of N_0, N_1, and N_2 are collected and its S/N ratio is calculated using the method described in Step 1. This S/N ratio will be used to check reproducibility. Let the target under the standard condition be denoted by m. Next, tune the output to match with the objective function. Let the results of N_0 under the optimum condition be denoted by y_1, $y_2, \ldots, y_k$, and consider them as levels of signal factor, as shown in Table 3.2.

Table 3.2   Data for tuning.

Target	m_1 m_2 ...... m_k
Output	y_1 y_2 ...... y_k

Designing an objective function is trying to make the output y of the users' signal M close to the target m. In many cases, the ideal function is expressed by the following equation:

$$y = \beta M \tag{3.1}$$

But this is not always the case; there are many different cases. Under the optimum condition, the output at N_0 is obtained as shown in Table 3.3. This table is used for tuning.

Table 3.3   Outputs under standard condition.

M (signal)	M_1 M_2 ... M_k
m (target)	m_1 m_2 ... m_k
y (output)	y_1 y_2 ... y_k

Actually, the results under N_1 and N_2 have been collected. But these results will be used for checking reproducibility, not for tuning.

If the target m is proportional to signal M, analysis is made using the levels of signal M, no matter what the value of β may be. The analysis of using signal M and the one using target m are the same. Here, the general case of calculation using target m is shown. This is known as the Taguchi method for tuning.

Under the standard condition N_0, if the outputs $y_1, y_2, \ldots, y_k$ agree with targets $m_1, m_2, \ldots, m_k$ respectively, no tuning is necessary. If y is approximately proportional to m with adequate precision, there are many approaches for adjusting the proportional constant β to be equal to 1. The method is as follows:

1. Use the signal M. The goal is to change the signal to be equal to the target, m, such as when M and m are proportional to each other. For example, if y is always larger than m by 5 percent, multiply M by 0.95.

2. Use one of the control factors (sometimes more than one) for tuning to adjust the proportional constant (denoted by β_1) to 1.

3. Use a design constant other than the control factors studied in the simulation for tuning.

Following is the method of tuning used when the relationship is not proportional. For this purpose, orthogonal expansion is used. This method of tuning will be an important engineering subject in the future.

Equations for Orthogonal Expansion

The orthogonal expansion for tuning is made with the proportional term as the first term. The equation up to the third order term is as follows:

$$y = \beta_1 m + \beta_2 \left(m^2 - \frac{K_3}{K_2} m \right) + \beta_3 \left[m^3 + \frac{K_3 K_4 - K_2 K_5}{K_2 K_4 - K_3^2} m^2 + \frac{K_4^2 - K_3 K_5}{K_3^2 - K_2 K_4} m \right] + \cdots \quad (3.2)$$

where $K_1, K_2, \ldots$ are written using the targets $m_1, m_2, \ldots, m_k$, which correspond to $M_1, M_2, \ldots, M_k$ respectively.

$$K_i = \frac{1}{k}(m_1^i + m_2^i + \cdots + m_4^i) \quad (i = 2, 3, \cdots) \quad (3.3)$$

Since m's are given, $K_2, K_3, \ldots$ are constants. Generally, the terms higher than the third order are unnecessary. In most cases, expansion up to the second order is considered.

From the above equations, orthogonal expansion is performed to obtain linear, quadratic, and cubic terms, and an ANOVA table is prepared, as shown in Table 3.4. This table is for tuning only.

Table 3.4 Analysis of variance (ANOVA) for tuning.

Source	f	S	V
$\beta_1 = f(M_1)$	1	$S\beta_1$	
β_2	1	$S\beta_2$	
β_3	1	$S\beta_3$	
e	k–3	Se	Ve
Total	k	S_T	V_T

f: degrees of freedom
S: sum of squares
V: variance

If tuning is done based on cubic terms, the error variance is estimated as V_e. The loss before tuning, denoted by L_0, is

$$L_0 = \frac{A_0}{\Delta_0^2} V_T$$

The loss after tuning is given by

$$L = \frac{A_0}{\Delta_0^2} V_e$$

If the tuning is made only by the linear term, the error variance is

$$V_e = \frac{1}{k-1} \left(S_{\beta 2} + S_{\beta 3} + S_e \right)$$

The details of orthogonal expansion and descriptions of terms in the equations will be made clear by the example below.

3.3 Design of Color Ribbon Shifting Mechanism by Simulation

This case study was presented in the eighth annual Taguchi Symposium in 1990 in the United States. This study has had a significant impact on industry in the United States. In this section, the data of N_0 were calculated from the average of N_1 and N_2 in the report and analyzed using dynamic characteristic.

The color ribbon shift mechanism of a printer guides four-color ribbons to the correct positions of the printing head. This mechanism was developed by Oki Electric Company in Japan in the late 1980s. The ideal function is based on the agreement of the amount of ribbon cartridge tip rotation with the amount of ribbon guide sliding. But there is actually a difference due to the movement transformation by the linkage. If the difference is enhanced, the function will be affected by a fiber running in the ribbon (by hitting the ribbon edge) or by color mixing (by hitting the adjacent color ribbon).

In this case, the signal factor is the rotating angle M. The target values are shown in Table 3.5. Troubles occur when the amount of shift exceeds 1.45 mm.

Table 3.5 Rotating angles and target values (5 levels).

Rotating angle (M)	1.3	2.6	3.9	5.2	6.5
Target value (mm)	2.685	5.385	8.097	10.821	13.555

Thirteen control factors were selected for parameter design in Table 3.6. These factors were assigned to orthogonal array L_{27}. However, it is recommended that L_{36} be used for the assignment of control factors.

Table 3.6 Factors and levels (F: degree; others: mm).

Factor level	1	2	3
A	6.0	6.5	7.0
B	31.5	33.5	35.5
C	31.24	33.24	35.24
D	9.45	10.45	11.45
E	2.2	2.5	2.8
F	45.0	47.0	49.0
G	7.03	7.83	8.63
H	9.6	10.6	11.6
I	18.0	20.0	22.0
J	80.0	82.0	84.0
K	23.5	25.5	27.5
L	61.0	63.0	65.0
M	16.0	16.5	17.0

Before compounding, the effects of control factors on the objective characteristic (angle of movement) were studied by fixing the control factors at the second level. Table 3.7.shows the results.

Table 3.7 Effects of noise factors.

Noise factor	A′	B′	C′	D′	E′	F′	G′	H′	I′	J′	K′	L′	M′
Acting direction	+	-	-	+	+	+	-	-	-	+	+	-	+

From the table, the combinations of positive and negative conditions were used to set two levels of compounded noise factors, as shown in Table 3.8.

In the report, the stability of rotating angles were improved, and then the tuning to targets was performed using simultaneous equations, which is rather tedious.

Table 3.8 Compounded noise factor levels.

Factor	N_1	N_2
A′	−0.1	+0.1
B′	+0.1	−0.1
C′	+0.1	−0.1
D′	−0.1	+0.1
E′	−0.05	+0.05
F′	−0.5	+0.5
G′	+0.1	−0.1
H′	+0.1	−0.1
I′	+0.1	−0.1
J′	−0.15	+0.15
K′	+0.15	−0.15
L′	+0.15	−0.15
M′	−0.15	+0.15

From the viewpoint of stabilizing the movement, we need to ensure that there are no differences between the movement under various noise conditions and the standard condition. Therefore, the output under the standard condition is set as the new signal factor, denoted by *M*, then the S/N ratio is calculated with the outputs under noise conditions. Since the program of calculation was not available, the average angles of N_1 and N_2 were used as the output of N_0. This method is correct only when the absolute values of N_1 and N_2 from the output under the standard condition are equal and different in their signs. The S/N ratio of using the output under the standard condition as the signal is called the standard S/N ratio. The S/N ratio of using the average as a substitute can be referred to as the substituted S/N ratio.

3.3.1 Calculation of Standard S/N Ratio and Optimization

Table 3.9 shows the amount of movement under the standard condition N_0 at each rotating angle and under N_1 and N_2. The results were from run No. 1 of orthogonal array L_{27}.

Table 3.9   Results of run no.1.

Rotating angle	1.3°	2.6°	3.9°	5.2°	6.5°	Linear equation
Standard condition (N_0)	3.255	6.245	9.089	11.926	14.825	L
N_1	2.914	5.664	8.386	11.180	14.117	463.694
N_2	3.596	6.826	9.792	12.672	15.533	524.735

Table 3.10   Decomposition of variation.

Source	f	S	V
β	1	988.430	988.430
$N \times \beta$	1	3.7696	3.769
e	8	0.2419	0.0302
(N)	9	4.011	0.4457
T	10	992.441	

The SN ratio, η, is calculated as

$$\eta = 10\log\frac{\frac{1}{2r}(S_\beta - V_e)}{V_N} = 3.51\text{db} \tag{3.4}$$

For run No.2 and other runs, the S/N ratios are similarly calculated using the amounts of movement under the standard condition. But here, the signal factor levels were calculated from the average of N_1 and N_2 of each run. Therefore, the signal factor levels are different for each of the 18 runs.

Table 3.11 shows the experimental layout and S/N ratios, Table 3.12 shows the level totals, and Figure 3.1 shows the factorial effects.

The calculation in this simulation shows the two-step design as a strategy. It also shows the way of providing the noise in simulation, greatly affecting U.S. research. In many cases, noise factors are assigned to an orthogonal array without compounding them. For example, three levels of noise factors are assigned to an L_{27} orthogonal array and all combinations with the inner orthogonal array L_{27} are run. Here, in calculating the S/N ratio, the signal factor is not the angle, but the output of an angle under the standard condition. The S/N ratios of 27 runs are calculated for conducting optimization. The calculation of sensitivity for linear and quadratic terms is illustrated in Section 3.3.2.

Table 3.11   Layout and S/N ratio using averages.

No.	A	B	C	D	E	F	G	H	I	J	K	L	M	η
	1	2	3	4	5		7	8	9	10	11	12	13	(db)
1	1	1	1	1	1	1	1	1	1	1	1	1	1	3.51
2	1	1	1	1	2	2	2	2	2	2	2	2	2	2.18
3	1	1	1	1	3	3	3	3	3	3	3	3	3	0.91
4	1	2	2	2	1	1	1	2	2	2	3	3	3	6.70
5	1	2	2	2	2	2	2	3	3	3	1	1	1	1.43
6	1	2	2	2	3	3	3	1	1	1	2	2	2	3.67
7	1	3	3	3	1	1	1	3	3	3	2	2	2	5.15
8	1	3	3	3	2	2	2	1	1	1	3	3	3	8.61
9	1	3	3	3	3	3	3	2	2	2	1	1	1	2.76
10	2	1	2	3	1	2	3	1	2	3	1	2	3	3.42
11	2	1	2	3	2	3	1	2	3	1	2	3	1	2.57
12	2	1	2	3	3	1	2	3	1	2	3	1	2	0.39
13	2	2	3	1	1	2	3	2	3	1	3	1	2	5.82
14	2	2	3	1	2	3	1	3	1	2	1	2	3	6.06
15	2	2	3	1	3	1	2	1	2	3	2	3	1	5.29
16	2	3	1	2	1	2	3	3	1	2	2	3	1	3.06
17	2	3	1	2	2	3	1	1	2	3	3	1	2	-2.48
18	2	3	1	2	3	1	2	2	3	1	1	2	3	3.86
19	3	1	3	2	1	3	2	1	3	2	1	3	2	5.62
20	3	1	3	2	2	1	3	2	1	3	2	1	3	3.26
21	3	1	3	2	3	2	1	3	2	1	3	2	1	2.40
22	3	2	1	3	1	3	2	2	1	3	3	2	1	−2.43
23	3	2	1	3	2	1	3	3	2	1	1	3	2	3.77
24	3	2	1	3	3	2	1	1	3	2	2	1	3	−1.76
25	3	3	2	1	1	3	2	3	2	1	2	1	3	3.17
26	3	3	2	1	2	1	3	1	3	2	3	2	1	3.47
27	3	3	2	1	3	2	1	2	1	3	1	3	2	2.51

Table 3.12 Level totals.

	1	2	3
A	34.92	27.99	20.01
B	24.26	28.55	30.11
C	10.62	27.33	44.97
D	32.92	27.52	22.48
E	34.02	28.87	20.03
F	35.40	27.67	19.85
G	24.66	28.12	30.14
H	29.35	27.23	26.34
I	28.64	27.21	27.07
J	37.38	28.48	17.06
K	32.94	26.59	23.39
L	16.10	27.78	39.04
M	22.06	26.63	34.23

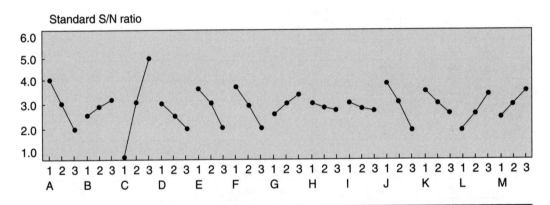

Figure 3.1 Response graphs of standard S/N ratio.

Table 3.13 Prediction and confirmation of the standard S/N ratio.

Condition	Prediction	Confirmation
Optimum condition	12.50 db	14.58 db
Initial condition	3.15 db	3.54 db
Gain	9.35 db	11.04 db

3.3.2 Analysis for Tuning

The outputs of N_0 under the optimum condition obtained in the previous section are shown in Table 3.14.

Table 3.14   Results of N_0 from simulation.

Signal factor M (angle)	1.3	2.6	3.9	5.2	6.5
Target m (mm)	2.685	5.385	8.097	10.821	13.555
Output y (mm)	2.890	5.772	8.600	11.633	14.948

From Table 3.14, a graph is drawn, as shown in Figure 3.2. Comparing the standard outputs under the optimum condition and the target values, it can be seen that their proportional constant is not equal to 1. The outputs also deviate with a curvature.

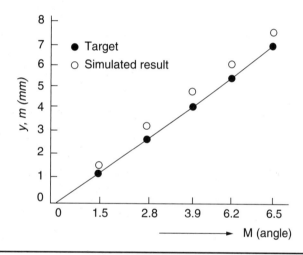

Figure 3.2   Standard ouputs under optimum conditions.

Since the proportional constant β_1 is greater than 1, correction is made on *M*. *M* is calibrated to be *M** using the following equation:

$$M* = \frac{1}{\beta_1} \times M \tag{3.5}$$

In some cases, the signal factor *M* cannot be calibrated to be *M**. When β is not equal to 1, correction is generally made using the signal factor. Sometimes control factor(s) may be used. The designer can freely use either way. Note that correction is normally made by the signal.

As mentioned before, the output under the standard condition *y* deviates from the target *m*. Tuning is done to minimize this deviation. In order to evaluate the precision of tuning, perform the orthogonal decomposition of variation of *y*'s to obtain the linear and quadratic terms of Equation (3.2).

The total variation *ST* has degrees of freedom *f* of 5, calculated as

$$S_T = 2.890^2 + \cdots + 14.948^2$$

$$= 473.8127 \qquad (f = 5) \tag{3.6}$$

The variation of the proportional term, $S_{\beta 1}$, is

$$S_{\beta 1} = \frac{(m_1 y_1 + m_2 y_2 + \cdots + m_5 y_5)^2}{m_1^{\ 2} + m_2^{\ 2} + \cdots + m_5^{\ 2}}$$

$$= \frac{(2.685 \times 2.890 + \cdots + 13.555 \times 14.948)^2}{2.685^2 + \cdots 13.555^2} \tag{3.7}$$

$$= 473.695$$

The coefficient of the proportional term, β_1, is calculated as

$$\beta_1 = \frac{m_1 y_1 + m_2 y_2 + \cdots + m_5 y_5}{m_1 + m_2 + \cdots + m_5}$$

$$= \frac{436.707653}{402.600925} \tag{3.8}$$

$$= 1.0847$$

For the tuning by signal, multiply $\frac{1}{1.0847}$ by the signal (angle). If tuning is to be made by a control factor, use the one that significantly affects β_1. The method is illustrated in Section 3.5.

To analyze the quadratic term, the following constants, K_1 and K_2, are calculated first.

$$K_2 = \frac{1}{5}(m_1^{\ 2} + m_2^{\ 2} + \cdots + m_5^{\ 2})$$

$$= \frac{1}{5}(2.685^2 + \cdots + 13.555^2) \tag{3.9}$$

$$= 80.520$$

$$K_3 = \frac{1}{5}(m_1^{\ 3} + m_2^{\ 3} + \cdots + m_5^{\ 3})$$

$$= \frac{1}{5}(2.685^3 + \cdots + 13.555^3) \tag{3.10}$$

$$= 892.8012$$

From Equation (3.2), the quadratic term is calculated as

$$\beta_2\left(m^2 - \frac{K_3}{K_2}m\right) = \beta_2\left(m^2 - \frac{892.8012}{80.520}m\right)$$

$$= \beta_2\left(m^2 - 11.0897m\right)$$

(3.11)

To calculate β_2 or the variation of quadratic term, the coefficients of the quadratic term, $w_1, w_2, \ldots, w_5$, that respectively correspond to $m_1, m_2, \ldots, m_5$ are calculated.

$$w_i = m_i^2 - 11.0897m_i \qquad (i = 1, 2, \cdots, 5)$$

(3.12)

$$w_1 = 2.685^2 - 11.0897 \times 2.685$$

$$= -22.567$$

$$w_2 = 5.385^2 - 11.0897 \times 5.385$$

$$= -30.720$$

$$w_3 = 8.097^2 - 11.0897 \times 8.097$$

$$= -24.232$$

$$w_4 = 10.821^2 - 11.0897 \times 10.821$$

$$= -2.9076$$

$$w_5 = 13.555^2 - 11.0897 \times 13.555$$

$$= 33.417$$

The linear equation of the quadratic term, L_2, is calculated using $w_1, w_2, \ldots, w_5$.

$$L_2 = w_1 y_1 + w_2 y_2 + \cdots + w_5 y_5$$

$$= -22.567 \times 2.890 + \cdots + 33.477 \times 14.948$$

$$= 16.2995$$

(3.13)

r_2 is the total of the squares of $w_1, w_2, \ldots, w_5$ calculated by the following equation:

$$r_2 = w_1^2 + w_2^2 + \cdots + w_5^2$$

$$= (-22.567)^2 + \cdots + 33.477^2$$

$$= 3165.33$$

(3.14)

The variation of the quadratic term is calculated by squaring L_2 divided by r_2. In general, the variation of a linear equation is calculated from the square of the linear equation divided by its number of units (total of the squares of coefficients). Therefore,

$$S_{\beta 2} = \frac{16.2995^2}{3165.33}$$

$$= 0.083932$$

(3.15)

The coefficient of quadratic term, β_2, is calculated by

$$\beta_2 = \frac{L_2}{r_2}$$

$$= \frac{16.2995}{3165.33}$$

$$= 0.005149$$

(3.16)

From the results of N_0 that are the standard outputs, the ANOVA table for the comparison with targets is constructed as shown in Table 3.15.

Table 3.15   ANOVA table for tuning (up to quadratic term).

Source	f	S	V
β_1	1	473.695	
β_2	1	0.083932	
e	3	0.033900	0.011300
T	5	473.812874	
(β_2+e)	(4)	(0.117832)	(0.029458)

The decomposition of variation for the comparison with the target function is an important step before tuning, since the precision of tuning can be predicted.

3.3.3 Economic Evaluation of Tuning

The economic evaluation of tuning is of absolute nature. It can be predicted before performing tuning.

Since the functional limit is 1.45 mm, its loss L is calculated from the loss function as

$$L = \frac{A_0}{\Delta_0{}^2} \sigma^2$$

$$= \frac{A_0}{1.45^2} \sigma^2$$

(3.17)

where A_0 is the loss in the market when the functional limit exceeds 1.45 mm. It is the cost of claim handling such as repair. Assume $A_0 = 30,000$ yen. σ^2 includes both the tuning error and the error in the S/N ratio.

It is difficult to evaluate the absolute value of the error of the S/N ratio. It is because the absolute values of environmental, deteriorating, and between-product variations are unknown. Therefore, the gain of the S/N ratio is relative. But the actual loss of tuning can be calculated by calculating the error variance as follows:

1. The error variance after tuning using only the linear term, $\sigma_1{}^2$, is calculated as

$$\sigma_1{}^2 = \frac{S_{\beta2} + S_e}{4}$$

$$= \frac{0.0893932 + 0.033930}{4}$$

(3.18)

$$= 0.029458$$

2. The error variance after tuning using linear and quadratic terms, $\sigma_2{}^2$, is calculated as

$$\sigma_2{}^2 = \frac{S_e}{3}$$

$$= \frac{0.0033930}{3}$$

(3.19)

$$= 0.001130$$

The error variances calculated from Equations (3.18) and (3.19) are used in Equation (3.17) to obtain the loss. The loss when only the linear term is used is calculated as

$$L_1 = \frac{30000}{1.45^2} \times 0.029458$$

$$= 420.3 \ \text{(yen)}$$

The loss when linear and quadratic terms are used is calculated as

$$L_2 = \frac{30000}{1.45^2} \times 0.001130$$

$$= 16.1 \text{ (yen)}$$

The improvement when linear and quadratic terms are used, compared to the case when only the linear term is used, is

$$420.3 - 16.1 = 404.2 \text{ (yen)}$$

Assuming a monthly production of 20,000 units, the quality improvement is about 8 million yen.

3.3.4 Tuning Method

Generally, tuning is done using the control factors, which affect β_1 and β_2. β_1 can be tuned by the use of signal factor. In such a case, tuning is done using the control factor(s), which affect β_2. In the past, tuning was done using either one factor at a time or the least squares method with multiple factors. In both cases, it was not quite successful because the success depends on the engineer's ability to select the tuning factors.

For the purpose of tuning methods, the linear and quadratic coefficients of each run in array L_{27} were calculated. Table 3.16 shows the level averages of coefficients, and Figure 3.3 shows their effects.

Table 3.16 Level averages of linear & quadratic coefficients.

	Linear Coefficient			Quadratic Coefficient		
	1	2	3	1	2	3
A	1.0368	1.0427	1.0501	−0.0079	−0.0094	−0.0107
B	1.0651	1.0472	1.0173	−0.0095	−0.0094	−0.0091
C	1.0653	1.0387	1.0255	−0.0124	−0.0091	−0.0064
D	1.0435	1.0434	1.0427	−0.0083	−0.0093	−0.0104
E	1.0376	1.0441	1.0478	−0.0081	−0.0094	−0.0105
F	1.0449	1.0434	1.0412	−0.0077	−0.0093	−0.0109
G	1.0654	1.0456	1.0185	−0.0100	−0.0092	−0.0088
H	1.0779	1.0427	1.0089	−0.0090	−0.0092	−0.0098
I	1.0534	1.0430	1.0331	−0.0094	−0.0093	−0.0093
J	1.0271	1.0431	1.0593	−0.0076	−0.0093	−0.0111
K	1.0157	1.0404	1.0734	−0.0083	−0.0094	−0.0103
L	1.0635	1.0405	1.0256	−0.0113	−0.0095	−0.0073
M	1.0295	1.0430	1.0570	−0.0101	−0.0095	−0.0084

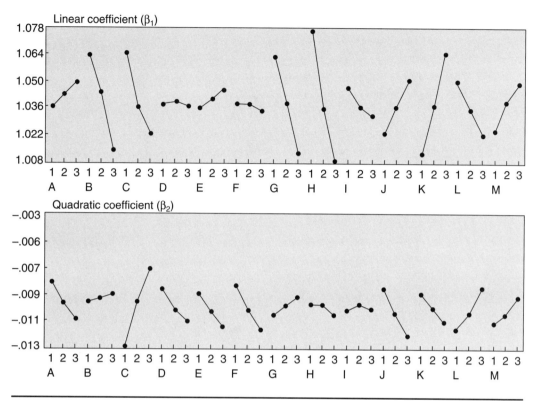

Figure 3.3   Response graphs of linear and quadratic coefficients.

The linear coefficient does not have to be tuned to 1. In many cases, the range of rotating angle can be changed for this purpose. In this case, the linear coefficient is about 8.5 percent larger. Therefore, the rotating angle is reduced by 8.5 percent. An important goal for tuning is to eliminate the quadratic term. The quadratic coefficient is $\beta_2 = 0.005$. We want to make $\beta_2 = 0$ without affecting the S/N ratio. From the response graph (Figure 3.1), the factors insignificant to the S/N ratio are *B, G, H,* and *I*. But these factors are not effective on β_2 (Figure 3.3); therefore, the use of these factors cannot minimize β_2. The next candidates are factors *K* or *L*. For example, move the first level of *K* toward the smaller direction. Such movement increases the linear coefficient. But because the linear coefficient can be adjusted by the signal factor, it is not going to create a problem. It is preferable to use only one factor to eliminate β_2. For this, tuning should be done under conditions that are close to the optimum. Tuning can be done using extrapolation.

4

Simulation Case Studies

This chapter presents three simulation-based case studies from U.S. and Japanese industries.

4.1 Case Study 1: Optimization of a Discrete Floating MOS Gate Driver

This case study was carried out by Thomas Hedges and John Schieffer of Delphi-Delco Electronic Systems Kokomo. We thank Thomas and John for presenting this case study in the 2003 robust engineering symposium.

4.1.1 Summary

By using robust design methods, an optimum circuit configuration was selected; it provided the fastest turn-on/turn-off time while minimizing variation with temperature and component variation. A significant performance improvement was achieved over the baseline design. The turn-on response variation was reduced by 50% (mostly delay) and the turn-on time was reduced by 70 to 80% of the initial circuit. The turn-off response variation was reduced by 16% (mostly saturation voltage), and the turn-off time was reduced by 20% of the initial circuit. The overall circuit response has been improved by eliminating all categories of unwanted outputs. The responses are much cleaner and exhibit less saturation voltage limitation, time delay, slew-rate limiting, and variation.

The optimum design met the required specification at a cost of one-fifth of the cost of the existing IC solution. The total time taken for this experiment was about one week, three days. This experiment yielded a design with much improved performance over the initial design in a similar time frame. Robust engineering techniques optimized the design cycle time by identifying circuit interactions that are not necessarily intuitive.

4.1.2 Background

One of the major functions of an engine control module (ECM) is the control of several types of solenoid such as fuel injectors. A simple solenoid consists of several turns (or loops) of wire around a bar of ferrous metal. A current passing through the wire induces a magnetic field, which forces the bar to move in the direction of the rotating magnetic field. Reversing the current's direction will reverse the direction of movement. Typically the bar will be spring-loaded, and controlling the average current through the solenoid in a single direction changes the relative position.

The magnetic properties of a solenoid mean that the current does not flow instantaneously like in a resistor, but instead rises and falls at a rate determined by the opposing magnetic fields. The average current is controlled by the pulse width modulation (PWM) of a switch, commonly a power MOSFET. The switch is turned on, allowing current to begin flowing; once the desired level is reached the switch is turned off and the current begins to fall. The ratio of ON time to OFF time (or pulse width) will determine the average current achieved.

The average current through the solenoid will vary with the work required by the solenoid (force and rate of movement), and this in turn drives the cost and size of the components in the drive circuitry. A power MOSFET is the preferred device for this kind of current modulation because of the device's low ON resistance and fast switching capability. In general, the size and cost of the power MOSFET will increase with the average

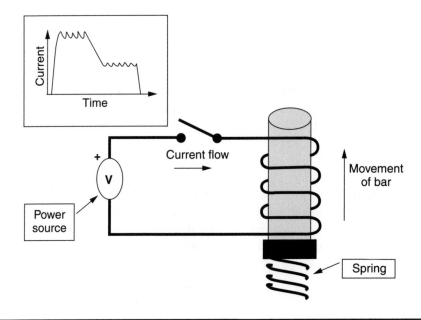

Figure 4. 1 A simple solenoid.

power dissipated by the part. The average power in a MOSFET has two components, "conduction losses" and "switching losses." The conduction losses are directly proportional to the load current and ON resistance of the device. The switching losses are directly proportional to the system voltage, load current, and the switching time of the device.

As can be seen from equation (4.1), for a given load current and system voltage, using a lower ON resistance part can reduce the conduction losses. This generally requires larger and more expensive devices for significant benefits. The other way to reduce power is by reducing switching times, which may be achieved with a high performance "gate driver" and without the need to use newer, more expensive technology.

$$P_{Conduction} = I_{RMS}^2 \cdot R_{ON}$$

$$P_{Switching} = \frac{n}{T} \cdot \left(\frac{I_{ON} \cdot V_{DS}}{2} \cdot t_{Off} + \frac{I_{Off} \cdot V_{DS}}{2} \cdot t_{On} \right) \tag{4.1}$$

The power MOSFET can be placed in the "high side" (positive) or the "low side" (negative) of the power source, or even in a combination of both. Figure 4.2 illustrates a high-side configuration. The high-side configuration is generally more challenging because of the need to provide a gate drive voltage, which is 10V to 15V higher than the main system voltage. Several topologies are available to perform this function, but a "bootstrap" or "floating MOSFET gate driver" is preferred because of cost. There are, however, several limitations of this circuit, particularly drive strength. Recognizing the popularity of this circuit topology, but also the shortcomings of it, several electronics suppliers offer integrated solutions (ICs) with very good performance. As should be expected, a premium is paid for the performance and convenience of the integrated solutions.

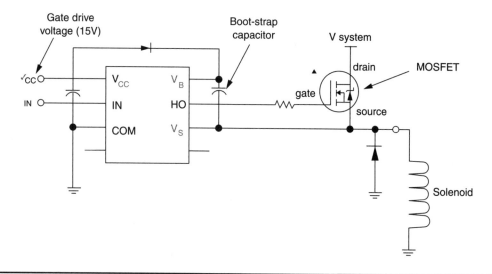

Figure 4.2 A floating MOS gate drive (IC).

4.1.3 Introduction

The main objective of this study was to develop a discrete floating MOS gate drive circuit with performance that was comparable to the existing IC solution. The major constraints were that an aggressive cost reduction must be achieved and minimal increase in circuit board must be maintained. The current design used 24 floating MOS gate driver ICs and so success would yield a very significant cost savings as well as a reusable "building block" that could be used in other designs.

An initial concept was developed using traditional methods, but this design still exhibited significant variation over the application operating range and consequently did not achieve the desired performance needed to replace the IC solution. At this point, the application of Taguchi robust design methods was used to fine-tune the performance and reduce variability of the basic concept so that it could meet the application requirements.

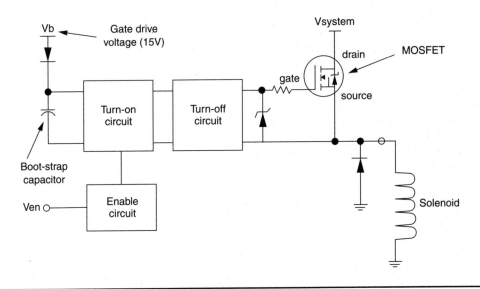

Figure 4.3   Baseline circuit topology.

4.1.4 Developing the Ideal Function

The ideal output response for this kind of circuit is to turn on the MOSFET instantaneously. As a practical matter, however, this is not achievable.

The MOSFET is turned on by charging the gate-to-source capacitance; an example waveform is shown in Figure 4.4.

So the ideal response of this circuit is a 0-1 step function for turn-on and 1-0 step function for turn-off. The obvious conclusion here would be to try to minimize the turn-on and turn-off times by using a "smaller-the-better" approach. The actual approach we took was to use a "dynamic" function that described the ideal circuit response (see Figure 4.5).

The ideal response was broken down into two parts; turn-on began from the instant the enable signal was asserted, t_{ON} (0), and ended 10μs later; the turn-off began when the enable signal was negated, t_{OFF} (0), and ended 10μs later. The 10μs period for each response

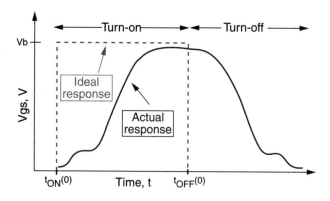

Figure 4.4 Ideal circuit response.

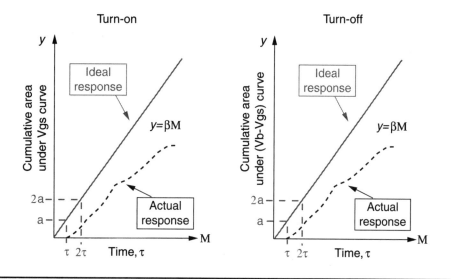

Figure 4.5 Dynamic ideal functions for turn-on and turn-off.

was chosen so as to allow the output to stabilize. By using this approach, two dynamic functions could be formulated, which completely described the "ideal" response:

$$M = t - t_{ON}(0)$$

$$Y_{Turn-On}(M) = \int_{t_{ON}(0)}^{M} V_{gs}(M).dM$$

$$M = t - t_{OFF}(0)$$

$$Y_{Turn-Off}(M) = \int_{t_{OFF}(0)}^{M} [Vb - V_{gs}(M)].dM$$

(4.2)

When applied to the ideal response, these functions would yield a straight line, which is ideally suited for the dynamic signal-to-noise calculation.

There are several undesirable features of the practical response of this circuit:

- Delay. Time from t_{ON} (0) until the output begins to move from its initial state.

- Low slew rate. This is the overall rate of change of the output, or the slope.

- Plateau length. This is the "flat spot" characteristic of a MOSFET.

- Droop. Applies to turn-on and is the amount the voltage drops from its maximum value within the event period ($10\mu s$).

- Saturation. This is the difference between *Vb* and the maximum V_{gs} for turn-on, and the difference between 0 (zero) and the minimum V_{gs} for turn-off.

By driving these ideal functions toward a straight line with a normalized slope of 1, all these undesirable features should be minimized as the response approaches a step response.

4.1.5 Noise Strategy

The predominant noise factors in this system are well known to be:

- Ambient operating temperature— –40° C, 25° C, 125° C

- Transistor current gain tolerance—Low, Nominal, High

These factors can be compounded into a single factor with three levels (N1, N2, N3), as shown in Table 4.1.

Table 4.1   Compounding of noise factors.

	Ambient Operating Temperature	Transistor Current Gain Tolerance
N1 – Nominal Response	25° C	Nominal
N2 – Slow Response	-40° C	Low
N3 – Fast Response	125° C	High

4.1.6 Control Factors and Levels

The control factors in this experiment can be categorized as:

- Key component nominal values

- Key component grade

- Subcircuit configurations

Before the final levels could be selected, some experimentation had to be done to test for "impossible combinations" or "boundary conditions." Much of this was learned during the initial concept development, but this exercise identified several boundary conditions that were unforeseen. Consequently, several control factor levels were adjusted. Table 4.2 shows control factors and their levels.

Table 4.2   Control factors and levels.

	Level 1	Level 2	Level 3
Rpu_bst	High	Low	-
Transistor Type	Low Gain	Medium Gain	High Gain
Turn-On Sub-Circuit Configuration	Type 1	Type 2	Type 3
Turn-Off Sub-Circuit Configuration	Type 1	Type 2	Type 3
Return-on	High	Medium	Low
Return-off	High	Medium	Low
Rs_en	High	Medium	Low
Cen	Low	Medium	High

Figure 4.6 is the parameter diagram (p-diagram) showing various elements for robust design experiments.

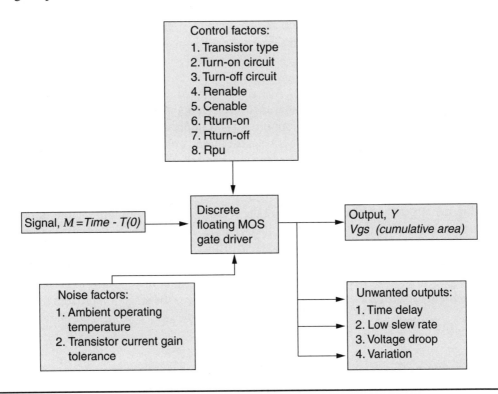

Figure 4.6   Parameter diagram.

4.1.7 Experiment Strategy and Measurement System

The experiment was performed using the Saber Simulation Environment. This method is more economical and efficient and allows the designer to access parameter limits that would not be available using a prototype approach.

After parameter design simulation results were confirmed, a "bread board" of the optimum and initial designs was constructed and tested with the worst-case conditions practically available (i.e., we cannot economically screen out hfe extremes in transistors.)

These real samples were used primarily to confirm the validity of the Saber model.

Parameter Design Experiment Layout

The L_{18} (2^1 x 3^7) orthogonal array was chosen for this experiment. Each run was composed of the three levels of compounded noise and 1000 signal levels, in increments of 10ns. Table 4.3 shows the experimental layout.

From Figure 4.7, it is clear that the real opportunity for improvement lies within the turn-on event. This holds true with observations made with the initial design and the nature of the two sub-circuit topologies. It can be seen that there is significant variation over the experimental range, and that the optimum circuit yields a very significant improvement for the turn-on event. Although a significant improvement was not anticipated for the turn-off event, it was important to monitor it because strong interactions were observed during the development of the initial concept and control factors. Figures 4.8 and 4.9 show response analysis for S/N ratios and sensitivities.

Two-Step Optimization

After studying the data, it was clear that there was an opportunity to significantly improve the turn-on event and relatively less opportunity to improve the turn-off event. In turn-on case, the factor E has significant effect because there is about 5 dB gain between E1 and E3. This gain is much higher than that of the most significant factor, D, in turn-off position. There are other factors in turn-on position that have about the same gains like factor D in turn-off position. This data, combined with the fact that the turn-off event was already meeting the target specification, weighted the selection of the optimum factors in favor of the turn-on event. In general, the factor that yielded the largest S/N ratio for turn-on was selected, unless that factor had a very negative effect on the beta of turn-on. The optimal factor combination, chosen this way, in turn-on position is: A2-B2-C2-D1-E3-F2-G1-H1. Despite the bias toward the turn-on event, the optimum factors still presented some improvement for the turn-off event. Table 4.4 summarizes the selection process of optimal design.

Table 4.3 Experimental layout.

L18 ($2^1 \times 3^7$)									M1			M2			.....	M1000			Ton		Toff	
No.	1	2	3	4	5	6	7	8	N1	N2	N3	N1	N2	N3	.....	N1	N2	N3	S/N	Beta	S/N	Beta
1	1	1	1	1	1	1	1	1	-	-	-	-	-	-	.....	-	-	-	216.57	1.83	217.35	2.01
2	1	1	2	2	2	2	2	2	-	-	-	-	-	-	.....	-	-	-	216.23	2.01	217.94	2.06
3	1	1	3	3	3	3	3	3	-	-	-	-	-	-	.....	-	-	-	217.88	2.06	217.31	1.98
4	1	2	1	1	2	2	3	3	-	-	-	-	-	-	.....	-	-	-	216.89	1.83	217.66	2.05
5	1	2	2	2	3	3	1	1	-	-	-	-	-	-	.....	-	-	-	222.37	2.35	218.25	2.08
6	1	2	3	3	1	1	2	2	-	-	-	-	-	-	.....	-	-	-	217.16	2.01	217.98	2.11
7	1	3	1	2	1	3	2	3	-	-	-	-	-	-	.....	-	-	-	213.53	1.60	218.20	2.10
8	1	3	2	3	2	1	3	1	-	-	-	-	-	-	.....	-	-	-	217.59	1.92	218.03	2.11
9	1	3	3	1	3	2	1	2	-	-	-	-	-	-	.....	-	-	-	222.21	2.49	217.95	2.11
10	2	1	1	3	3	2	2	1	-	-	-	-	-	-	.....	-	-	-	220.27	2.18	218.01	2.14
11	2	1	2	1	1	3	3	2	-	-	-	-	-	-	.....	-	-	-	216.95	2.02	217.22	2.05
12	2	1	3	2	2	1	1	3	-	-	-	-	-	-	.....	-	-	-	215.17	0.52	218.79	2.16
13	2	2	1	2	3	1	3	2	-	-	-	-	-	-	.....	-	-	-	220.08	2.12	218.14	2.09
14	2	2	2	3	1	2	1	3	-	-	-	-	-	-	.....	-	-	-	218.21	2.00	218.04	2.11
15	2	2	3	1	2	3	2	1	-	-	-	-	-	-	.....	-	-	-	219.26	2.20	218.13	2.11
16	2	3	1	3	2	3	1	2	-	-	-	-	-	-	.....	-	-	-	217.42	1.91	218.02	2.13
17	2	3	2	1	3	1	2	3	-	-	-	-	-	-	.....	-	-	-	221.96	2.32	217.96	2.08
18	2	3	3	2	1	2	3	1	-	-	-	-	-	-	.....	-	-	-	217.38	2.02	218.17	2.09

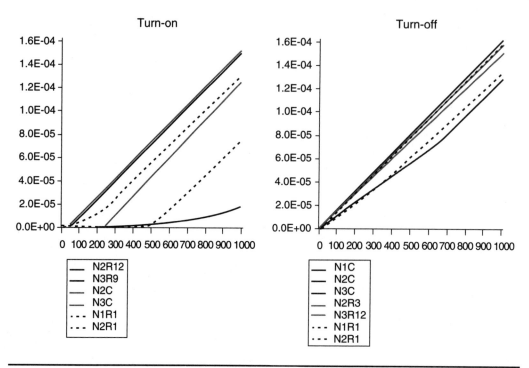

Figure 4.7   Turn-on and turn-off events.

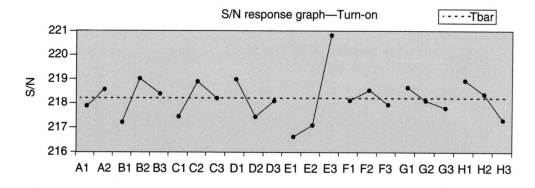

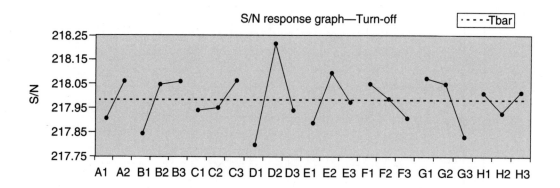

Figure 4.8   Response analysis for S/N ratios.

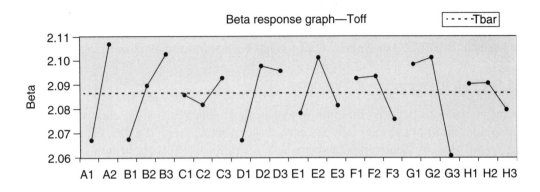

Figure 4.9 Response analysis for sensitivities.

Table 4.4 Selection of optimal design.

	A	B	C	D	E	F	G	H
Initial design	1	1	1	1	1	1	1	1
To maximize s/n for ton	2	2	2	1	3	2	1	1
To maximize s/n for toff	2	3	3	2	2	1	1	1
To maximize beta for ton	1	2	2	1	3	2	2	2
To maximize beta for toff	2	3	3	2	2	2	2	1
Optimum design	2	2	2	1	3	2	2	1

4.1.8 Confirmation

The predictions for the optimal design were as expected; a significant improvement of the S/N ratio for turn-on was predicted, as was a relatively small improvement of the S/N ratio for turn-off. The same trend was also true for the beta. The optimum design confirmed very well with an actual gain of 6.141 dB for turn-on, which is approximately a 50% reduction in variability. The turn-off response, although relatively insignificant, still produced a gain of 1.57 dB, or a 16% reduction in variability. The same kind of improvement was confirmed for beta, with a 41% increase in beta for turn-on and a 7% increase for turn-off. Table 4.5 summarizes results of confirmation experiments.

Table 4.5 Results of conformation experiments.

Turn-on	Prediction		Confirmation	
	S/N Ratio	Beta	S/N Ratio	Beta
Initial design	216.511	1.681	216.574	1.833
Optimum design	224.459	2.939	222.715	2.587
Gain	7.948	1.258	6.141	0.754

Turn-off	Prediction		Confirmation	
	S/N Ratio	Beta	S/N Ratio	Beta
Initial design	217.484	2.040	217.346	2.010
Optimum design	217.964	2.103	218.916	2.156
Gain	0.480	0.063	1.569	0.146

The effects of robust optimization can be seen very clearly in the actual circuit response waveforms. The response is visibly "squarer" (more like the ideal step), the delay has been cut in half, and the "plateau" region has been shortened by as much as two-thirds.

4.1.9 Conclusions

Strong interactions between the turn-on and turn-off subcircuits were clearly identified. (The optimum turn-on circuit may actually cause problems with the turn-off circuit, and vice versa). Most of the circuit parameters have a significant effect on the turn-on response, but they have a relatively insignificant effect on the turn-off response. Contrary to initial assumptions, it was found that the highest gain transistors (most expensive) were not necessarily better, due to turn-on/turn-off circuit interactions.

4.2 Case Study 2: Direct Injection Diesel Injector Optimization Using Robust Engineering

This case study was carried out by Desire Djomani and Pierre Barthelet of Delphi Automotive Systems, Europe, and Michael Holbrook of Delphi Automotive Systems, Flint, MI. We thank these authors for presenting in the 1999 robust engineering symposium.

4.2.1 Summary

Delphi Automotive Systems is entering the direct injection diesel business, which requires a significant shift in technologies from the current diesel injection approach. The injector itself is the key to mastering this goal and its high sensitivity to sources of variation makes robust engineering a valuable approach to optimization.

A robust engineering dynamic experiment based on a numerical model of the injector allowed us to achieve the following:

- 4.46 dB (decibels) improvement in the signal to noise ratio through parameter design. This represents a reduction of about 40% in the variability of injected quantity.

- An improvement of about 26% in the predicted manufacturing process end-of-line first-time quality (percentage of good injectors at the end of the line).

4.2.2 Background

The common rail direct injection diesel fuel system is an important technology for Delphi. For this reason, a product and process engineering team, dedicated to the design and implementation of the best possible common rail system with respect to both product and process, was set up at the European Technical Center. The direct injection diesel common rail system is composed of the following core components of the engine management system:

- Injectors

- High-pressure pump

- Fuel rail and tubes

- High-pressure sensor

- Electronic control module

- Pressure control system

The main challenge with diesel common rail systems as opposed to indirect diesel injection systems is the continual high operating pressures. Current common rail systems are designed to operate with pressure levels of 1350 to 1600 bars. Figure 4.10 shows a sample injector and its key variability sources. The injector is the most critical and the most complex element of the system. A diesel common rail system will not be successful if the injectors are not world-class in terms of quality and reliability.

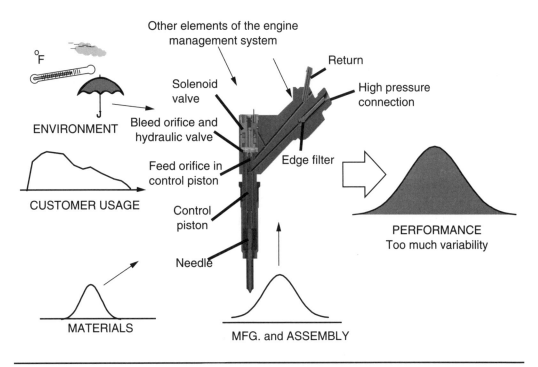

Figure 4.10   Injector and key sources of variability.

The injector complexity is due to very tight manufacturing tolerances and challenging customer requirements for injected quantity. These issues are confirmed by the problems reported by competitors. Some of them experienced very high scrap levels in production. An alternative approach is to build quality into the product at an early stage of design.

4.2.3 Objectives of This Study

A simulation model was developed, improved, and used to perform the orthogonal array experiments. Because of the very high confidence level in the simulation model (see Figure 4.15), we decided to use hardware only for the confirmation runs.

The main objectives of this study were:

- Reduce the part-to-part and shot-to-shot variation in injected quantity.

  - Part-to-part variation is variation among several injectors.

  - Shot-to-shot variation is variation from one injection to the next within the same injector.

- Decrease sensitivity to manufacturing variation and be able to reduce cost by increasing component tolerances as appropriate.

- Provide graphical tools to increase understanding of downstream quality drivers in the design.

The labeling used in the experiment is the following

A	**A′**
Control factor for parameter design	Control factor variation considered as a noise factor

4.2.4 Simulation Model Robustness

A direct injection diesel injector for a common rail system is a complex component, with high-precision parts and demanding specifications. To simulate such a component means representing the physical transient interactions of a coupled system including a magnetic actuator; fluid flows at high pressure, possibly with cavitation phenomena; and moving mechanical parts. The typical time scale for operation is a few microseconds to a few milliseconds.

Because pressure wave propagation phenomena are important in the accurate representation of injector operation, the simulation code cannot be limited to the injector itself, but must also include the common rail and the connection pipe from the rail to the injector (Figure 4.11).

The rail and the connection line are standard hydraulic elements, in which the model calculates wave propagation using classical methods for solving wave equations. The internal structure of the injector is illustrated on Figure 4.12. We can distinguish two hydraulic circuits and one moving part (plus the mobile part of the control valve). The first hydraulic circuit feeds the control volume at the common rail high pressure through a calibrated orifice. The pressure P_C in the control volume is controlled by activating the electromechanical control valve and bleeding off a small amount of fluid. The duration of electrical activation,

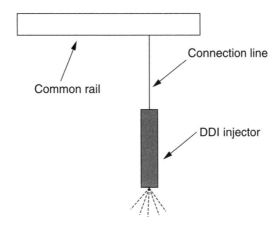

Figure 4.11 Modeled system.

called pulse width, is calculated by the engine control module (ECM), depending upon driver demand, rail pressure, and engine torque needs. The other hydraulic circuit feeds the nozzle volume at a pressure P_N that remains close to common rail pressure. Using internal sealing, the area stressed by the pressure is larger on the control volume side than on the nozzle side. Thus, as long as P_C and P_N remain equal, the needle is pushed against the nozzle seat and the injector is closed. To start an injection event, the control valve is activated, which lowers the pressure in the control chamber until the force balance on the needle changes sign. Then the needle moves up, and injection occurs. To close the injector, the control valve is closed and the pressure builds up again in the control chamber until the force balance on the needle changes sign again and the needle moves down and closes.

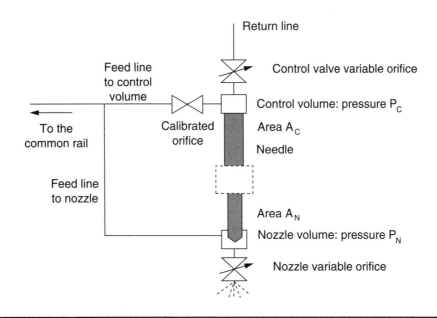

Figure 4.12 Schematic of the injector.

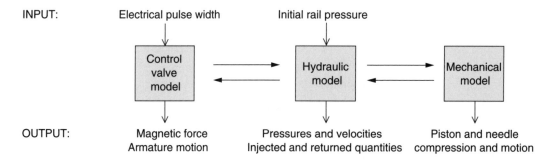

INPUT: Electrical pulse width   Initial rail pressure

Control valve model → Hydraulic model → Mechanical model

OUTPUT: Magnetic force   Pressures and velocities   Piston and needle
         Armature motion   Injected and returned quantities   compression and motion

Figure 4.13   Structure of the mathematical model.

The structure of the mathematical model of the injector can be deduced from its physical structure (Figure 4.13). Three sub-models are coupled:

- Electromechanical control valve

- Hydraulic circuits

- Mechanical moving parts

Model inputs are:

- Duration of electrical activation of electromagnetic actuator

- Rail pressure

Model outputs include time variation of:

- Magnetic force

- Fuel pressure and velocity in lines

- Flows through orifices

- Displacement of moving parts

The behavior of a direct injection diesel injector can be characterized by a so-called mapping, which gives the injected fuel quantity versus pulse-width and rail pressure (Figure 4.14).

Given the initial rail pressure and the pulse width, the model is expected to accurately predict the quantity of fuel that should be injected.

Approach to Optimization

The difficulty in building and then optimizing such a model is that some features strongly affect the results. Lack of precision about their model representation can affect results unacceptably. Experimental investigations have thoroughly studied the characteristics of internal flows in key parts like the control valve and the nozzle. From these experiments, empirical equations have been fitted and then implemented in the model. Finally, the transient nature of the flows is also a problem because most of the experiments are done statically.

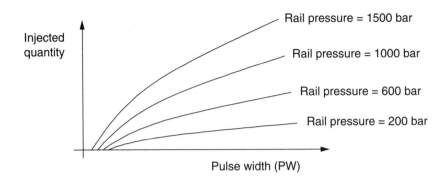

Figure 4.14 Schematic representation of injector mapping: injected quantity versus pulse width for various rail pressure levels.

In the end, after implementing the most realistic physical representation of variables, based either on experiments or on theoretical calculation, injector model optimization is a feedback loop between model results and experimentally observable injection parameters, like injected quantity, injection timing, and control valve displacement. Engineering judgment is then necessary to assess the cause of any discrepancy and to improve or even change the physical representation of variables shown to be inadequate.

Results

Figure 4.15 shows the correlation between model and experiment for injected quantity, for rail pressures and pulse widths covering the full range of injector operation, for three different injectors with different settings of control factor values. The agreement between

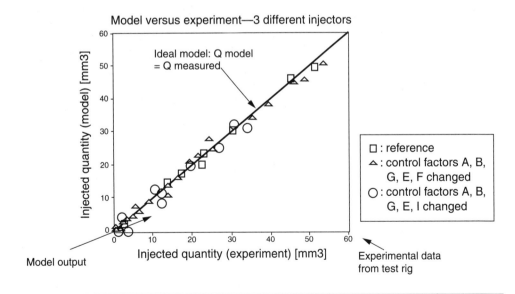

Figure 4.15 Comparison model data versus experimental data for various rail pressure, pulse width and injector control factor setting.

model and hardware is good over the full range of operation. Figure 4.15 is the basis of the high confidence level we have in the model outputs.

4.2.5 Parameter Design

The direct injection diesel injector has several performance characteristics:

- Recirculated quantity

- Total opening time

- Delay of main injection

- Injected quantity

In the traditional approach, these performance characteristics would require individual optimizations and trade-offs based on experimental results. In such a case, the power of a carefully chosen ideal function is invaluable. For an injection system, the customer requirement can be expressed as the quantity of fuel required for good combustion at a given operating point. By considering the customer need as a signal, we can compute through the simulation model, under noise conditions, what the actual injector will deliver. This last value is the y-axis of the ideal function. A perfect injector will have a slope of 1, with the actual quantity equal to the desired value. Figure 4.16 shows the behavior of the ideal function.

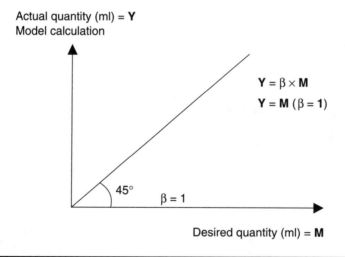

Figure 4.16   Ideal function.

A design that exhibits the ideal function is likely to be acceptable for any of the performance characteristics listed above.

Signal and Noise Strategies

Signal Levels

Five levels of desired injected quantity were selected based on customer specifications: 2 ml, 5 ml, 15 ml, 25 ml, and 40 ml.

Noise Strategy

Table 4.6 shows the impact of the noise factors on the injected quantity. A (+) indicates that an increase in the noise factor will increase the injected quantity (direct relationship). A (–) indicates that a decrease in the noise factor will increase the injected quantity (inverse relationship).

The compounded noise level 1 ($N1$) groups all the noise factor levels that have the effect of reducing the injected quantity. The compounded noise level 2 ($N2$) groups the noise factor levels that have the effect of increasing the injected quantity.

Table 4.6 List of noise factors

Noise factor	Level 1	Level 2	Relationship with injected quantity	Compounded noise level 1 (N1)	Compounded noise level 2 (N2)	Rationale
B′	–10	+ 10	+	Level 1	Level 2	Mfg
C′	–5	+ 5	+	Level 1	Level 2	Age
D′	–2	+ 2	+	Level 1	Level 2	Mfg, Age
E′	–3	+ 3	–	Level 2	Level 1	Mfg, Age
F′	–3	+ 3	–	Level 2	Level 1	Age
G′	–3	+ 3	+	Level 1	Level 2	Mfg, Age
H′	–4	+ 4	–	Level 2	Level 1	Age
I′	–30	+ 30	+	Level 1	Level 2	Mfg
J′	–3	+ 3	+	Level 1	Level 2	Age
L	0.6	1	+	Level 1	Level 2	Mfg, Age
M	–10	+ 10	+	Level 1	Level 2	System
N	0	0,03	+	Level 1	Level 2	Mfg
O	2	5	+	Level 1	Level 2	Mfg

Legend: Mfg = Manufacturing variation; Age = Aging; System = Influence of other components

B′, C′ . . . J′ are noise factors obtained by considering variation (from manufacturing or other sources) of the corresponding control factors. L, M, N, and O are noise factors not derived from control factors. We expect these noises to be present during product usage. Table 4.7 shows control factors and their levels.

An $L_{27} (3^{13})$ orthogonal array was used to perform the experiment. Two columns were unused. Figure 4.17 is the parameter diagram for this study.

Table 4.7   Control factors and levels (current design levels are in bold type; Xs in level 2 column are reference values).

Factor	Level 1	Level 2	Level 3
A	-16.6 %	X	+ 16.6 %
B	**-11.1%**	X	+ 11.1%
C	-16.6 %	X	+16.6 %
D	**-11.1%**	X	+ 11.1%
E	- 28.6%	X	**+ 28.6%**
F	- 18.5%	X	+ 18.5%
G	- 18.2%	X	**+ 22.7%**
H	+ 33.3%	X	+ 66.6%
I	- 11.1%	X	**+ 11.1%**
J	- 8.62%	X	**+ 6.9%**
K	-2.3%	X	**+ 2.3 %**

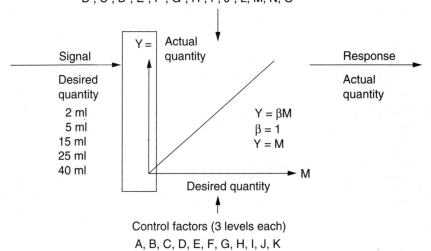

Noise factors (compounded to 2 levels)
B', C', D', E', F', G', H', I', J', L, M, N, O

Signal

Desired quantity

2 ml
5 ml
15 ml
25 ml
40 ml

$Y =$ Actual quantity

Desired quantity

$Y = \beta M$
$\beta = 1$
$Y = M$

M

Response

Actual quantity

Control factors (3 levels each)
A, B, C, D, E, F, G, H, I, J, K

Figure 4.17   Parameter diagram.

Table 4.8 Experimental layout.

#	\multicolumn{13}{c}{Control factor array}	Signal	2 ml		5 ml		15 ml		25 ml		40 ml		S/N	β

#	A	B	C	D	E	F	G	H	I	J	K	12	13	Noises	N1	N2	N1	N2	N1	N2	N1	N2	N1	N2	S/N	β
1	1	1	1	1	1	1	1	1	1	1	1	1	1													
2	1	1	1	1	2	2	2	2	2	2	2	2	2													
3	1	1	1	1	3	3	3	3	3	3	3	3	3													
25	3	3	2	1	1	3	2	3	2	1	2	1	3													
26	3	3	2	1	2	1	3	1	3	2	3	2	1													
27	3	3	2	1	3	2	1	2	1	3	1	3	2													

(The Signal/Noise data region is blank, labelled **DATA**.)

Data Analysis and Two-Step Optimization

The data were analyzed using the dynamic signal to noise ratio with the following formula:

$$\eta = 10 \log \left[\frac{(S_\beta - Ve)}{r\ Ve} \right]$$

S_β = Sum of squares of distance between zero and the least square best fit line (forced through zero) for each data point

Ve = Mean square (variance);

r = Sum of squares of the signals

The optimal parameter combination was selected through two-step optimization. Usually, in two-step optimization we select an optimal factor setting based on factor levels that provide maximum S/N ratio at first. In the second step we use one factor or two to adjust the process to the desired setting. Here for optimal combination (as shown in Figure 4.18 and Table 4.9), all factor levels with higher S/N ratios, barring the factor E, were selected. This factors level combination is A3-B2-C3-D3-F2-G1-H3-I1-J1-K3. The factor E has almost no impact on S/N ratios. However, it has a significant impact on sensitivity (E1 has highest sensitivity), which is required for process setting. Because of this reason E1 has been chosen as optimal setting for factor E. Hence the optimal combination in this case was A3-B2-C3-D3-E1-F2-G1-H3-I1-J1-K3.

As shown in Table 4.11, the model confirms the expected improvement with a slight difference. Neither the optimum nor the current design combinations were part of the control factor orthogonal array. The initial hardware testing on the optimized configuration shows promising results. The hardware confirmation was completed before the end of 1999. Figure 4.19 shows a graphical comparison between optimal design and initial design.

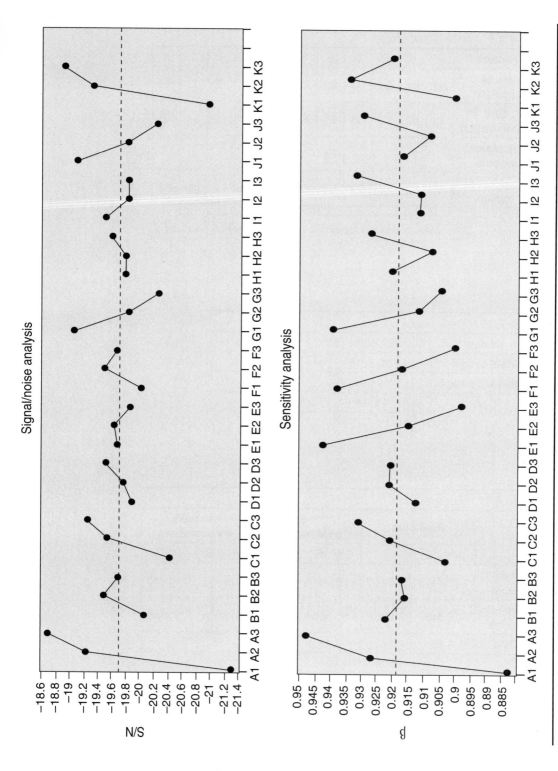

Figure 4.18 Signal to noise ratio and sensitivity plot.

Table 4.9   Two-step optimization.

Factors	A	B	C	D	E	F	G	H	I	J	K	
Initial design	A2	B1	C1	D1	E3	F2	G3	H2	I3	J3	K3	
S/N maximization	A3	B2	C3	D3	E?	F2	G1	H3	I1	J1	K3	←1st step
Adjustment for beta					E1							←2nd step
Optimized design	A3	B2	C3	D3	E1	F2	G1	H3	I1	J1	K3	

Design change required   Design change required

Table 4.10   Prediction.

Design	Signal / noise (dB)	β (Slope)
Initial design	- 20.7118	0.8941
Optimized design	- 15.0439	1.0062
Gain	+ 5.66	0.1121

Table 4.11   Confirmation.

	Predicted		Model confirmation		Hardware confirmation	
	S/N (dB)	β	S/N (dB)	β	S/N (dB)	β
Initial design	- 20.7118	0.8941	- 20.2644	0.9150	Ongoing	Ongoing
Optimum design	- 15.0439	1.0062	- 15.8048	0.9752	Ongoing	Ongoing
Gain	5.66	0.1121	4.46	0.06		

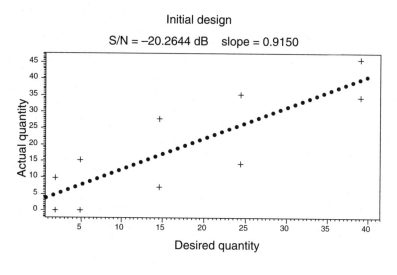

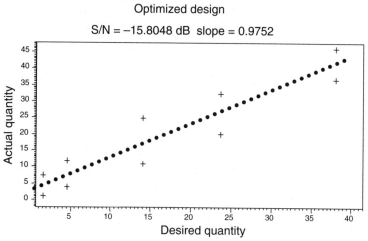

Figure 4.19 Graphical results initial design compared to optimized design for parameter design.

4.2.6 Discussions on Parameter Design Results

- B and C are control valve parameters. The design change on these parameters suggested by parameter design will improve injected quantity, part-to-part variation, and shot-to-shot variation. The simulation model confirms these improvements. Hardware confirmation is ongoing.

- A, D, E, G, H, I, J are hydraulic parameters. Implementing the changes suggested by parameter design will decrease sensitivity to most of the noise factors and to pressure fluctuations in the system.

- An improvement in signal to noise ratio can be directly translated into a reduction in variability.

$$\text{Variability improvement} = (1/2)^{(\text{Gain}/6)}(\text{initial variability})$$

Gain = signal to noise ratio gain in decibels; in our case, the model confirmed gain is 4.46 dB (see Table 4.11). We are making an almost 40% reduction in variability from the initial design. It was anticipated that the variability reduction would translate to a 16 to 26% increase of the fraction of parts inside injected quantity tolerances at the end of the manufacturing line.

In this study, it was possible to simulate control factor manufacturing variation as noise factors. The ability to consider manufacturing variation is an important advantage of simulation-based robust engineering as compared to full hardware-based robust engineering.

4.3 Case Study 3: Robust Design of Transistors

This case was conducted by Sumio Hirai and Masaaki Koga of Miyazaki Oki Electric Company, Japan. We thank the authors for presenting this study in the 1990 robust engineering symposium.

4.3.1 Introduction

In designing a MOSLSI system, it is very important to understand the electrical characteristics of a MOS transistor (MOSFET).

Important factors used to control the electrical characteristics of a MOS transistor are threshold voltage, drain to source current, channel conductivity, and MOS load capacity. The performance of a MOS transistor is greatly affected by manufacturing conditions. It is very difficult to manufacture stable MOS transistor of electrical characteristics under fluctuations in manufacturing conditions.

There is a strong correlation between product quality and drain to source current. It is, therefore, important to control drain to source current variability in order to improve the reliability of product function.

Rather than attempting to control the manufacturing environment, it is better to know whether it is possible to determine an optimum condition that will minimize drain to source current variability in the face of fluctuating manufacturing conditions. This was accomplished through a computer simulation study using a model of MOS transistor drain to source current and an L_{36} ($2^{11} \times 3^{12}$) orthogonal array.

4.3.2 Objective of the Study

The objective of the study is to determine a stable MOS transistor manufacturing condition for drain to source current that will allow us to hit a specified current target with minimal variability.

Figure 4.20 shows the correlation between product yield and the drain to source current of the MOS transistor. Figure 4.21 shows the cross section of a MOS Transistor. From the viewpoint of the MOS IC process, the drain to source current (I_D) is controlled by the gate length (L), the gate film thickness (t_{oxi}), and the impurity depth (X_j).

A drain to source current I_D of 5.6 mA is desirable. However, it is difficult to maintain the stability of this current condition because the manufacturing conditions vary.

In order to minimize the variability of drain to source current I_D, control label manufacturing conditions were assigned to an L_{36} orthogonal array, and drain to source current was calculated by means of a mathematical model. A nominal-the-best type characteristic

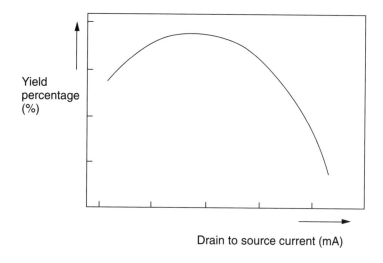

Figure 4.20   Correlation between product yield and drain to source current.

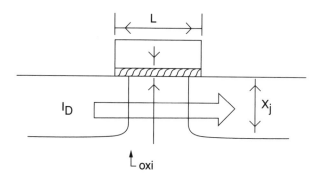

Figure 4.21   Cross-section of a MOS transistor.

was used to evaluate quality (i.e., stability of current performance under varying conditions), and sensitivity analysis was used to adjust the mean to the target. The target current is

$$I_D = 5.6 \pm 0.3 \text{ (mA)} \tag{4.3}$$

In other words, the objective of the study was to determine a manufacturing condition that will allow us to maintain the target current of 5.6 mA with minimal variability.

4.3.3 A Model for Calculating Current

Equation 4.4 for the calculation of current is as follows:

$$I_D = \frac{W}{L} \mu n \text{Cox} \left\{ (V_G - v_{FB} - 2\phi_F)V_D - \frac{1}{2}V_D^2 \right.$$

$$\left. - \left[\frac{2}{3} \frac{\sqrt{2Ks.eo.q.NA}}{\text{Cox}} \left\{ (2 + 2\phi = +V_D)^{3/2} - (2\phi_F)^{3/2} \right\} \right] \right] \tag{4.4}$$

where

$$\text{Cox} = \frac{Kox.\varepsilon o}{t_{oxi}}$$

$$L = Lgate - 2xj$$

$$Xj = \left[\left(-\ln \frac{N\sqrt{2\pi(\Delta R^2_{pp} + 2Df.t)}}{Nop} \right) x2(\Delta R^2 pp + 2Df.t) \right]^{\frac{1}{2}} + Rpp$$

$$N_A = \frac{N_{OB}}{\sqrt{2\pi}\Delta R_{PB}} \exp\left\{ -\frac{(toxi-R_{PB})^2}{2\Delta R^2_{PB}} \right\} + N$$

$$\phi_F = \frac{KT}{q} \ln \frac{N_A}{Ni}$$

$$V_{FB} = -\frac{KT}{q} \ln \frac{N_A.N_D}{N^2 i}$$

$$Df=Do \exp\left(-\frac{\Delta E}{KT} \right) \rightarrow Df = 11.154 \exp\left(-\frac{5.926x10^{-19}}{KT_P} \right)$$

The constant terms in Equation 4.4 are as follows:

μ_n	:	Electron mobility	1100 cm^2/sec
V_G	:	Gate voltage	5.0V
V_D	:	Drain voltage	5.0V
K_S	:	Relative dielectric constant of silicon	11.7 F/cm
εo	:	Dielectric constant in vacuum	8.854×10^{-14}
q	:	Electron charge	1.602×10^{-19}C
K_{ox}	:	Relative dielectric constant of oxide film	3.9
K	:	Boltzman's constant	1.38×10^{-23} j/deg
T	:	Absolute temperature	300^0 K
Ni	:	Intrinsic carrier concentration	1.45×10^{10} cm^{-3}
N_D	:	Impurity density of Gate	5.50×10^{20} cm^{-3}

Table 4.12 shows the impurity distribution of the ion injection.

Table 4.12: Projected range (R_p) and its standard deviation (ΔR_p).

On	P+		B+	
Energy	$\mathbf{R_{PP}}$	$\mathbf{\Delta R_{PP}}$	$\mathbf{R_{PB}}$	$\mathbf{\Delta R_{PB}}$
20 Kev	0.0253	0.0119	0.0662	0.0283
40	0.0486	0.0212	0.1302	0.0443
60	0.0730	0.0298	0.1903	0.0556

4.3.4 Experimental Details

Selection of Factors and Layout of Experiment

Control Factors

Factors that might affect I_D in Equation 4.4 and that can be varied in the manufacturing process were selected for study. These are the control factors. Table 4.13 shows the control factors for the study.

Noise Factors

Table 4.14 shows the noise factors in manufacturing equipment, the manufacturing environment, and so on. Three levels of noise factors were studied.

Table 4.13   Control factors and levels.

	Factor		Level 1	Level 2	Level 3
A	Gate film thickness	toxi	A_1	A_2	A_3
B	Boron dose amount	N_{OB}	B_1	B_2	B_3
C	Boron acceleration voltage	R_{PB}, ΔR_{PB}	C_1	C_2	C_3
D	Gate Width	W	D_1	D_2	D_3
E	Gate length	L gate	E_1	E_2	E_3
F	Phosphorus dose amount	N_{OP}	F_1	F_2	F_3
G	Phosphorus acceleration voltage	R_{PP}, ΔR_{PP}	G_1	G_2	G_3
H	Diffusion time	t	H_1	H_2	H_3
I	Diffusion temperature	T_P	I_1	I_2	I_3

Table 4.14   Noise factors with three levels.

	Factor		Level 1	Level 2	Level 3
A	Gate film thickness		−10%	0	10%
B	Boron dose amount		−5%	0	5%
D	Gate Width		−10%	0	10%
E	Gate length		−10%	0	10%
F	Phosphorus dose amount		−5%	0	5%
H	Diffusion time		−1%	0	1%
J	Wafer impurity concentration	N	N_1	N_2	N_3

Level 1 and Level 3 are percent derivations from Level 2.

Experimental Layout

The nine three-level control factors (A, B, . . . , I) were assigned to an L_{36} inner array and the seven three-level noise factors were assigned to an L_{36} outer array (see Table 4.15). This experimental layout was used to determine the variability in current I_D caused by noise factors in the outer array for various combinations of control factor levels in the inner array. The inner array gives 36 experimental runs. Each run allows us to evaluate the effect of noise on current I_D variability for a particular combination of control factor levels. For each run of inner array there are 36 runs in the outer array. For each run of the inner array, the S/N ratios and sensitivities are calculated based on data obtained in all 36 noise combinations of outer array.

Table 4.15   Experimental layout for control and noise factors.

Outer array
Noise factor

No.	1	2	3	4	· · · ·	35	36

Outer array noise factor columns (L36):

	A 1	B 2	D 3	E 4	F 5	H 6	J 7	e 8	e 9	e 10	e 11	e 12	e 13
No. 1	1	1	1	1	1	1	1	1	1	1	1	1	1
2	2	2	2	2	2	2	2	2	2	2	2	2	1
3	3	3	3	3	3	3	3	3	3	3	3	3	1
4	1	1	1	1	2	2	2	2	3	3	3	5	1

Inner array
Control factor

L36

SN ratio
sensitivity

(dB)

No.	A 1	B 2	C 3	D 4	E 5	F 6	G 7	H 8	I 9	e 10	e 11	e 12	e 13
1	1	1	1	1	1	1	1	1	1	1	1	1	1
2	2	2	2	2	2	2	2	2	2	2	2	2	2
3	3	3	3	3	3	3	3	3	3	3	3	3	3
4	1	1	1	1	2	2	2	2	3	3	3	3	1
5	2	2	2	2	3	3	3	3	1	1	1	1	1
6	3	3	3	3	1	1	1	1	2	2	2	2	1
7	1	1	2	3	1	2	3	3	1	2	2	3	1
.													
.													
35													
36													

L36

Results

36 × 36 = 1296

Data Analysis

For each of the 36 experimental runs of the inner array, 36 current I_D values (y1, y2, ..., y36) are calculated based on conditions of the outer array.

$$S_m = \frac{(\mathbf{y}_1 + \mathbf{y}_2 + ------ + \mathbf{y}_{36})^2}{36}$$

$$Ve = \frac{1}{35}\left(\mathbf{y}_1^2 + \mathbf{y}_2^2 + ---- \mathbf{y}_2^2\right) - \mathbf{Sm}$$

Hence

$$\text{S/N ration: } \eta = 10 \log \frac{\frac{1}{36}(\mathbf{Sm} - \mathbf{Ve})}{\mathbf{Ve}}$$

$$\text{Sensivity: } S = 10 \log \frac{1}{36}(\mathbf{Sm} - \mathbf{Ve})$$

Table 4.16 summarizes the results of the calculations for the signal to noise (S/N) ratio and for Sensitivity S for each of the 36 runs.

Table 4.16   Results of S/N ratio and sensitivity calculation.

No.	SN ratio η (dB)	Sensitivity S (dB)	No.	SN ration η (dB)	Sensitivity S (dB)
1.	14.375	18.346	19	13.946	24.026
2.	12.400	20.038	20	2.725	25.507
3.	8.672	22.284	21	11.589	15.945
4.	10.326	21.515	22	14.749	23.989
5.	13.236	16.715	23	10.832	19.329
6.	10.846	22.794	24	5.037	15.966
7.	13.493	30.914	25	10.897	22.090
8.	12.697	13.753	26	13.430	16.188
9.	3.526	5.494	27	5.273	16.930
10.	11.528	30.003	28	13.537	24.086
11.	9.875	22.445	29	11.562	23.001
12.	11.781	5.649	30	5.800	5.202
13.	11.392	19.112	31	14.345	26.894
14.	11.162	18.065	32	11.707	9.003
15.	10.842	19.756	33	7.227	23.860
16.	5.273	34.856	34	13.819	20.449
17.	11.350	18.212	35	3.067	36.352
18.	11.498	7.251	36	11.617	9.493

In order to determine which factors affect variability and which affect the mean, an analysis of variance (ANOVA) was performed for the S/N ratio and for sensitivity. Tables 4.17 and 4.18 show the ANOVA tables for the S/N ratio and sensitivity, respectively.

Table 4.17   ANOVA tables for S/N ratio.

	Factor	f	SS	MS	ρ%
A:	Gate film thickness	2	80.8442	40.4221	18.6
B:	Boron dose amount	2	1.3799	0.6900	
C:	Boron acceleration voltage	2	12.9533	6.4766	2.1
D:	Gate Width	2	1.6452	0.8226	
E:	Gate length	2	70.3860	35.1930	16.1
F:	Phosphorus dose amount	2	4.3323	2.1662	
G:	Phosphorus acceleration voltage	2	2.7753	1.3876	
H:	Diffusion time	2	29.3990	14.6995	6.1
I:	Diffusion temperature	2	160.6910	80.3455	38.1
e:	Error	17	45.7783	2.6928	
e′:	(Pooled error)	25	55.9110	2.2364	19.0
		35	410.1845		100.0

Table 4.18   ANOVA tables for sensitivity.

	Factor	f	S	V	ρ%
A:	Gate film thickness	2	659.3697	329.6848	32.1
B:	Boron dose amount	2	10.2896	5.1448	
C:	Boron acceleration voltage	2	195.4775	97.7387	9.2
D:	Gate Width	2	521.8624	260.9312	25.3
E:	Gate length	2	333.1167	166.5583	16.0
F:	Phosphorus dose amount	2	1.8453	0.9227	
G:	Phosphorus acceleration voltage	2	6.1259	3.0629	
H:	Diffusion time	2	1.6229	0.8115	
I:	Diffusion temperature	2	193.8292	96.9146	9.1
e:	Error	17	101.0258	5.9427	
e′:	(Pooled error)	25	120.9095	4.8364	8.3
		35			100.0

f: degrees of freedom; SS: sum of squares; MS: mean squares;
S: combination ratio

Determination of the Optimum Condition

Next, the optimum levels of control factors in the study are determined. Response tables allow us to compare factor level averages for the S/N ratio and for sensitivity. Table 4.19 shows the response tables with level averages of control factors for both the S/N ratio and sensitivity.

Table 4.19   Factor level averages for S/N and sensitivity.

Level factor	η (S/N)			S		
	1	2	3	1	2	3
A	12.31	10.34	8.64	24.69	19.88	14.22
B	10.70	10.29	10.29	20.35	19.20	19.24
C	9.68	10.45	11.15	16.30	21.35	21.14
D	10.47	10.15	10.67	14.69	20.14	23.97
E	8.46	11.21	11.61	23.51	19.18	16.10
F	10.21	10.92	10.16	19.33	19.58	19.88
G	10.72	10.06	10.50	19.86	19.02	19.22
H	11.69	9.63	9.96	19.33	19.61	19.85
I	12.24	11.57	7.46	7.13	18.95	22.71
	$\overline{m}=10.43$ dB	$\overline{m}=19.60$ dB				

Response graphs allow us to visually assess the effects of control factors. The response graphs in Figure 4.22 show the effects of control factors.

From the response graphs the optimum condition was selected:

$$A1\ (B1)\ C3\ (D3)\ E3\ (F2)\ (G1)\ H1\ I1$$

We can estimate the S/N ratio for this condition as

$$\overline{\mu} = (12.31 + 10.70 + \ldots + 12.24) - (8 \times 10.43) = 18.57\ (dB)$$

Since the target value is 5.6 mA, the standard deviation for the optimum condition is estimated by

$$\eta = 10\ LOG\ \frac{m^2}{\sigma^2} = 10\log\frac{5.6^2}{\sigma^2} = 18.57 (dB)$$

$$\sigma = \pm 0.660\ (mA)$$

The condition currently in use is that in run No. 2 of the inner array, as shown in Table 4.15; its S/N ratio improved by 6.17 (dB). From the existing to the optimum condition, its standard deviation was reduced by a fraction of 4.41.

The sensitivity at the optimum condition is estimated by

$$\overline{\mu s} = (24.69 + 2035 + \ldots + 17.13) - (8 \times 19.60) - 25.35\ (dB)$$

$$S = 10\log m^2 = 25.35\ (dB) \rightarrow m = 18.54\ (mA)$$

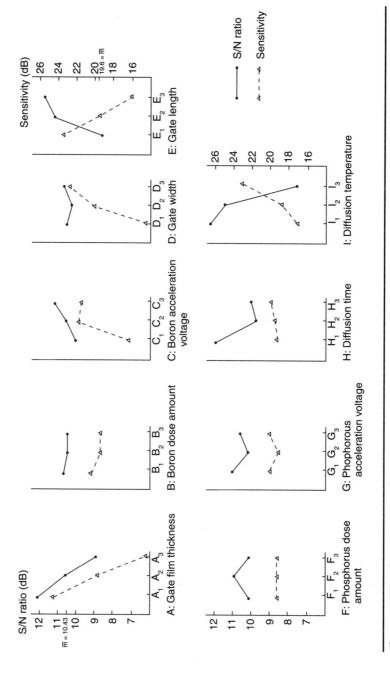

Figure 4.22 Response graphs.

Comparing this estimate with the target value we see that it is necessary to reduce the sensitivity by

$$14.96 - 25.35 = -10.39 \text{ (dB)}$$

This is equivalent to a reduction of 12.91 (mA) in terms of current.

The Optimum Condition after Adjusting Sensitivity

We want to adjust the mean to the target value without affecting variability. We must thus be able to adjust the sensitivity without affecting the S/N ratio too greatly. The following adjustment was made:

	S	η
D3→ D1;	−9.28 (dB)	−0.20 (dB)
B1→ B2;	−1.15 (dB)	−0.41 (dB)
	−10.43 (dB)	−0.61 (dB)

With this, the optimum condition now becomes:

A1   B2   C3   D1   E3   F2   G1   H1   I1

Its S/N ratio and sensitivity are estimated as:

$$\text{S/N ratio} \quad : \quad \eta = 17.96 \text{ (dB)}$$
$$\text{Sensitivity} \quad : \quad S = 14.92 \text{ (dB)}$$

This gives a 5.56 (dB) improvement in the S/N ratio, or a 3.60-fold reduction in error variance. The mean and the standard deviation for this condition are:

$$m = 5.57 \text{ (mA)}$$
$$\sigma = \pm\, 0.708 \text{ (mA)}$$

This was accomplished by using only two factors, B and C, to adjust the current to the target value. Because these factors had a lower effect on the S/N ratio, adjustment could be made while maintaining a small drain current variability.

Confirmation Using Model Simulation

S/N ratio and sensitivity estimates were calculated using the adjusted optimum condition for control factors as the nominal condition around which conditions were varied as per the outer array. From these results, the S/N ratio and sensitivity were calculated.

$$\text{SN ratio} \quad : \quad \eta = 14.779 \text{ (dB)} \qquad \sigma = \pm 0.962 \text{ (mA)}$$

$$\text{Sensitivity} \quad : \quad S = 14.440 \text{ (dB)} \qquad m = 5.275 \text{ (mA)}$$

Table 4.20 shows the ANOVA table for this condition.

Table 4.20 ANOVA table.

Factor	f	SS	MS	p (%)
A	2	9.1930	4.5965	28.3
B	2	0.0329	0.0164	
D	2	6.8780	3.4390	21.2
E	2	8.8978	4.4489	27.4
F	2	0.0026	0.0013	
H	2	0.0053	0.0026	
J	2	7.0745	3.5372	21.8
e	21	0.3111	0.0148	
e′	27	0.3519	0.0130	
	35	32.3953		100.0

f: degrees of freedom
SS: sum of squares
MS: mean squares
p: combination ratio
e: error
e′: pooled error

From the results of the ANOVA (Table 4.20), factors A, D, E, and J are seen to be significant for reducing variability. Because the condition presently has a smaller variability than the ranges shown in Table 4.12, we can expect more drain current stability. If the linear and quadratic effects of those factors were calculated, we could be even clearer about which items to further control.

4.3.5 Conclusions

Results of the study led to the following conclusions:

1. After the optimum condition was selected, the S/N ratio was improved by 6.17 (dB); the error variance was reduced by a fraction of 4.41. The current at that condition was 18.5 (mA).

2. After adjusting the sensitivity, the S/N ratio became 17.96 (dB). Compared to the previous condition, this was an improvement of 5.56 (dB). There was a 3.61-fold reduction in the error variance. The average current was then 5.57 (mA).

3. After sensitivity adjustment, an average current of m = 5.28 (mA) and a standard deviation of σ = ± 0.962 (mA) were obtained using the model. If the variability of gate film thickness, gate width, gate length, and wafer impurity concentration were reduced, it is possible that even more stable current can be maintained.

4. Only two control factors out of the nine in the study were needed to adjust the current to the target value. For factors diffusion time and diffusion temperature, which had little effect on S/N and sensitivity, lower cost levels were selected.

5. By using simulation, factors affecting variability can easily be determined at the design stage. Less expensive materials and conditions can also be selected, thereby achieving cost savings without affecting quality. This is an efficient and economical approach for achieving product stability.

SECTION II

Application of Robust Engineering Methods for Software Testing and Software Algorithm Optimization

5

Robust Software Testing

U ser-friendly software should perform its intended function under all usage conditions, known as active signals. Irrespective of the usage conditions, the user expects the desired results from the software just by following steps in the software's user manual. Therefore, the software designers should consider all the user conditions and test the software under them. It is not adequate to test the software under each of these conditions independently, because of the presence of interactions between them. To study these interactions, we need to test the software under all combinations of the user conditions, which will be very large and may not be feasible, if there are many conditions. Hence, there is a need to develop a method in which the number of combinations to be tested is minimal and adequate. In this chapter such a test procedure is developed by using the principles of robust engineering. The procedure is described with case studies. The method uses orthogonal arrays (OAs) to study the effect of two-factor (active signal) interactions. Usually, it is sufficient to test two-factor interactions because effects of higher order interactions are small and can be neglected.

5.1 Introduction

Good software should perform its intended function under all combinations of the user conditions. These user conditions are referred to as active signals and are used to get the desired output. Two examples of active signals are inserting an ATM card, punching the personal identification number (PIN), and selecting the desired transaction; and typing the address of an airline ticket–booking Web site and moving the mouse and using the keyboard to select flight schedules and get a price. For given software the user conditions are unique and may be very large in number. Usually, the designer tests the software's performance under the user conditions separately (like one factor at a time experiments). Even after such tests, the software sometimes fails because of the presence of interactions between the active signals. The presence of interactions can be explained by considering a train ticket reservation system.

Suppose a customer wants to buy two tickets and he opts for a window seat. Based on these requirements (signals), the software gives an output (ticket) with two window seats, which the customer may not prefer (usually he prefers two seats next to each other). This type of situation arises because of interactions. Therefore, the software designer must study all the interactions and take appropriate corrective actions before the release of the software. To be sure of the interaction effects, the software should be tested under various combinations of the signals.

The different states of the signal are referred to as the different levels. For a given signal the number of levels may be very high. In the case of the ATM transaction example, the levels for PIN may be from 0001 to 9999. If the number of such signals is very high, the number of possible combinations will be in billions. Since it is not feasible to test the software under all the combinations, a procedure must be found to minimize the number of combinations. This procedure should also be adequate for finding the effects of the signals and their interactions. In this chapter, such a method is developed by using the principles of robust engineering. The objective of this procedure is to obtain all possible two-factor interaction effects by conducting almost the same number of experiments as in the case of one-factor-at-a-time experiments. Since in most of the cases higher order interactions (higher than the second order) are not important, it is sufficient to test only the two-factor interactions.

5.2 Robust Engineering Methods for Software Testing

In this section, we will explain how the robust engineering methods can be used for testing software. This method of testing considers all the active signals. The important principles of robust engineering for software testing are:

1. Measurement of the performance of the software under different combinations of the user conditions/active signals

2. Use of orthogonal arrays to study two-factor interactions

Since there will be several levels of the usage conditions, it is adequate to limit the number of levels to two or three. These levels should be selected in such a way that the entire spectrum of usage conditions are covered. Usually, the levels, like low, middle, and high, could be selected. Figure 5.1 is a p-diagram that shows the typical software testing arrangement used for this approach. In this figure the noise factors correspond to the hardware conditions for the software. For the ATM example, the noise factor is the condition of the machine (old or new). Noise factors are not necessary for all software testing applications, so it is shown in a dotted box.

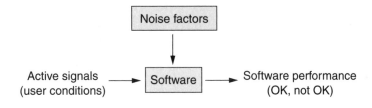

Figure 5.1 P-diagram for software testing.

Role of the Orthogonal Arrays

The purpose of using the orthogonal arrays in the robust design or the design of experiments is to estimate the effects of several factors and required interactions by minimizing the number of experiments. In the case of software testing, the purpose of using the OAs is to study all the two-factor interactions with a minimum number of experiments. In fact the number of combinations with OAs is almost equal to the number of experiments to be conducted with one-factor-at-a time.

Let us suppose that there are 23 active signals, 11 with two levels and the remaining 12 with three levels. If we want to study all the two-factor combinations, the total number of experiments in this case would be:

The number of two-level factor combinations	$= 4 \times (^{11}C_2)$	$= 220$ combinations
The number of three-level factor combinations	$= 9 \times (^{12}C_2)$	$= 594$ combinations
The number of two-level and three-level factors	$= 6 \times 11 \times 12$	$= 792$ combinations

Total	1606

Depending on the number of signal factors and their levels, a suitable OA is selected. For this example, if a suitable OA is used the number of combinations to be run would be 36. The OAs are typically denoted as L_a ($2^b \times 3^c$) where L denotes the Latin square design; a is the number of runs (combinations); b is the number of two-level signal factors, and c is the number of three-level signal factors. The array to be used for this example is L_{36} ($2^{11} \times 3^{12}$).

5.3 Method of Software Testing

For the purpose of explanation the same example of 23 signals is used. Let A, B, C, . . . , L, M, . . . ,U, V, W represent these 23 factors. The signal factors are allocated to the different columns of the L_{36} array as shown in Table 5.1. In the array the numbers 1, 2, 3 correspond to the different levels of the signals. The 36 combinations in Table 5.1 have to be run to obtain the effect of two-factor interactions. The response for each combination is 0 or 1. 0 means the software function is satisfactory, and 1 means the software has bugs.

Table 5.1   Signal factor allocation in L_{36} ($2^{11}X3^{12}$) array.

Signal factor	A	B	.....	L	M	.....	V	W	
Run\column	1	2	.....	12	13	.....	22	23	Response
1	1	1		1	1	.....	1	1	0 or 1
2	1	1		2	2	.....	2	2	0 or1
3	1	1		3	3	.....	3	3	0 or 1
4	1	1		1	1	.....	3	3	0 or 1
5	1	1		2	2	.....	1	1	0 or 1
6	1	1		3	3	.....	2	2	0 or 1
7	1	1		1	1	.....	2	3	0 or 1
8	1	1		2	2	.....	3	1	0 or 1
9	1	1		3	3	.....	1	2	0 or 1
10	1	2		1	1	.....	3	2	0 or 1
11	1	2		2	2	.....	1	3	0 or 1
.....	...	...	.....	...	...	.....	...	...	...
32	2	2		2	1	.....	2	2	0 or 1
33	2	2		3	2	.....	3	3	0 or 1
34	2	2		1	3	.....	3	1	0 or 1
35	2	2		2	1	.....	1	2	0 or 1
36	2	2		3	2	.....	2	3	0 or 1

5.3.1 Study of Two-Factor Interactions

Since the L_{36} array contains two-level and three-level factors, the following three types of two-factor interactions have to be studied:

1. Interaction between two-level factors

2. Interaction between three-level factors

3. Interaction between two-level and three-level factors

If A and B are two factors, the total number of a particular two-factor combination in an OA can be obtained by the following equation:

$$n_{ij} = \frac{n_{i.} \times n_{.j}}{N} \qquad (5.1)$$

where n_{ij} = the number of combinations of ith level of A and j^{th} level of B

$n_{i.}$ = the number of ith levels of A in a column that is assigned to A

$n_{.j}$ = the number of jth levels of B in a column that is assigned to B

N = total number of experimental runs in the array

5.3.2 Construction of Interaction Tables

For the purpose of discussion, let us consider the two-level factors A and B. These factors are assigned to the columns 1 and 2 of the OA. For these factors, the possible combinations are A1B1, A1B2, A2B1, and A2B2. Where A1 and A2 correspond to the first and second level of factor A and B1 and B2 are the first and second levels of the factor B. The number of these combinations can be obtained by Equation 5.1. For this example, the number of combinations of A1B1 is equal to (18 x 18)/36, which is 9. Similarly, the number of other combinations is also equal to 9. For checking the effect of interactions, we have to check how many times the software had failed in a given combination. If the software fails at all times, there is something wrong with that combination and the software designer has to fix this combination. In this example, for a particular combination if the software fails all the times (9 times), the software designer has to look into this combination. Since the responses for the combinations of the OAs are 0s or 1s, the number of 1s will determine the combination (interaction) to be fixed. The number of ones can be obtained by constructing the interaction tables. In L_{36} array the number of such tables is $^{11}C_2$, which is 55. For the two factors A and B, such a table looks like Table 5.2.

Table 5.2   Interaction table for two-level factors.

Factor A/Factor B	B1	B2
A1	No. of 1s	No. of 1s
A2	No. of 1s	No. of 1s

In a similar way, interaction tables for three-level factors and a combination of two-level and three-level factors can be constructed. Examples of three-level factor interaction and two-level and three-level factor interaction are shown in Tables 5.3 and 5.4, respectively. The combinations with all ones are to be fixed by the software designer.

Table 5.3   Interaction table for three-level factors.

Factor L/Factor M	M1	M2	M3
L1	No. of 1s	No. of 1s	No. of 1s
L2	No. of 1s	No. of 1s	No. of 1s
L3	No. of 1s	No. of 1s	No. of 1s

Table 5.4   Interaction table for three-level factors.

Factor A/Factor W	W1	W2	W3
A1	No. of 1s	No. of 1s	No. of 1s
A2	No. of 1s	No. of 1s	No. of 1s

The total number of interaction tables for L_{36} array is = 55(two-level factors) + 66 (three-level factors) + 132 (two-level and three-level factors) = 253. Thus, using L_{36} array we can study all 1606 combinations by conducting only 36 experiments and constructing the interaction tables.

From the above discussions, the steps required to test software can be summarized as follows:

1. Identification of active signals and their levels

2. Selection of a suitable OA for testing

3. Conducting the test for different combinations of an OA

4. Constructing the interaction tables

5. Identification of significant interactions (by counting the number of 1s)

It should be noted that this method helps in reducing most of the bugs in given software. In some cases, even after applying this method the software may still have a few bugs because of the presence of higher order interactions. Even if the number of active signals is very high, orthogonal arrays of higher size can be constructed to accommodate the signals.

5.4 Case Study 1: Efficient Method for Software Debugging with the Orthogonal Array

This case study was performed by Jyunichi Deguch, Kazuhiro Kajimoto, and Kei Takada of Seiko Epson Company, Japan. We thank them for allowing us to use this study in the book.

5.4.1 Summary

Most of the cost associated in software is in debugging. Many studies of debugging tools in software engineering say they are difficult to use. In this study, robust engineering methods are used to perform software debugging. The signal factors were assigned to an L_{18} orthogonal array, and the combinations were tested using the procedure outlined earlier in the chapter. The fÀ-version of software that was developed in Seiko Epson was used for testing. With 18 combinations of L_{18} array, it was possible to discover several bugs. In this case study, the detailed method of testing of fÀ-version of software is explained.

5.4.2 Introduction

Debugging is a very important activity in software development and requires most of the time spent on the project. When bugs are found after the project is shipped, the reputation of a company goes down drastically. In recent years, through advances in Internet technology, it is possible to distribute a beta version of the software to users to obtain their feedback. Using their feedback, one can test the software more efficiently and modify its features. However, it is important to develop robust software with minimum bugs before shipping it to the user. There is no standardized way to test the software. When the person in charge of debugging changes, the method of debugging will also change and, therefore, the quality of software will change. Therefore, there is a need to develop a method that gives minimum bugs at the lowest possible cost and is independent of the person in charge of development.

5.4.3 Use of Orthogonal Array for Debugging

The proposed method is as follows. This method is to evaluate a system's objective function to many signals (user commands), by the use of the design of experiments technique of the Taguchi methods. The experiment allocates the item (the signal factor, user command) that users can set up to the orthogonal array. Next, software is tested with all combinations of the orthogonal array. If the output is different from the signals intended by user, bugs exist in the software and the response is "1." When the output is correct, there is no error and the response is "0." The data are analyzed through analysis of variance (ANOVA) to identify the combinations and factors responsible for bugs.

Experimental Details

For debugging software, eight signal factors were selected and were assigned to L_{18} $(2^1 \times 3^7)$ array. The selection of levels for signal factors is done as follows: If the range of factors is 0~100 like a continuous variable, the levels 0, 50, and 100 are selected; for discrete with alternate selection from 5 patterns 1~5, three levels are selected. Those factors with two levels can be assigned to a three-level column by dummy treatment (dummy levels are denoted with '). The factors and levels are given in Table 5.5. Here factors and levels are not shown because of proprietary reasons.

Table 5.5   Signal factors and levels.

	1	2	3
A	A1	A2	
B	B1	B2	B3
C	C1	C2	C3
D	D1	D2	D3
E	E1	E2	*E2'*
F	F1	F2	*F1'*
G	G1	G2	*G1'*
H	H1	H2	H3

' indicates dummy level.

Table 5.6 shows factor allocation and test results for L_{18} $(2^1 \times 3^7)$ array.

Table 5.6 Debugging with L_{18} $(2^1 \times 3^7)$ array.

	A	B	C	D	E	F	G	H	Result
1	1	1	1	1	1	1	1	0	0
2	1	1	2	2	2	2	2	2	0
3	1	1	3	3	2′	1′	1′	3	1
4	1	2	1	1	2	2	1′	3	1
5	1	2	2	2	2′	1′	1	1	0
6	1	2	3	3	1	1	2	2	0
7	1	3	1	2	1	1′	2	3	0
8	1	3	2	3	2	1	1′	1	0
9	1	3	3	1	2′	2	1	2	0
10	2	1	1	3	2′	2	2	1	0
11	2	1	2	1	1	1′	1′	2	0
12	2	1	3	2	2	1	1	3	1
13	2	2	1	2	2′	1	1′	2	0
14	2	2	2	3	1	2	1	3	1
15	2	2	3	1	2	1′	2	1	0
16	2	3	1	3	2	1′	1	2	0
17	2	3	2	1	2′	1	2	3	0
18	2	3	3	2	1	2	1′	1	0

′ indicates dummy levels.

Analysis of Experimental Results

The results of the L_{18} $(2^1 \times 3^7)$ array are given in Table 5.7. The calculation of effects of factors A and B are as follows: The number of bugs with the combination of A1B1 is summed up, and the number of bugs with A1B2, A1B3, A2B1, A2B2, A2B3 is summed up, in a similar way. This calculation is carried out with all factor combinations from A to H. The success or failure of a combination is evaluated in the following way: if you consider H3, it has four failures out of six trials where it is present (Table 5.6). However, the bug is not entirely caused by H3. So, let us look at the H and G two-way table. The bug occurs 100 percent of the time when H3 is present with G1 (G3) and H3. (G1 and G3 are the same level because G3 is a dummy level of G1. Since G has only two levels, it was assigned to a three-level column of the L_{18} array with the dummy level, which is G1). When there is such interaction effects, they need to be addressed so that software is minimally affected by bugs.

Table 5.7 Combinations of orthogonal array.

	B1	B2	B3	C1	C2	C3	D1	D2	D3	E1	E2	*E2'*	F1	F2	*F1'*	G1	G2	*G1'*	H1	H2	H3	Total
A1	1	1	0	1	0	1	1	0	1	0	1	1	0	1	1	0	0	2	0	0	2	2
A2	1	1	0	0	1	1	0	1	1	1	1	0	1	1	0	2	0	0	0	0	2	2
B1				0	0	2	0	1	1	0	1	1	1	0	1	1	0	1	0	0	2	2
B2				1	1	0	1	0	1	1	1	0	0	2	0	1	0	1	0	0	2	2
B3				0	0	0	0	0	0	0	0	0	0	0	0	0	0	0	0	0	0	0
C1							1	0	0	0	1	0	0	1	0	0	0	1	0	0	1	1
C2							0	0	1	1	0	0	0	1	0	1	0	0	0	0	1	1
C3							0	1	1	0	1	1	1	0	1	1	0	1	0	0	2	2
D1										0	1	0	0	1	0	0	0	1	0	0	1	1
D2										0	1	0	1	0	0	1	0	0	0	0	1	1
D3										1	0	1	0	1	1	1	0	1	0	0	2	2
E1													0	1	0	1	0	0	0	0	1	1
E2													1	1	0	1	0	1	0	0	2	2
E2'													0	0	1	0	0	1	0	0	1	1
F1																1	0	0	0	0	1	1
F2																1	0	1	0	0	2	2
F1'																0	0	1	0	0	1	1
G1																			0	0	2	2
G2																			0	0	0	0
G1'																			0	0	2	2
Total for H																			0	0	4	4

From Table 5.7, it is clear that the following combinations need to be looked into and addressed:

B1H3, B2H3, B2E2, C3H3, D3H3, F2H3, and G1H3

5.4.4 Comparison between Old Method and This Method

A discussion of the comparison between the old method and this method is provided in a tabular form in Table 5.8. This discussion is reported by people who conducted this study.

Table 5.8 Comparison between old method and this method.

	Old method	Orthogonal array
Efficiency of the discovery of bugs	• Lot of tests are carried out • Independent effects	• Fewer trails • Independent and combined effects
Area coverage	• Empirically decided • Not all user conditions are considered	• By using the orthogonal array, it is decided objectively • The balance of the combination is good • Checks over a wide area are possible
Software inspection inspection resources	• Very tedious check sheet and report with many pages • Need to conduct all combinations in the check sheet	• Test engineer decides factors and levels. The combination is selected using OAs • The number of combinations is small with a large number of factors
Detect ability	• Each level is inspected with one at a time test. Therefore, not easy to find combined effects.	• Through this analysis, bugs and contributing effects are identified based on data
Decision making	• It is easy since it does not evaluate combination effect	• Need to make two-way tables and make a decision

5.4.5 Conclusions

This method of testing was applied to the software developed by another company. The team conducting the test identified bugs. That means we can use this method to assess the robustness of our competitor's system and perform benchmarking.

Seiko Epson reported that users have sued some companies over bugs. Fortunately, this company has not been sued by users. Seiko Epson recognizes the criticality of introducing a robust testing method to avoid such situations, and the company is planning to introduce this method in all testing activities.

5.5 Case Study 2

This study was conducted by Masahiko Suginuwa and Kazuya Inoue of Omron Company in Japan.

The software performance was to be analyzed with 23 signals. These signals were identified as A, B, C, . . . ,U, V, W. For these factors suitable levels were selected. Table 5.9 shows some of the signal factors with chosen levels.

Table 5.9 Signal factors and number of levels.

Signal	A	L	M	N	O	P	B	...	W	K
Number of levels	2	3	3	3	3	3	2	...	3	2

The factors A, B, C, . . . , U, V, W were assigned to the different columns of L_{36} array as described before. The results of the 36 combinations are shown in Table 5.10.

Table 5.10 Results of the different combinations of L$_{36}$ array.

Experiment no	1	2	3	4	5	6	7	8	9	10	11	12	13	14	15	16	17	18
Response	1	0	0	0	1	1	0	1	0	0	1	1	0	0	0	0	0	0
Experiment no	19	20	21	22	23	24	25	26	27	28	29	30	31	32	33	34	35	36
Response	0	0	0	1	0	1	0	0	0	0	1	0	1	0	0	0	0	0

0: performance OK
1: performance not OK

5.5.1 Analysis of Results

With the help of the results of Table 5.11, the two-way interaction tables were constructed. As mentioned before, for the signals in L$_{36}$ array, the total number of two-way tables is 253. Out of all the two-factor combinations, only two combinations were considered important, as both had 100 percent errors. These combinations are K2W1 and Q1S1. These combinations are shown with arrows in Table 5.11. The combinations of K and W and Q and S are separately shown in Tables 5.12 and 5.13.

Table 5.11 Main table showing two-way interactions.

	B1	B2	...	C1	C2	...	D1	D2	...	S1	S2	S3	...	W1	W2	W3
A1	4	2		5	1		3	3						4	1	1
A2	2	2		1	3		2	2						3	1	0
B1				3	3		3	3						4	2	0
B2				3	1		1	3						3	0	1
C1							3	3						4	1	1
C2							3	1						3	1	0
...																
...																
K1														1	0	0
K2												→		6	2	1
...																
...																
Q1										4	0	0				
Q2							→			1	1	0				
Q3										1	1	2				
...																
S1																
S2																
S3																
...																
V1														3	0	1
V2														3	1	0
V3														1	1	0

Table 5.12 Combinations of K & W.

	W1	W2	W3	Total
K1	1	0	0	1
K2	6	2	1	9
Total	7	2	1	10

Table 5.13 Combinations of Q & S.

	S1	S2	S3	Total
Q1	4	0	0	4
Q2	1	1	0	2
Q3	1	1	2	4
Total	6	2	2	10

In Table 5.12 the different combinations of K and W are obtained (from the L_{36} array) as follows: K1W1 from runs 1, 15, 16, 20, 27, 34; K1W2 from runs 2, 13, 17, 21, 25, 35; K1W3 from runs 3, 14, 18, 19, 26, 36; K2W1 from runs 5, 8, 12, 24, 29, 31; K2W2 from runs 6, 9, 10, 22, 30, 32; K2W3 from runs 4, 7, 11, 23, 28, 33.

The combinations of Table 5.13 are obtained in a similar way. The combinations Q1S1 (which has 100 percent errors) is obtained from runs 1, 6, 11, 23 of the L_{36} array.

5.5.2 Debugging the Software

After identifying the significant interactions, suitable corrective actions were taken. After taking the corrective actions again, 36 runs of the L_{36} array were conducted. It was found that in these runs all the responses were 0s indicating that there were no bugs in the software.

5.6 Different Testing Procedures

The method of software testing differs depending on the type of software application. A description of different methods is given below:

5.6.1 Printer Driver Type

There are many inputs. The output is just one response, success or failure. This type is most easy to inspect. For example, the signal factor of "the kind of paper" or "the enlargement" or "the reduction" or "the monochrome color" is selected in the case of the printer driver.

A test engineer does the printing job with the combination from the orthogonal array. The signal factor and the result that was printed are compared. If the quality of printing meets standards and satisfies the test engineer, the output becomes "0." If the result is different from the intended output, the output becomes "1." The analysis is carried out by using 0 and 1.

5.6.2 Robot Control Software Type

Suppose the robot's task is to "Move a block" or "Move a stick." When there is a failure it can be due to the block or stick. In this case, we need to judge whether it is necessary to record a response separately for "block position" and "stick position."

For example, "the position of the block" and "the position of the stick" are allocated to the orthogonal array as input command. Then we record "correctness of block position" and "correctness of stick position." Sometimes we need to evaluate more than one task for each combination of the orthogonal array. However, the number of combinations remains the same. Seiko Epson Company is applying this approach to test software for robotics.

5.6.3 Word Processor Software Type

The function of the software for a word processor is very complicated. The word processor not only writes letters but also prints pictures and draws tables. The pictures and tables must be arranged as required by the user. In such a case, we need to look at one function at a time. The signal factor (input command) that relates to the function is inspected. The output is compared with the specifications. We can test functions one by one, just as we did for the simple case of the printer driver discussed earlier.

5.7 Testing of Copy Machine Operation

The software testing procedure can be easily extended for testing other products. We describe the steps to be followed with a copy machine as an example.

> **Step 1: Determine factors and levels.** Factors are operation variables and levels are alternatives for operations. Assign them to an Orthogonal Array as shown in table 5.14.

Table 5.14 Assignment of factors and levels.

	Factors	Level 1	Level 2	Level 3
A	Staple	No	Yes	
B	Side	2 to 1	1 to 2	2 to 2
C	Number of copies	3	20	50
D	Number of pages	2	20	50
E	Paper tray	Tray 6	Tray 5 (LS)	Tray 3 (OHP)
F	Darkness	Normal	Light	Dark
G	Enlarge	78%	100%	128%
H	Execution	At machine	From PC	Memory

$L_{18} (2^1 \times 3^7)$

Response:

$$y = \begin{cases} 0 \text{ if no problem} \\ 1 \text{ if trouble} \end{cases}$$

> **Step 2: Run the test.** Test each run of orthogonal array as shown in Table 5.15. The response, y, is either 0 or 1 where $y = 1$ when trouble exists and $y = 0$ otherwise.

> **Step 3: Construct a response table.** A response table is constructed by adding 1s for each combination of two factors, A x B, A x C, . . . , G x H. It is okay to do this without assigning interactions.

Table 5.15 $L_{18}(2^1 \times 3^7)$ experimental setup.

	A	B	C	D	E	F	G	H	
	1	2	3	4	5	6	7	8	1=Trouble
1	1	1	1	1	1	1	1	1	0
2	1	1	2	2	2	2	2	2	0
3	1	1	3	3	3	3	3	3	0
4	1	2	1	1	2	2	3	3	0
5	1	2	2	2	3	3	1	1	1
6	1	2	3	3	1	1	2	2	1
7	1	3	1	2	1	3	2	3	0
8	1	3	2	3	2	1	3	1	0
9	1	3	3	1	3	2	1	2	0
10	2	1	1	3	3	2	2	1	0
11	2	1	2	1	1	3	3	2	0
12	2	1	3	2	2	1	1	3	0
13	2	2	1	2	3	1	3	2	0
14	2	2	2	3	1	2	1	3	0
15	2	2	3	1	2	3	2	1	1
16	2	3	1	3	2	3	1	2	0
17	2	3	2	1	3	1	2	3	0
18	2	3	3	2	1	2	3	1	0

Step 4: Look for 100 percent failure combination. Please refer to table 5.16. Since there are nine combinations of BiCj, there are two runs of B2C3 condition in L18. The total failure is two under B2C3, that indicates 100 percent failure for B2C3. Likewise, 100 percent failure occurred for B2F3, B2G2, C3G2, H1F3. Now the software developer must investigate these combinations. In general, for the combination AiBj to generate 100 percent failure the total must be: Size of Array / # of combinations AiBj. For this example, for A1B1 to become a 100 percent failure, the total must be 3 (18 / 6 = 3).

Table 5.16 Analysis of test results (two-way tables).

	A 1	B 2	C 3	D 4	E 5	F 6	G 7	H 8	
1	1	1	1	1	1	1	1	1	0
2	1	1	2	2	2	2	2	2	0
3	1	1	3	3	3	3	3	3	0
4	1	2	1	1	2	2	3	3	0
5	1	2	2	2	3	3	1	1	1
6	1	2	3	3	1	1	2	2	1
7	1	3	1	2	1	3	2	3	0
8	1	3	2	3	2	1	3	1	0
9	1	3	3	1	3	2	1	2	0
10	2	1	1	3	3	2	2	1	0
11	2	1	2	1	1	3	3	2	0
12	2	1	3	2	2	1	1	3	0
13	2	2	1	2	3	1	3	2	0
14	2	2	2	3	1	2	1	3	0
15	2	2	3	1	2	3	2	1	1
16	2	3	1	3	2	3	1	2	0
17	2	3	2	1	3	1	2	3	0
18	2	3	3	2	1	2	3	1	0

	A1	A2
B1	0	0
B2	2	1
B3	0	0

	A1	A2	B1	B2	B3
C1	0	0	0	0	0
C2	1	0	0	1	0
C3	1	1	0	2	0

	A1	A2	B1	B2	B3	C1	C2	C3
D1	0	1	0	1	0	0	0	1
D2	1	0	0	1	0	0	1	0
D3	1	0	0	1	0	0	0	1

	A1	A2	B1	B2	B3	C1	C2	C3	D1	D2	D3
E1	1	0	0	1	0	0	0	1	0	0	1
E2	0	1	0	1	0	0	0	1	1	0	0
E3	1	0	0	1	0	0	1	0	0	1	0

	A1	A2	B1	B2	B3	C1	C2	C3	D1	D2	D3	E1	E2	E3
F1	1	0	0	1	0	0	0	1	0	0	1	1	0	0
F2	0	0	0	0	0	0	0	0	0	0	0	0	0	0
F3	1	1	0	2	0	0	1	1	1	1	0	0	1	1

	A1	A2	B1	B2	B3	C1	C2	C3	D1	D2	D3	E1	E2	E3	F1	F2	F3
G1	1	0	0	1	0	0	1	0	0	1	0	0	0	1	0	0	1
G2	1	1	0	2	0	0	0	2	1	0	1	1	1	0	1	0	1
G3	0	0	0	0	0	0	0	0	0	0	0	0	0	0	0	0	0

	A1	A2	B1	B2	B3	C1	C2	C3	D1	D2	D3	E1	E2	E3	F1	F2	F3	G1	G2	G3
H1	1	1	0	2	0	0	1	1	1	1	0	0	1	1	0	0	2	1	1	0
H2	1	0	0	1	0	0	0	1	0	0	1	1	0	0	1	0	0	0	1	0
H3	0	0	0	0	0	0	0	0	0	0	0	0	0	0	0	0	0	0	0	0

The two-way response tables can also be shown in terms of percentage of failures, as shown in Table 5.17.

Step 5: Investigate those combinations with 100 percent failures. In this step the combinations responsible for bugs are investigated.

Table 5.17 Two-way response tables (in terms of percent failures).

	A1	A2	B1	B2	B3	C1	C2	C3	D1	D2	D3	E1	E2	E3	F1	F2	F3	G1	G2	G3
B1	0%	0%																		
B2	67%	33%																		
B3	0%	0%																		
C1	0%	0%	0%	50%	0%															
C2	33%	0%	0%	50%	0%															
C3	33%	33%	0%	100%	0%															
D1	0%	33%	0%	50%	0%	0%	0%	50%												
D2	33%	0%	0%	50%	0%	0%	50%	0%												
D3	33%	0%	0%	50%	0%	0%	0%	50%												
E1	33%	0%	0%	50%	0%	0%	0%	50%	0%	0%	50%									
E2	0%	33%	0%	50%	0%	0%	0%	50%	50%	0%	0%									
E3	33%	0%	0%	50%	0%	0%	50%	0%	0%	50%	0%									
F1	33%	0%	0%	50%	0%	0%	0%	0%	0%	50%	0%	50%	0%	0%						
F2	0%	0%	0%	0%	0%	0%	0%	100%	50%	0%	50%	0%	0%	0%						
F3	33%	33%	0%	100%	0%	0%	50%	50%	0%	0%	0%	0%	0%	50%						
G1	33%	0%	0%	50%	0%	0%	50%	0%	50%	50%	0%	0%	50%	50%	0%	0%	50%			
G2	33%	33%	0%	100%	0%	0%	0%	50%	0%	0%	50%	50%	0%	0%	50%	0%	50%			
G3	0%	0%	0%	0%	0%	0%	0%	0%	0%	0%	0%	0%	0%	0%	0%	0%	0%			
H1	33%	33%	0%	100%	0%	0%	50%	50%	50%	50%	0%	0%	50%	50%	0%	0%	100%	50%	50%	0%
H2	33%	0%	0%	50%	0%	0%	50%	0%	0%	0%	50%	50%	0%	0%	50%	0%	0%	0%	50%	0%
H3	0%	0%	0%	0%	0%	0%	0%	0%	0%	0%	0%	0%	0%	0%	0%	0%	0%	0%	0%	0%

When Some Runs Are Not Feasible

Suppose there are some infeasible combinations due to the nature of the testing. For example, in making flight reservation with an airline, "return date" is not applicable when booking a one-way trip. In the previous example, if E3:OHP is used B2: 1side 2side, and B3: 2side 2 side are not applicable, then simply record "Not applicable in response table" as shown in Table 5.18. However, if you want to test whether the system behaves correctly in such infeasible situations, you can ignore this. You need to make a technical judgment.

Table 5.18   Tables for infeasible runs.

	B1	B2	B3
E1	0	1	0
E2	0	1	0
E3	0	1	0

⇨

	B1	B2	B3
E1	0	1	0
E2	0	1	0
E3	0	NA	NA

5.8 Conclusions

From the above discussions, the following conclusions can be drawn:

- Principles of robust engineering can be applied for efficient software testing that eliminates most of the bugs.

- The user conditions are viewed as the active signals.

- It is important to test the performance of the software under different combinations of user conditions because of the presence of interactions between the active signals.

- Orthogonal arrays are used in studying all the two-factor interactions by conducting almost the same number of experiments as one-factor-at-a-time experiments do.

- Even if the number of active signals is very high, orthogonal arrays of higher size can be constructed to accommodate these signals.

- This software testing procedure can be easily extended to testing other products.

6

Software Algorithm Optimization

In Chapter 5, we discussed software testing using robust engineering methods. In this chapter we will discuss how to optimize software algorithms. The optimization procedure is similar to that of optimizing product/process by using simulation-based robust engineering. We will describe the procedure of optimizing software algorithms is described with the help of case studies.

6.1 Case Study 1: Robust Formation of Mobile Wireless Networks

This case study was carried out by Dr. Ning H. Lu of ITT A/CD, Advanced Systems. We thank the author for presenting this case study in the 2000 robust engineering symposium.

6.1.1 Summary

This case study is related to the application of a network formation algorithm for an ad hoc mobile wireless network. Here, an approach to optimizing the network formation algorithm is presented. The proposed algorithm was derived from a gradient search technique. The Taguchi robust design approach was used to optimize the algorithm so that the underlying network performance is least sensitive to changing environments and other uncontrollable factors. Results show that the Taguchi robust design approach increases the normalized system throughput performance by more than 50% without a loss in robustness. Future research activities will focus on a rule-based learning mechanism that can easily be adapted to new operating scenarios and/or operational needs. Furthermore, we will consider the development of a real-time automated Taguchi optimization module (ATOM) that resides on every node and operates on the local noise factors and exchanges relevant information on a global basis to enhance the overall system performance.

6.1.2 Introduction

Network formation is the first step of creating a self-organizing mobile wireless network, upon which communications among mobile nodes can be made. How well the network is formed directly impacts the throughput performance and the stability of the network. The formation process is considered to be the most crucial and difficult phase of ad hoc mobile networking. This is because during the formation process it has the least amount of information about the network. This study first characterizes the network formation and then develops a self-forming algorithm to solve problems. A two-tier network hierarchy [1–4], consisting of self-organized tier-1 cells interconnected through a self-configured backbone, was used as the networking baseline. The proposed self-forming algorithm was derived from a gradient search technique. The Taguchi robust design approach was used to optimize the self-forming algorithm so that the underlying network performance is least sensitive to changing environments and other uncontrollable factors. We first conducted the matrix experiment based on the L_{18} ($1^2 \times 7^3$) orthogonal array with eight control factors and dynamic signals, characterized the sensitivity due to variations of the control factor levels, and then determined optimum factor levels for our design.

This section of the chapter is organized as follows. Section 6.2 reviews the background and states the problem formulation. Section 6.3 addresses the problems and issues of designing such a system and presents the gradient search approach. Section 6.4 summarizes the results of self-forming algorithm. Finally, in Section 6.5 concluding remarks are provided, future research topics are identified, and a system architecture for the real-time ATOM is proposed.

6.1.3 Problem Formulation

The challenges of ad hoc mobile wireless networking are numerous. These include dynamically managing network resources to support end-to-end quality of service (QoS)–based services, matching information to users needs, and facilitating robust operations. To support such a QoS-based system, we must have an efficient and effective resource management mechanism that tracks the status of resources and anticipates the supply and demand. It can then allocate the available resources most effectively to the user. Our solution to this problem is based on a cell-based resource management concept in which a network is made by a collection of dynamically formed cells with each cell fully aware of its resources.

Effective resource management is essential to the quality and efficiency of system performance to support a wide range of services with different requirements. For example, the key components of communications resources in a local cell are timing, code, frequency, spatial, processing, bandwidth, energy, and so forth. The radio resource management function keeps track of the status of these resources and allocates resources according to user needs. One component of radio resources is power control. The principal objective is to provide each node with a quality of service that does not interfere with other nodes.

The Network Formation Algorithm

Cell-based formation dynamically organizes the mobile nodes into a set of cells covering an entire node population. A distributed, self-organizing, cell-based formation approach was developed for this task. Basically, each cell has a cell coordinator that is dynamically elected by the members in the cell. A cell coordinator allocates resources, such as time slots, power, codes, frequency channels, and spatial sectors, to the nodes within the cell. Since every node in a cell is directly linked to the cell coordinator, each cell coordinator also serves as a local broadcast node. This provides an effective framework for organizing a dynamic mobile wireless network. The network formation algorithm (Lu, 1999) based on the gradient search technique (Lu, 1998) is described below:

1. Initialize the search procedure with appropriate preference settings (e.g., the maximum number of cell members per cell, the maximum cell radius, etc.)

2. Compute the gradient of transconductance versus the radio density relative to a given node.

3. Search for the best set of cell coordinators while satisfying the preference constraints.

4. Affiliate members to the respective cell coordinators while providing the best fit to the organizational constraints.

5. Compute and identify the second best cell coordinator as its backup for each cell and their member sets.

6. Repeat procedures 2 through 5.

6.1.4 Robust Design

The Taguchi robust design approach was used to analyze the error sensitivity due to noise factors and to determine the most robust settings for system parameters. The goal was to make the design least sensitive to changing environments while minimizing degradations due to noise factors that are impossible to control or expensive to control.

Traditionally, for full system tradeoffs, engineers analyze varying levels of one factor or few factors at a time against constant levels of the other factors for various scenarios until all combinations have been exhausted. This full factorial design, examining every possible permutation of the combined factors, would normally require extensive efforts. For a relatively complex system, full factorial design very quickly becomes too large, too unwieldy, and far too expensive and/or time-consuming. Thus, to analyze controlling the performance factors for the desired system optimality is particularly difficult because of the dimension of the problem. Furthermore, to gain insight of the problem, experimentation must be done with parameters jointly controlled.

The matrix experiment defined by the Taguchi robust design approach was particularly effective in solving this problem. It exploits orthogonality of the factor space and uses the variability concept of desirables to significantly reduce the size and dimension of the problem. It uses interactions between control factors and noise factors to the output S/N ratio. When the trade-off confirms, there shall be no severe interaction among control factors to the variability of the desirables in the face of noises. The matrix experiment consists of a minimum set of tests that completely characterize a system under evaluation. The test matrix is organized as orthogonal arrays, allowing the influence effects of several control factors to be characterized and optimized jointly and efficiently, and it defines the minimum set of tests. The minimum set of tests spanning the total test space provides a significant reduction in the number of experiments required. Compared to a full factorial experiment, the number of test cases required for the matrix experiment is much fewer. The orthogonal arrays form the test cases such that the system response function can be analyzed individually for each of the orthogonal components. We considered the matrix experiment based on the L_{18} $(1^2 \times 7^3)$ orthogonal array with eight control factors, which will be detailed below.

System Process Diagram (P-Diagram)

Since cells are formed on the basis that all cell members are within direct communication range of the cluster head, network formation is thus influenced by factors including RF transmit power/range, terrain conditions, node density, EMI conditions, mobility, antenna orientation, and the cell's traffic patterns. The cell structure hides intracell topology from the units outside the cell, which maximizes frequency reuse, network throughput, and energy efficiency. The system process diagram (P-diagram) is shown in Figure 6.1, highlighting the main functions of the system, the input, the output, key noise factors, and control factors.

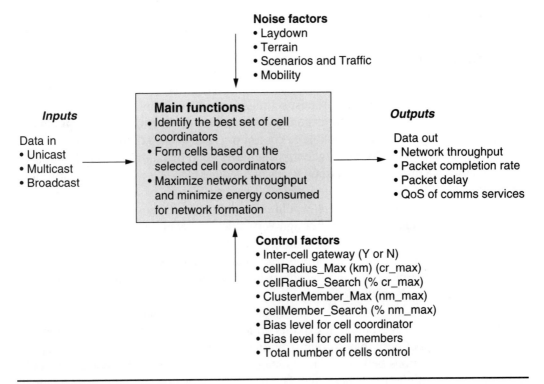

Figure 6.1 The system process diagram.

Ideal Function

Since the objective is to maximize the network throughput while ensuring energy efficiency, the ideal function (IF) can be formulated as the network throughput normalized by the total broadcast energy required for a fully connected network. That is,

$$I.F. = \frac{T}{\sum_{i=1}^{n} E_i} \tag{6.1}$$

The IF has desirable energy transfer characteristics. Therefore, this is a dynamic response problem, and the objective is to maximize the sensitivity of the IF (i.e., the larger-the-better problem shown in Figure 6.2).

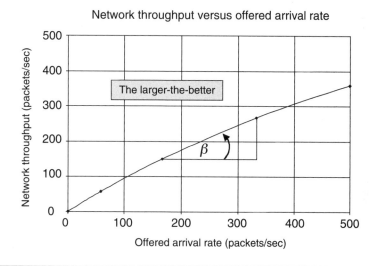

Figure 6.2   Ideal function.

Signal Strategy and Noise Strategy

To properly stress the experiment and evaluate for a wide range of operating conditions, we have considered the following signal and noise strategy:

1. Signal strategy: Various input offered loads in packets per second

   - 100 packets/sec (normalized load: $M1 = 0.2$)

   - 200 packets/sec (normalized load: $M2 = 0.4$)

   - 300 packets/sec (normalized load: $M3 = 0.6$)

- 400 packets/sec (normalized load: $M4 = 0.8$)

- 500 packets/sec (normalized load: $M5 = 1.0$)

2. Noise strategy: Compounded noise effect from noise factors such as the effects from laydown, terrain, node density, EMI conditions, mobility, antenna orientation; the resultant effect is the loss between transmitters and receivers.

Factor Levels and Matrix Experiments

We conducted the matrix experiment based on the L_{18} $(1^2 \times 7^3)$ orthogonal array with eight control factors and dynamic signals. The eight control factors used in our analysis and their factor levels are shown in Table 6.1.

Table 6.1 $\quad L_{18}$ $(1^2 \times 7^3)$ orthogonal array with eight control factors.

L_{18}	Experiment condition matrix								Control factors
	1	2	3	4	5	6	7	8	

Experiment number	A	B	C	D	E	F	G	H
1	1	1	1	1	1	1	1	1
2	1	1	2	2	2	2	2	2
3	1	1	3	3	3	3	3	3
4	1	2	1	1	2	2	3	3
5	1	2	2	2	3	3	1	1
6	1	2	3	3	1	1	2	2
7	1	3	1	2	1	3	2	3
8	1	3	2	3	2	1	3	1
9	1	3	3	1	3	2	1	2
10	2	1	1	3	3	2	2	1
11	2	1	2	1	1	3	3	2
12	2	1	3	2	2	1	1	3
13	2	2	1	2	3	1	3	2
14	2	2	2	3	1	2	1	3
15	2	2	3	1	2	3	2	1
16	2	3	1	3	2	3	1	2
17	2	3	2	1	3	1	2	3
18	2	3	3	2	1	2	3	1

Control factors

- Inter-cell gateway (Y or N)
- cellRadius_Max (km) (cr_max)
- cellRadius_Search (% cr_max)
- CliusterMember_Max (nm_max)
- cellMember_Search (% nm_max)
- Bias level for cell coordinator
- Bias level for cell members
- Total number of cells control

Control factors and levels					
Control factors			Levels		
Factor	Factor description	1	2	3
A	InterCluster gateway	No	Yes	
B	ncr_max	1.25	1.50	1.75
C	ncr_norm	0.50	0.65	0.80
D	nm_max	1.50	2.00	2.50
E	nm_norm	0.50	0.65	0.80
F	bias_ch	0.70	0.85	1.00
G	bias_cm	0.70	0.85	1.00
H	Cluster # control	0.75	1.00	1.25

As indicated, nm_max and ncr_max denote the maximum members in a cell and the maximum cell radius, respectively; nm_search and ncr_search correspond to the initial search values for these two variables.

System Analysis Model

Figure 6.3 shows the system analysis model that was used to evaluate the system performance. The network formation result was generated with MATLAB tools. The algorithm has been tested and verified via Monte Carlo simulations.

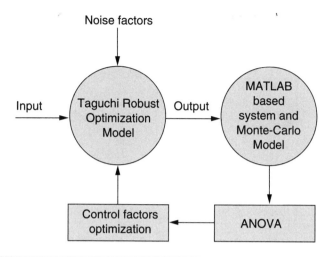

Figure 6.3   The system analysis model.

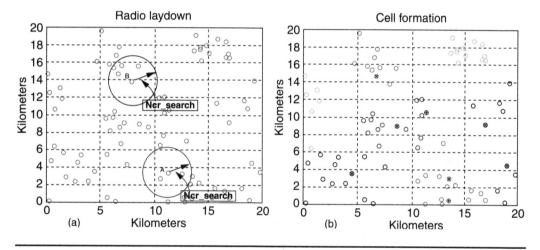

Figure 6.4   The radio laydown and network formation results.

Parameter Design

Let's consider a random deployment of 80 radios in an area of 20 km by 20 km, as shown in Figure 6.4a. The radio density is therefore 0.2 radios/km^2. Figure 6.4b illustrates the network formation result, which was generated with MATLAB tools. The algorithm has been tested and verified via Monte Carlo simulations. The gradient search method consistently forms a set of cells that meet the objective function while satisfying the imposed constraints. The Taguchi robust design approach was then used to analyze the error sensitivity due to noise factors and to determine the most robust settings for key system parameters.

The following summarizes the results of applying the Taguchi robust design approach to our problem. Table 6.2 shows the matrix experiment defined by the orthogonal arrays.

Table 6.2 Simulation results of matrix experiments.

L_{18}	M1 0.2		M2 0.4		M3 0.6		M4 0.8		M5 1	
	N1	N2	N1	N2	N1	N2	N1	N2	N1	N2
1	9.9419	10.8581	20.8171	22.6029	29.8085	32.6715	41.0630	44.6370	54.3762	59.1238
2	14.5952	15.9248	28.4790	30.9010	43.1190	46.5010	57.8107	62.4893	74.0261	79.2739
3	12.6523	13.4277	24.5412	26.1588	35.5407	37.9593	48.8941	51.9259	61.6863	66.1137
4	15.1653	16.2947	28.7807	31.0793	47.4301	50.7499	62.3499	66.4701	77.4300	83.5300
5	11.5527	12.3873	23.0441	24.8159	36.2633	38.5367	44.8809	48.1391	57.1351	61.3449
6	10.4338	11.2462	20.6284	22.2716	30.3705	32.3295	39.0019	42.1581	51.0285	54.7115
7	12.8036	13.8164	24.9099	26.8701	37.5069	40.3331	55.9549	59.4451	62.9225	66.9375
8	8.5436	9.1564	17.2155	18.5445	26.9879	29.1921	35.8691	38.8309	46.0784	49.8616
9	9.1096	9.7904	18.8919	20.3481	29.9060	31.9740	37.8650	40.3150	47.1538	50.5462
10	10.1501	11.1099	18.6509	20.6491	29.1049	31.8951	36.0649	39.7151	46.2437	51.2163
11	37.9112	41.4488	80.5221	87.2779	109.3731	119.8269	155.9612	170.0188	204.7728	221.7072
12	47.4030	53.6370	77.2330	89.4670	142.4737	160.6263	156.9903	180.5497	220.5412	250.9988
13	33.2306	36.7894	69.1543	76.0457	104.7022	114.6578	141.7119	156.9481	179.3586	197.4814
14	49.8046	56.4754	88.4022	100.7978	147.3777	166.2823	196.5741	222.4259	195.2340	225.0460
15	23.8127	25.9873	46.4313	50.1687	70.7233	76.9567	96.2238	103.2962	114.4103	124.1497
16	34.7918	38.4882	74.2825	81.9975	96.2787	107.4613	136.5544	151.3656	171.2419	190.8581
17	34.7854	38.7346	75.4320	83.5080	116.3193	128.0207	146.4825	163.2375	182.1632	199.7168
18	25.0072	26.9728	50.7751	54.4049	81.2276	86.4524	104.0987	111.5813	126.1842	135.4558

L_{18}	Experiment condition matrix								100 Monte Carlo simulation runs	
	1	2	3	4	5	6	7	8		
Experiment number	A	B	C	D	E	F	G	H	Beta	$S/N=10\text{Log}(B^2/V)$ (dB)
1	1	1	1	1	1	1	1	1	54.7809	28.3569
2	1	1	2	2	2	2	2	2	75.7137	31.3442
3	1	1	3	3	3	3	3	3	63.1890	31.9337
4	1	2	1	1	2	2	3	3	80.2562	30.8682
5	1	2	2	2	3	3	1	1	59.4734	30.7145
6	1	2	3	3	1	1	2	2	52.2188	30.8857
7	1	3	1	2	1	3	2	3	67.0145	27.7590
8	1	3	2	3	2	1	3	1	47.0975	30.1412
9	1	3	3	1	3	2	1	2	49.2793	31.1193
10	2	1	1	3	3	2	2	1	48.7770	28.1808
11	2	1	2	1	1	3	3	2	206.2755	27.9924
12	2	1	3	2	2	1	1	3	229.5033	23.5610
13	2	2	1	2	3	1	3	2	186.2159	28.9726
14	2	2	2	3	1	2	1	3	238.1117	31.2597
15	2	2	3	1	2	3	2	1	121.6650	30.2178
16	2	3	1	3	2	3	1	2	179.9265	27.2031
17	2	3	2	1	3	1	2	3	194.1809	28.2826
18	2	3	3	2	1	2	3	1	133.4549	30.5889
The overall mean value (dB)									115.9519	29.4101

Each row indicates a test with the specified control factor levels. It shows a tremendous benefit that the 18 designed experiments can completely characterize the system under evaluation. The factor effects on beta and the S/N ratio are shown in Figure 6.5.

Factor effects on beta

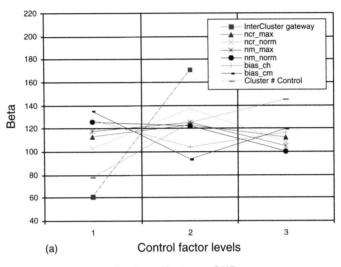

(a)

Control factor levels

Factor effects on SNR

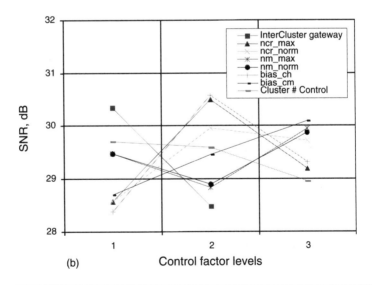

(b)

Control factor levels

Figure 6.5 Factor effects on beta and S/N ratio.

Optimal Factor Settings and Confirmation

The optimal control factor levels and performance predictions are summarized in Table 6.3. Confirmation runs were conducted. Simulation results show that the Taguchi robust design approach increases the normalized system throughput performance by more than 50% without a loss of system robustness.

Table 6.3 Optimum control factor settings and confirmation results.

Configuration	Factor levels	Prediction	Confirmation
Optimum	$A_2 B_2 C_2 D_2 E_1 F_1 G_1 H_3$	277.46	281.32
Initial	$A_2 B_2 C_1 D_2 E_3 F_1 G_3 H_2$	182.16	186.22
Delta performance on beta		52.32%	51.07%

Configuration	Factor levels	SNR (dB)	Confirmation
Optimum	$A_2 B_2 C_2 D_2 E_1 F_1 G_1 H_3$	27.36	27.69
Initial	$A_2 B_2 C_1 D_2 E_3 F_1 G_3 H_2$	28.37	28.97
Delta performance on SNR (dB)		−1.02	−1.28

6.1.5 Real-Time Automated Taguchi Optimization Module (ATOM)

Future research activities will focus on a rule-based learning mechanism that can easily be adapted to new operating scenarios and/or operational needs. Furthermore, we will consider the development of a real-time automated Taguchi optimization module (ATOM) that operates on the local noise factors and exchanges information on a global basis to enhance the overall system performance.

Figure 6.6a illustrates the situation that where the region of interest is large the optimized performance will be somewhat robust over the whole region. If the knowledge of the system realizes that the region of interest is actually smaller than originally thought, the optimized performance will be better if the uncertainty can be narrowed down by using the information provided. Figure 6.6b shows the real-time fractal optimization module within our system, which is replicated in each fractal node. A self-learning mechanism (e.g., neural network–based) with the real-time TOM enhances the dynamic part of the system. With the unprecedented communications capability, the event space indicators are fed back to each fractal node with its local parameters for joint and simultaneous system optimization.

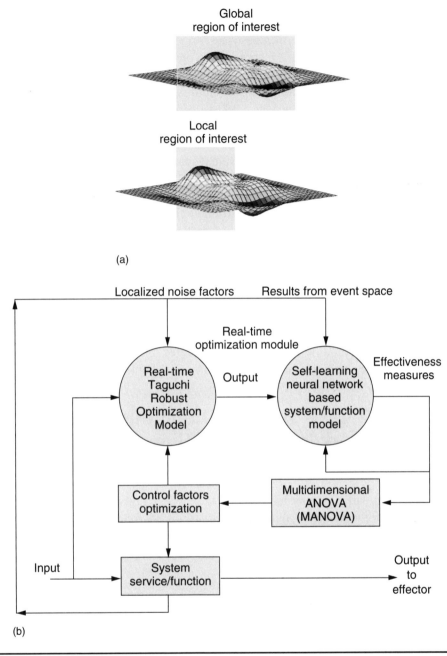

Figure 6.6 The real-time automated Taguchi optimization module (ATOM) concept.

6.1.6 Concluding Remarks

In this case study, an application of a network formation algorithm for an ad hoc mobile wireless network was considered. An approach to optimizing the network formation algorithm was studied. The proposed algorithm was derived from a gradient search technique. A two-tier network hierarchy consisting of automatically formed cells interconnected through a self-configured backbone was used as a network baseline. Dynamic network formation hides intracell topology from the units outside of the cell, so as to maximize network throughput and minimize overall message delay. The proposed algorithm also provides maximum frequency reuse of the signal space to further increase the overall network capacity. The Taguchi robust design approach was used to optimize the self-forming algorithm such that the underlying network performance is least sensitive to the variation in operating environments and other uncontrollable factors. We first conducted the matrix experiment based on the L_{18} ($1^2 \times 7^3$) orthogonal array with eight control factors and dynamic signals, characterized the sensitivity due to variations of the control factor levels, and then determined optimum factor levels for our design. Simulation results show that the Taguchi robust design approach increases the normalized system throughput performance by more than 50% without a loss in system robustness. Future research activities will focus on a rule-based learning mechanism that can easily adapt to new operating scenarios and/or operational needs. Furthermore, we will consider the development of a real-time automated Taguchi optimization module (ATOM) that operates on the local noise factors and exchanges information on a global basis to enhance the overall system performance.

6.2 Case Study 2: Direct Injection, Spark Ignition Gasoline Engine Development Using Taguchi Methods

This case study was carried out by John R. Jaye of Chrysler Corporation, Advanced Systems. We thank the author for presenting this case study in the 1998 robust engineering symposium.

6.2.1 Summary

Direct injection, spark ignition (DISI) gasoline engines have the potential to significantly improve automobile fuel economy. The development of such engines is significantly more difficult than conventional port fuel injected engines due to an increase in the number of engine control and design variables. This difficulty is further compounded by increasingly stringent emission standards. The following study applies outer and inner L_{18} arrays for software (control) and hardware (design) to the emissions and performance development of a prototype DISI engine.

6.2.2 Introduction

DISI gasoline engines are in the process of development around the world because they offer the potential for improved performance, lower fuel consumption, and lower emissions. These improvements are needed primarily because of increasingly strict emission regulations. Marketplace pressures for power, performance, and fuel economy are also part of the push to direct injection.

Most gasoline engines have the fuel injector upstream of the engine intake valves (usually described as port fuel injection, see Figure 6.7a). Injection is generally started well before the intake valves open, and fuel is resident for some time in the port with air before being introduced into the combustion chamber. This type of fuel system is almost universal in gasoline-powered automobiles. Some of the problems with this type of system arise from poor evaporation of the fuel (especially when the engine is cold) and minimizing the fuel transport lag as the speed and load of the engine are changed. These problems can be difficult to overcome as emission standards become more stringent.

Direct injection engines have the tip of the fuel injector mounted in the combustion chamber (see Figure 6.7b), much like diesel engines. Fuel is injected after the intake valves close. The mixture of air and fuel is ignited by spark plugs as in conventional gasoline engines. This arrangement eliminates fuel transport lag. Since the amount of time available for injection is significantly shorter, improved injection systems deliver significantly smaller fuel droplets. Injecting the fuel inside the chamber can increase the amount of air ingested, cool the air through evaporation of the fuel, and increase the speed of the combustion process. All of these effects are important in reducing emissions and increasing power and fuel economy.

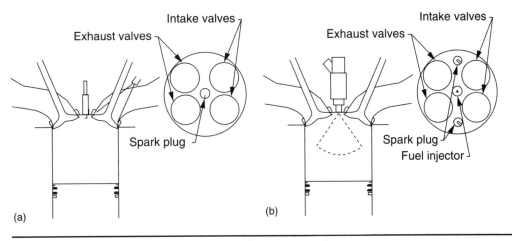

Figure 6.7 Port fuel injection and direct fuel injection diagrams.

Development of direct injection engines is more difficult than conventional port fuel injected engines because the number of engine design and engine control variables increases. In particular, injection system characteristics are critical to the success of a DISI engine. Also, the mixture quality of the fuel and air before ignition can be dramatically different than with conventional port fuel injected engines.

To address the development problem, Taguchi test techniques were adopted for the testing of a prototype DISI engine. The purpose of the test was threefold:

1. Determine which engine design and control variables are the primary factors in controlling the performance and emission characteristics of a prototype DISI engine.

2. Determine whether Taguchi test techniques are suitable for this type of engine development.

3. Complete the entire test project in two months.

The test design is composed of an outer L_{18} array of six engine control variables and an inner L_{18} array of six engine hardware variables. L_{18} arrays were chosen for this work because of the desire for primary effect information, curvature information, and speed. This test design resulted in 324 individual tests. A "one at a time" test of these variables would be impractical (11 variables at three levels and one variable at six would require more than 1 million tests).

Of concern with this test design are interactions. Engine hardware and control variables can interact very strongly, especially with DISI engines.

6.2.3 Engine and Experiment Description

The engine used for this test was a production Chrysler 2.4-liter engine modified to run as a single-cylinder engine. The cylinder head was modified to accept a centrally mounted fuel injector and dual spark plugs. The head was also modified so that the intake ports were bifurcated, and a throttle was installed in the rearward port to control airflow (not shown). The engine speed for the test was 1600 RPM and the load was held at 44 psi IMEP (indicated mean effective pressure, proportional to torque/displacement). This is an engine operating point, which represents city driving and portions of the federal test procedure. Emissions, performance, and combustion information were recorded for all test points. Of particular interest were the following measurements:

ISFC—indicated specific fuel consumption, a measure of thermal efficiency; units of lb/ihphr (pounds per indicated horsepower x hour)

ISCNOx—indicated specific oxides of nitrogen (NOx) emissions, a regulated emission; units of gm/ihphr (grams per indicated horsepower x hour)

ISHC—indicated specific hydrocarbon (HC) emissions, a regulated emission; units of gm/ihphr

COV of IMEP—covariance of IMEP, a measure of combustion consistency, in percent

The term indicated means the total work done by the engine (output plus losses). By presenting data based on indicated terms, comparisons and predictions can be made for multicylinder engines.

Each measurement is to be minimized for best engine performance and emissions.

Control Factors

The inner array for the test included the following hardware factors:

Injector cone angle	A, A - 20, and A - 40 degrees
Injector static flow rate	1, 1.3, and 1.6 normalized flow rate
Port throttle position	open, half, and closed
Spark plug gap	D, D + .010, and D + .020"
Plug protrusion	E, E + 3, and E + 6mm
Plug position	both, left, and right

These factors were chosen because they strongly effect how the fuel and air is introduced, mixed, and ignited in the combustion chamber. Injector cone angle and flow rate combinations can result in a wide range of droplet sizes and injection time periods. In addition, the cone angle affects the placement of the fuel in the cylinder. The port throttle position determines if the airflow rotates inside the combustion chamber around the central axis ("swirl," closed port position) or along the plane perpendicular to that axis ("tumble," open port position). The half position will have a flow field with attributes of swirl and tumble. The spark plug gap controls ignitability under differing operating conditions. The plug protrusion is a measure of how far into the chamber the gap is located. Plug position was also included to determine if there are spatial differences in the fuel/air mixture inside the cylinder.

The outer array for the test included the following software factors:

Injection timing	G, G - 60, G - 120, G - 180, G - 240, and G - 300 degrees before top center
EGR	H + 0, H + 4, and H + 8%
Fuel/air ratio	I, I - .010, and I - .020
Fuel rail pressure	J, J + 500, and J + 1000 psi
Dwell	K, K + 1.5, and K + 3 milliseconds
Spark advance	L, L + 15, and L + 30 degrees before top center

These factors were chosen because they strongly affect the performance and emissions of the engine and because they are easily controlled. Injection timing affects the residence time of the fuel in the chamber before ignition. Six levels were selected for this factor due to its importance on performance. EGR (exhaust gas recirculation) affects the amount of burned gases and temperature in the chamber. Fuel/air ratio and spark advance affect, individually and separately, all aspects of engine combustion and performance. The fuel rail pressure affects the injection duration and the fuel droplet size. Dwell refers to the length of time the spark is present in the spark plug gap and affects formation of the flame. The arrays are shown in Tables 6.4 and 6.5.

Table 6.4   Hardware array.

	Empty	Cone angle	Flow	Port throttle	Plug gap	Plug protr	Plug posit	Empty
1	1	A	1.0	1	D	E	Both	1
2	1	A	1.3	.5	D+.01	E+3	Left	2
3	1	A	1.6	0	D+.02	E+6	Right	3
4	1	A-20	1.0	1	D+.01	E+3	Right	3
5	1	A-20	1.3	.5	D+.02	E+6	Both	1
6	1	A-20	1.6	0	D	E	Left	2
7	1	A-40	1.0	.5	D	E+6	Left	3
8	1	A-40	1.3	0	D+.01	E	Right	1
9	1	A-40	1.6	1	D+.02	E+3	Both	2
10	2	A	1.0	0	D+.02	E+3	Left	1
11	2	A	1.3	1	D	E+6	Right	2
12	2	A	1.6	.5	D+.01	E	Both	3
13	2	A-20	1.0	.5	D+.02	E	Right	2
14	2	A-20	1.3	0	D	E+3	Both	3
15	2	A-20	1.6	1	D+.01	E+6	Left	1
16	2	A-40	1.0	0	D+.01	E+6	Both	2
17	2	A-40	1.3	1	D+.02	E	Left	3
18	2	A-40	1.6	.5	D	E+3	Right	1

Table 6.5   Control array.

	Inj. tmg.	EGR	F/A	Rail press.	Dwell	Spark	Empty
1	G	H	I	J	K	L	1
2	G	H+4	I-.01	J+500	K+1.5	L+15	2
3	G	H+8	I-.02	J+1000	K+3	L+30	3
4	G-60	H	I	J+500	K+1.5	L+30	3

(continued)

(continued)

Table 6.5 Control array.

	Inj. tmg.	EGR	F/A	Rail press.	Dwell	Spark	Empty
5	G-60	H+4	I-.01	J+1000	K+3	L	1
6	G-60	H+8	I-.02	J	K	L+15	2
7	G-120	H	I-.01	J	K+3	L+15	3
8	G-120	H+4	I-.02	J+500	K	L+30	1
9	G-120	H+8	I	J+1000	K+1.5	L	2
10	G-180	H	I-.02	J+1000	K+1.5	L+15	1
11	G-180	H+4	I	J	K+3	L+30	2
12	G-180	H+8	I-.01	J+500	K	L	3
13	G-240	H	I-.01	J+1000	K	L+30	2
14	G-240	H+4	I-.02	J	K+1.5	L	3
15	G-240	H+8	I	J+500	K+3	L+15	1
16	G-300	H	I-.02	J+500	K+3	L	2
17	G-300	H+4	I	J+1000	K	L+15	3
18	G-300	H+8	I-.01	J	K+1.5	L+30	1

Test Results

During the test work, some hardware and software combinations proved to be inoperable (the engine stalled or was too unstable for reliable measurements). This was the case with some late injection timings (120 and 60 deg) and some left plug position settings. Test data for these points were assigned very high values since minimization of responses was the goal. Interpretation of the S/N data must be made with care since assigned values for inoperable test points have no variability.

The hardware response graphs for ISFC are shown in Figure 6.8. The graph includes the average ISFC response data, the 95% and 75% confidence bands from ANOVA, and the S/N ratio data. Strong and very nonlinear responses resulted for cone angle, port position, and plug position. Gap and injector flow rates show a generally linear trend. Plug protrusion shows little influence on results. There is also a significant amount of noise and/or interactions as indicated by the results from the unused columns. S/N results show similar trends except for protrusion, gap, and flow rate.

The test results can also be presented as software responses due to the nature of the test design. Figure 6.9 shows this data for ISFC. Note the overwhelming response of injection timing on the results. This strong a response was not expected before testing began.

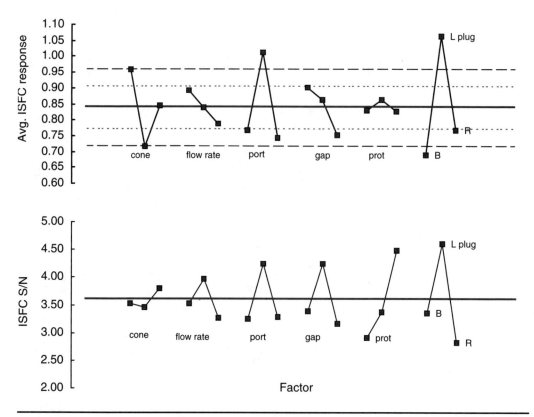

Figure 6.8 ISFC average and S/N response curves for hardware factors.

Response graphs for ISCNOx, ISHC, and COV of IMEP are included in the Appendix A. Interestingly, the trends for all four test measurements are the same. This implies that with this engine, low emissions, low fuel consumption, and low variability in operation will result with the optimum hardware and software combination. This is a very surprising result and counters most experience with engine design and development.

From the test results, the optimum factors for lowest emissions and best fuel consumption are:

A - 20 cone angle	G or G - 60 injection timing
1.6 flow rate	H EGR
Both ports	I F/A
D + .02" gap	J + 500 rail pressure
E + 6mm protrusion	K + 3ms dwell
Both spark plugs	L + 15 spark advance

In addition to the surprising emissions and fuel consumption results noted above, the test produced other results of interest:

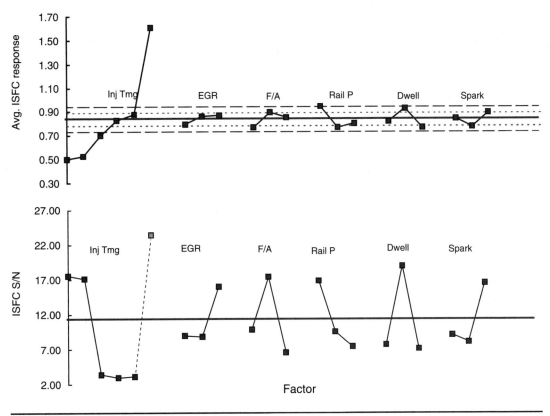

Figure 6.9 ISFC average and S/N response curves for software factors.

- The flow rate response on performance and emissions is opposite of the expected response. Higher flow rate injectors have bigger fuel droplets, and bigger droplets are historically associated with high emissions and poor fuel economy.

- The poor performance exhibited with the left plug is difficult to explain given that the fuel spray and combustion chamber are symmetrical.

- The response characteristics of the port throttle position are unexpected based on previous experience.

- Plug protrusion was thought to be an important factor before the test.

Confirmation Test Results

The first set of confirmation test results are shown in Figure 6.10. This test examined the flow rate (1.3 versus 1.6 flow rate) result as well as the parallel emissions and performance

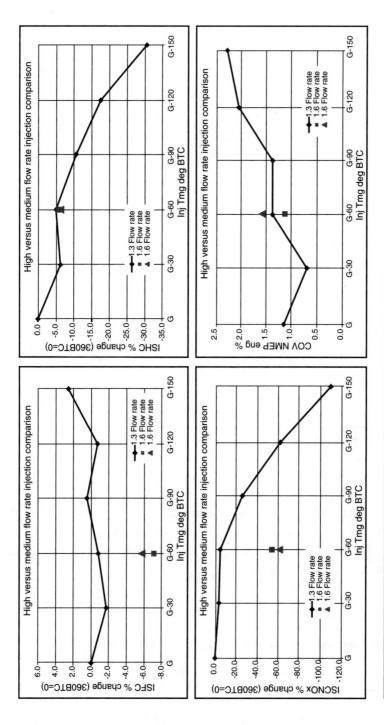

Figure 6.10 Confirmation test results for emissions, performance, and injector flow rate.

result. The tests were performed using traditional engine test techniques and results are shown as a function of injection timing. The predicted lower fuel consumption and lower NOx emissions with the highest flow rate injector were confirmed. Lower HC and COV of IMEP results did not occur, however. This suggests that there is an interaction present and that further tests will be required. The results are still very encouraging since there was no degradation in HC and COV of IMEP with the higher flow rate injector.

The L_{18} test that most closely resembled the optimum factor combination exhibited similar ISFC, COV of IMEP, and ISCNOx response trends as shown in Figure 6.10. The L_{18} response for ISHC did not show the reduction in HC levels that were found in the confirmation testing.

A 3D computational fluid dynamic (CFD) simulation made after the test was completed confirmed that higher injector flow rate is a benefit.

Traditional test techniques were also used to confirm the effects of fuel/air ratio and EGR on performance and emissions. Though these factors are of small influence in this test, they are used here as another confirmation of the testing technique. Each of these factors affects engine operation in specific ways regardless of the engine type. Rail pressure and spark advance responses mirrored known operating characteristics.

Figures 6.11, 6.12, and 6.13 show the results of the fuel/air and EGR confirmation tests for the optimum hardware configuration. Spark advance was constant for all results, and fuel/air is shown from I to I − .01. The ISFC results (Figure 6.11, upper graph) show that EGR degrades performance slightly and that fuel/air ratio improves performance slightly. The fuel/air result is not the trend predicted from the L_{18} tests. The ISCNOx test results (Figure 6.11, lower graph) do show that the L_{18} results were predictive (increasing, then decreasing ISCNOx as the fuel/air ratio is reduced; decreasing ISCNOx as EGR is increased). The ISHC and COV of IMEP results shown in Figure 6.13 demonstrate that the L_{18} predictions for these values were not correct (refer to Appendix I). The L_{18} results indicate that both should increase as the control factor levels increase. The confirmation test results show that ISHC decreases for both fuel/air and EGR and that COV of IMEP is insensitive to the control factor levels.

Test work conducted on an optical access engine confirmed the plug position results. The image was made by looking up through a quartz window in the piston. The intake valves are at the top of the image, and the edge of the left spark plug can just be seen on the far left of the image (the window did not allow for full viewing of the chamber). The majority of the fuel is around the right spark plug, as predicted by analysis of the test results. Further work with 3D CFD modeling confirmed the L_{18} and optical test results.

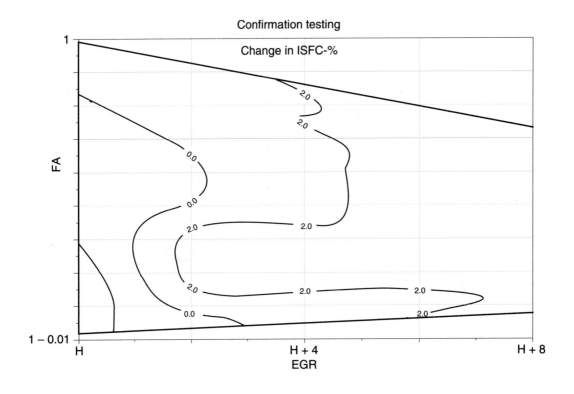

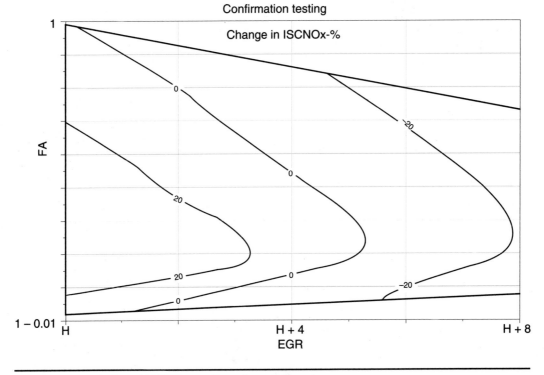

Figure 6.11 ISFC and ISCNOx confirmation test results.

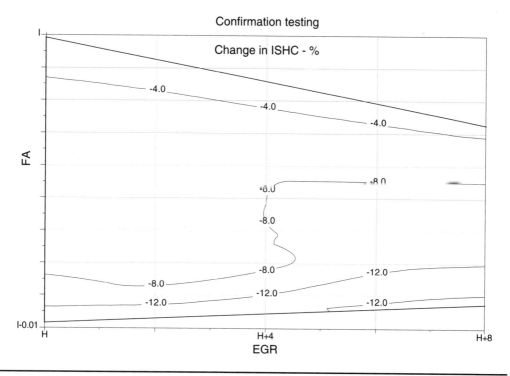

Figure 6.12 ISHC of IMEP confirmation test results.

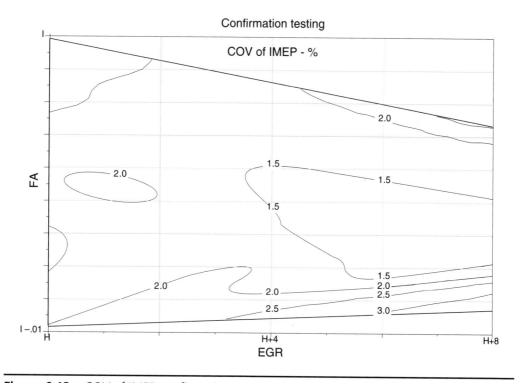

Figure 6.13 COV of IMEP confirmation test results.

6.2.4 Conclusions

The results from this project have demonstrated that L_{18} Taguchi methods can be used in the development of a prototype DISI engine. Of particular note:

- 12 engine design and control factors were tested, and main effects determined for each factor.

- The total time for the test, including confirmation tests, was two months. Traditional test techniques would require significantly longer time.

- The course of testing revealed results that would not have been found if traditional test techniques had been used.

- Hardware and software combinations were found in which fuel economy was improved and NOx emissions were reduced with no penalty to HC emissions or combustion stability.

6.3 Case Study 3: Robust Testing of Electronic Warfare Systems

Stan Goldstein and Tom Ulrich of ITT Avionics in Clifton, NJ, have conducted this case study. We thank them for presenting in the 2000 robust engineering conference. This case study is not related to software algorithm optimization but serves as an example of the robust testing method described in Chapter 5.

6.3.1 Summary

The process of development testing for electronic warfare (EW) systems can be both expensive and time consuming since the number of individual radar emitter types and modes is large. Robust engineering methods have been applied to development testing of EW systems whereby the confirmed test cycle time has been significantly decreased by a factor of 4 to 1, while providing equivalent diagnostics of system performance. This has been accomplished through the use of Taguchi robust engineering methods including an L_{18} experimental matrix to define a robust subset of radar emitter types. Ongoing test results including overall mean and factor-based signal to noise (S/N) ratios have been effectively used as a measure of system performance improvement.

The Taguchi L_{18} array has demonstrated the capability to test more system functionality in significantly less time than conventional methods.

6.3.2 Statement of Business and Experimental Objectives

ITT Avionics, a division of ITT Industries, is a developer of electronic warfare systems for domestic and foreign military use. The development of EW systems includes testing and evaluation of new systems against a wide and varied range of radar emitter types, taking a significant amount of time and effort. In order to minimize development time, while improving product quality and performance, Taguchi robust engineering methods were implemented. The objective is to reduce EW system test time for a large quantity of emitters by defining a reduced set of orthogonal emitter types.

6.3.3 Experimental Approach Used (Array, Signal, Noise Groups)

Most Taguchi engineering methods employ control factors used to determine the sensitivity of system performance to various design parameters. In this situation, the approach is to evaluate a systems performance against a wide variety of simulated field conditions (noise factors) in a time-efficient manner. A secondary goal is to determine system deficiencies in order to develop a more robust system design. A third result of the task was to yield a single measure of system performance (mean S/N ratio) to track hardware and software improvements.

Since the objective of this task is cause detection, a group of noise factors were selected in lieu of control factors to define the selected orthogonal array.

The purpose of an EW system is to search for various radar systems (emitters) in its operational environment, determine location, and classify function by measuring various radiated parameters and received characteristics. If a radar site is considered hostile, then effective measures are taken by the EW system to mitigate the emitter's function. This is illustrated in Figure 6.14, "Electronic Warfare Scenario." As an example, airport radar systems may be searching for aircraft, whereas a hostile emitter site may be seeking to launch and control armaments. The determination of radar type (airport, hostile, etc.) and radar mode (search, acquisition, track) is therefore a critical function. The scope of this project is limited to assessing EW system performance to identify a radar system and its mode.

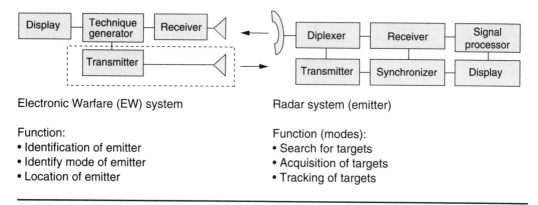

Electronic Warfare (EW) system

Function:
• Identification of emitter
• Identify mode of emitter
• Location of emitter

Radar system (emitter)

Function (modes):
• Search for targets
• Acquisition of targets
• Tracking of targets

Figure 6.14   Electronic warfare scenario.

The electronic warfare system makes these critical determinations by measuring various characteristics of the radar's transmitted signal. Measuring the signal amplitude from two or more EW system receive antennas permits the determination of radar position by determining the angle of arrival (AOA). Measuring transmitted parameters from the radar such as the frequency, pulse, scan type, and amplitude help determine the type and mode of the radar system. These parameters become noise factors for orthogonal array determination.

The challenge for this project is selecting a signal (limited group of emitters) that represent the functional variation of the entire ensemble of radar types. The transfer function is to identify each emitter in the signal set without error. The Taguchi problem type was selected to be "maximum-the-best," given that correct identification of the emitter is considered to be a correct signal and that any error in the system output is considered noise. The system must detect all signals without radar type or mode identification error.

It is recognized that the EW system will need to be tested against the entire group of radar systems. However, since software upgrades are made on a near weekly basis, the 16 hours required to evaluate the entire ensemble of emitter types becomes expensive and time consuming. The goal of this project was therefore to cut the weekly 16-hour test time by at least half while maintaining test integrity.

P-Diagram of the System

Figure 6.15 illustrates the P-diagram for this project. The input signal is the domain of emitters as described by the L_{18} experimental matrix. The output signal is the correct identification of each radar emitter and mode that the EW system is subjected to. The control factors consist of the EW system hardware and software configuration that is tested in a

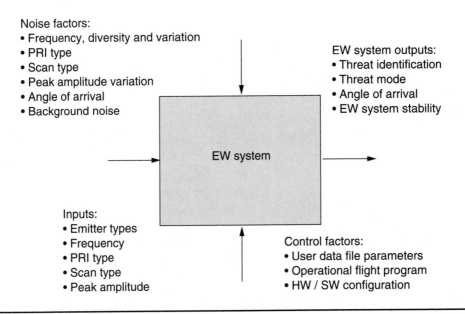

Figure 6.15 P-diagram for robust testing of EW systems.

particular system configuration. The system configuration is variable depending on project phase due to improvements in hardware and software.

Noise factors are those that define the variable domain of conditions that the EW system is subjected to. This will include the variation in emitter characteristics over the domain of all emitter types, the variation of emitter position including angle of arrival and signal amplitude, variation in emitter mode, and background noise.

Selection of Orthogonal Array

The selection of array size was based on the determination of one two-level factor and seven three-level factors. They are summarized in Table 6.6.

Table 6.6 Factors and levels.

Factor	Level 1	Level 2	Level 3
Freq. diversity	Single	Multiple	-----
Frequency	Low	Mid	High
PRI type	CW	Stable	Agile
Scan type	Steady	Circular	Raster
Peak power	Nominal	Medium	Low
AOA *	Boresite	Offset 1	Offset 2
Illumination	Short	Medium	100 %
Background *	None	Low density	High density

The L_{18} array was selected because it can accommodate one two-level factor and up to seven three-level factors. Selection of an L_{18} array will also yield growth for two three-level factors noted with an asterisk. The next issue in developing this project was selection of 18 emitters from a group in the order of 100 in size.

Selection of Robust Emitter Set from the Large Domain of Emitter Types

Selection of emitters started with the characterization of each radar system in the total domain in terms of the noise factors and parameters selected. Hence, each of the 18 experiments defined by the L_{18} array would consist of a different set of emitter characteristics. Table 6.7, "Selection of 18 Robust Emitters," illustrates the selection process for Experiment 2. The principle characteristics were single RF frequency, high RF frequency, stable PRI, circular scan, and short illumination time. The difficulty in choosing emitters from the ensemble available was that only a few provided a perfect match to the Taguchi defined set. This problem was handled by calculating the shortest distance for each emitter in the ensemble against the 18 defined experiments.

Table 6.7 Selection of eighteen robust emitters.

Experiment	Item	Mean distance	RF diversity	RF	PRI type	Scan type	Peak power	Illumination
2	76	1	Single	High	Stable	Circular		Medium
			Single	High	Stable	Circular		Short

	Item	Item Distance	RF Diversity	RF	PRI Type	Scan Type	Peak Power	Illumination
	66	4	0	1	1	1		1
	70	2	0	0	1	0		1
	74	2	0	1	0	0		1
	76	1	0	0	0	0		1
	80	3	0	0	1	1		1
	82	3	0	1	1	1		0
	83	2	0	0	0	1		1
	84	2	0	0	0	1		1
	88	4	1	1	1	0		1
	90	3	0	0	1	1		1

Table 6.7 shows that for Experiment 2, the shortest distance exists for Item Number 76, with the only incorrect parameter being short illumination time, hence a distance of 1. Item 76 was therefore selected for Experiment 2. Peak power is adjusted for each experiment and therefore not considered in the selection process. Note that "0" indicates an exact correlation to the desired parameter, while a "1" indicates no match. All experiments were selected in the same manner.

Table 6. 8 presents the entire set of 18 test emitters. Several experiments exactly match the orthogonal requirement with an item distance of zero. Several emitters such as Item 76 used in Experiment 2 are not quite orthogonal. That is, the distance is other than 0, either 1 or 2. The correct or desired parameter is located in the center of each parameter box, while the parameter exhibited by the emitter is located under. The count of valid parameter matches and incorrect matches are summed at the bottom of each factor column.

The important point to be made here is that an array selected for the purpose of cause detection need not be exactly orthogonal to be effective.

Table 6.8 L_{18} Orthogonal array for robust testing of EW systems.

| Experiment | ITEM number | Distance item (mean) | Expert array laboratory performance: Column factor and parameter assigned | | | | | | | | Observation |
			A RF diversity	B RF	C PRI type	D Scan type	E Peak power	F	G Illumination	H	m_i = (defects)
1	10	0	Single	High	CW	Steady	Nominal	F1	100%	H1	1.000
2	76	1	Single	High	Stable	Circular	Medium	F2	1 Medium short	H2	0.000
3	80	0	Single	High	Agile	Raster	Low	F3	Short	H3	6.000
4	61	1	Single	Mild	CW	Steady	Medium	F2	1 Short 100%	H3	0.000
5	12	1	Single	Mild	Stable	1 Circular steady	Low	F3	100%	H1	4.000
6	70	2	Single	1 Mid high	Agile	Raster	Nominal	F1	1 Medium short	H2	0.000
7	88	0	Single	Low	CW	Circular	Nominal	F3	Medium	H3	2.000
8	147	0	Single	Low	Stable	Raster	Medium	F1	Short	H1	0.000
9	141	1	Single	1 Low mid	Agile	Steady	Low	F2	100%	H2	2.000
10	82	2	1 Multiple single	1 High mid	CW	Raster	Low	F2	Medium	H1	3.000
11	5	2	Multiple	1 High low	Stable	1 Steady circular	Nominal	F3	Short	H2	2.000
12	88	2	Multiple	1 High mid	Agile	Circular	Medium	F1	1 100% short	H3	4.000
13	66	0	Multiple	Mid	CW	Circular	Low	F1	Short	H2	2.000
14	59	1	1 Multiple single	Mid	Stable	Raster conical	Nominal	F2	100%	H3	0.000
15	149	2	Multiple	Mid	Agile	1 Steady raster	Medium	F3	1 Medium short	H1	4.000
16	32	1	1 Multiple single	Low	CW	Raster conical	Medium	F3	100%	H2	1.000
17	134	1	Multiple	Low	Stable	Steady	Low	F1	1 Medium 100%	H3	0.000
18	155	1	1 Multiple single	Low	Agile	Circular	Nominal	F2	Short	H1	0.000
	Item mean	1.00									
Total fault analysis	Valid (mean)	15.75	14	13	18	15	18	18	12	18	
	Incorrect (mean)	2.25	4	5	0	3	0	0	6	0	

F1: Boresite; F2: Offset 1; F3: Offset 2
H1: None; H2: Low density; H3: High density

Signal to Noise Ratio Used as a Result of the Ideal Function Developed

The ideal transfer function for this problem is to correctly identify each emitter and its mode without error over the domain of emitter types. Each emitter is tested and evaluated to determine if its radar type is correct, radar mode is correct, and angle of arrival is correct. Any incorrect output is assigned a count of one per incorrect output. Since there may be subjective considerations during this evaluation, the operator further places a "color" valuation to the experiment in the form of green, yellow, or red (defect count of 0, 1, or 2 respectively). Green is a stable signal with no variations or anomaly. Yellow may indicate some concern regarding timeliness or stability of the identification, while red indicates a more serious malfunction, such as multiple emitter types identified for the one emitter tested.

Typical emitter performance evaluation is graded per the example in Table 6.9.

Table 6.9   Evaluation of emitter performance.

Experiment (emitter)	Type defects	Mode defects	AOA defects	Color defects	Total defects
1	0	0	1	0	1
2	0	0	0	0	0
3	2	2	0	2	6

The S/N ratio for this experiment is calculated using the relationship:

$$S/N = -20 \log \left[\frac{\text{total defects}}{n+1} \right] \qquad (6.2)$$

Since the problem type is "maximum the best," the S/N ratio for a perfect system is 0 dB. Any error in performance yields a negative S/N ratio. The relationship including "defects plus one" is used since the Log (0) is undefined, and Log (1) is zero. The value for n is 18 to compute the entire array S/N ratio, while n may vary from mean parameter count (6 or 9) because certain emitters were not perfect orthogonal fits. As an example, the RF diversity factor is segmented with $n = 5$ for the parameter "multiple" and $n = 13$ for the parameter "single."

A sample calculation is shown here for computing the S/N ratio for RF diversity. Since this is a two-level factor, an orthogonal array would contain nine entries for the parameter "single" and nine for the parameter "multiple." Since only five of the experiments contain the parameter "multiple," only those parameters are used for the S/N ratio calculation. These include experiments 11, 12, 13, 15, and 17. Hence:

$$\text{S/N ratio} = 20 \, \text{Log} \, [(M_{11} + M_{12} + M_{13} + M_{15} + M_{17}) / 5 + 1]$$

$$\text{S/N ratio} = 20 \, \text{Log} \, [(2 + 4 + 2 + 4 + 0) / 5 + 1] = -10.6 \, \text{dB}$$

For the parameter "single":

$$\text{S/N ratio} = 20 \text{ Log } [(M_1 + M_2 + M_3 + M_4 + M_5 + M_6$$
$$+ M_7 + M_8 + M_9 + M_{10} + M_{14} + M_{16} + M_{18}) / 13 + 1]$$

$$\text{S/N ratio} = 20 \text{ Log } [(1 + 0 + 6 + 0 + 4 + 0 + 2 + 0 + 2 + 3 + 0 + 1 + 0) / 13 + 1] = -7.8 \text{ dB}$$

Improvement in S/N Ratio by Confirmation and the Associated Business Impact

The reduction in test time has surpassed the goal of a 50% decrease in weekly test time. The 18 emitters can be tested in only four hours, a reduction of four to one in effort. This is quite significant given that the sensitivity to test results did not yield any additional system weakness when the monthly test sequence was conducted. The monthly test sequence extended over a 16-hour period, with a number of emitters remaining to be evaluated.

Table 6.10, "System performance summary," shows test results during several weeks of development, but it does not represent the final system configuration. Several important results are observed from this table:

1. The overall S/N ratio increases from −9.4 dB to −5.0 dB. This yields a steady improvement per system upgrade, which can be used to track system performance.

2. From the first test conducted, the system demonstrated a sensitivity to input signal peak power. This is significant because peak power is one parameter that is not normally evaluated in the conventional sequence due to the large quantity of emitters tested. Test 2 shows an improvement in mean SNR not consistent in sequence with the remainder of the group. Upon investigation, it was determined that correct peak power levels were not maintained for that group.

    It is therefore concluded that the Taguchi Method identified, early in the development process, a system sensitive parameter that would not normally have been recognized.

3. The Taguchi method provides a perspective of system performance, perhaps not readily evident when testing a group of independent emitter types. That is the correlation of EW system sensitivity to the specific noise factors selected.

4. Additional tests may be added to the L_{18} Taguchi matrix to provide an added level of robustness to the project. As noted in Table 6.6, emitter angle of arrival and background noise have been noted as noise factors but not yet implemented. Angle of arrival testing will consist of placing the emitter at three different angular positions from the EW system. Background noise has been defined to simulate unknown emitter types.

Table 6.10 System performance summary.

Factor / Parameter	Test 1	Test 2	Test 3	Test 4	Test 5	Test 6
Mean SNR	−9.4 dB	−8.2 dB	−8.7 dB	−6.9 dB	−5.8 dB	−5.0 dB
RF diversity - Single - Multiple	RF diversity −8.9 −10.6	RF diversity −5.0 −13.3	RF diversity −7.8 −10.6	RF diversity −5.0 −10.6	RF diversity −5.3 −6.9	RF diversity −3.3 −8.3
RF freq. - Low - Mid - High	RF freq. −8.8 −10.9 −7.4	RF freq. −2.0 −9.5 −9.1	RF freq. −8.8 −10.6 −5.3	RF freq. −4.9 −8.8 −5.3	RF freq. −3.5 −7.5 −4.4	RF freq. 0.0 −8.8 −0.0
PRI type - CW - Stable - Agile	PRI type −9.5 −8.2 −10.0	PRI type −2.5 −9.5 −10.5	PRI type −8.0 −6.0 −11.3	PRI type −4.4 −8.0 −8.0	PRI type −1.3 −8.0 −6.7	PRI type −6.0 −2.5 −6.0
Scan type - Steady - Circular - Raster	Scan type −13.3 −7.6 −7.0	Scan type −5.1 −11.6 −7.0	Scan type −7.6 −8.3 −9.6	Scan type −6.0 −9.5 −5.5	Scan type −6.8 −7.6 −3.5	Scan type −5.1 −6.8 −3.5
Peak power - Nominal - Medium - Low	Peak power −4.4 −8.5 −13.0	Peak power −6.7 −10.9 −6.0	Peak power −5.3 −8.0 −11.7	Peak power −5.3 −6.7 −8.5	Peak power −1.3 −7.4 −7.4	Peak power 0.0 −4.4 −8.5

6.3.4 Conclusions

An L_{18} Taguchi matrix has been successfully employed to yield a robust test methodology for EW systems. The robust group of 18 emitter types coupled with operationally based noise factors has surpassed the capability established by testing each radar type individually. Analysis of the L_{18} test results compared with test results from the entire domain of emitters demonstrates that the L_{18} can find more system sensitivities than testing the entire ensemble of emitters in a conventional manner.

What is more, the L_{18} array used contained experiments (emitters) that were "not quite orthogonal," thereby permitting a selection of emitters from a standard group. This eliminated the time and effort to generate simulations for a new emitter set.

The Taguchi L_{18} array has effectively demonstrated the capability to test more system functionality in significantly less time than conventional methods.

SECTION III

Design of Information Systems
for Pattern Analysis

7

Use of Robust Engineering Methods for Designing Information Systems

7.1 Introduction

A baby can recognize its mother's face. A dog can recognize its master's voice. They seem to have some information system and mechanism by which they can compare faces or voices so as to accurately determine their mother's face or master's voice. What is really happening here is the study of patterns, generated by combinations or interactions of several variables. Unfortunately, in the real world, we don't have good information systems governed by an appropriate theory by which we can recognize patterns based on the information in the variables and make accurate predictions. If there were such systems, probably one could have taken actions based on patterns to avoid incidences like events on September 11, stock market collapses, weather irregularities, wrong health diagnosis, and product failures. Development of such systems remains quite difficult.

Making accurate predictions based on existing information is also important in today's world of business as it enhances market share by way of increased customer confidence. Sometimes, these predictions would also help create markets. Usually, predictions have to be based on the information on multiple characteristics (or variables) defining the systems. Such systems are called multidimensional systems. A multidimensional system could be an inspection system, a sensor system, a company diagnosis system, a stock market prediction system, a weather forecasting system, or a medical diagnosis system. While dealing with these systems, inaccurate diagnosis or predictions could occur because of inadequate multidimensional measurement capabilities.

In this article, we propose a methodology by which a multivariate measurement scale can be constructed to understand behavior of different patterns, which will in turn, help measure or predict various conditions of the multivariate systems so the observer can take appropriate corrective actions. In statistical literature there exists a measure called the Mahalanobis distance, which measures distances in multivariate systems by considering correlations between the variables. These correlations are an approximate measurement of the interactions between the variables. Because of this reason, we use the Mahalanobis distance to represent patterns corresponding to combinations of the variables. Here, the Mahalanobis distance is used for the construction of the scale, and the principles of robust engineering or Taguchi methods are used to estimate the accuracy of the scale. Hence this technique is referred to as Mahalanobis-Taguchi strategy (MTS). We will also describe a means to validate the measurement scale. Using such a scale one can determine whether a particular product will be returned from the customer, whether a patient needs immediate surgery, whether something abnormal is going to take place, or whether it's worthwhile investing money in a company. Unlike most of the methods, MTS is data analytic, meaning that MTS can be applied irrespective of the type of input variables and their distributions.

7.2 What Is MTS?

MTS is a pattern analysis technique, which is used to make predictions through a multivariate measurement scale. Patterns are difficult to represent in quantitative terms and are extremely sensitive to correlations between the variables. The Mahalanobis distance, which was introduced by an Indian statistician, P. C. Mahalanobis, measures distances of points in multidimensional spaces. The Mahalanobis distance has been extensively used in areas like spectrographic applications and agricultural applications. This distance is proved to be superior to other multidimensional distances like Euclidean distance because it takes correlations between the variables into account. For this reason we use Mahalanobis distance (actually, a modified form of the original distance) to represent differences between individual patterns in quantitative terms.

For any scale, one must have a reference point from which the measurements can be made. While it is easier to obtain a reference point for the scale with a single characteristic, it is not possible to obtain a single reference point when we are dealing with multiple characteristics. Therefore, in MTS the reference point corresponding to multiple variables is obtained with the help of a group of observations that are as uniform as possible and still able to distinguish patterns through Mahalanobis distance. These observations are modified so that their center is located at the origin (zero point) and the corresponding Mahalanobis distances are scaled so as to make average distance of this group unity. The zero point and unit distance thus obtained are used as reference points of the scale, and the distances are measured from this point. This set of observations is often referred to as "Mahalanobis space" or "unit group" or "normal group." Selection of this group is entirely at the discretion of the decision maker conducting the diagnosis. In manufacturing applications, this group might correspond to parts having no defects; in a medical diagnosis application, this group might consist of a set of people without any health problems, and in stock market predictions, this group could correspond to companies having average steady growth in a three-year period. The observations in this group are similar and not the same. Judicious selection of this group is extremely important for accurate diagnosis or predictions.

After developing the scale, the next step is the validation of the scale, which is done by the help of observations that are outside the Mahalanobis space. In this stage, we are, in a way, validating the Mahalanobis space (that is, if it provides a good base or reference point for future predictions/measurements) and hence the accuracy of the scale. This is important because no method is considered good if it does not perform the intended function with observations that are not considered while developing the method. For the observations outside the Mahalanobis space, the distances are measured from the center of the normal group based on means, standard deviations, and correlation structure of this group. If the scale is good, the distances of these observations must match with the decision maker's judgment. In other words, if an observation does not belong to a normal group, it should have larger distance. Here we introduce a measure called signal to noise (S/N) ratio for assessing the accuracy of the scale. S/N ratio captures the correlation between the true or observed information (that is, input signals) and the output of a system in the presence of uncontrollable variation (that is, noise). In MTS, S/N ratio is defined as the measure of accuracy of predictions. A typical multidimensional predictive system that is used in MTS can be described using Figure 7.1.

As mentioned above, the output or prediction accuracy should have a good correlation with the input signal, and S/N ratios measure this correlation. The predictions are made based on the information on the variables defining the system and should be "accurate" even in the presence of noise factors such as different places of measurement, operating conditions, and so forth. For example, in a rainfall prediction system the input would be actual rainfall, and the output would be the Mahalanobis distance calculated from the variables affecting the rainfall. In this case, the S/N ratio measures correlation between actual rainfall and the Mahalanobis distance.

If the accuracy of predictions is satisfactory, we will identify a useful subset of variables that is sufficient for the measurement scale while maintaining good prediction accuracy. Our experience shows that in many cases, the accuracy with useful variables is better than the accuracy with the original set of variables. However, in some cases the accuracy with useful variables might be less—which might be still desirable as it helps reduce cost of inspection or measurement. In multidimensional systems the total number of combinations to be examined would be of the order of several thousands, so it is not possible to examine all combinations. Here, we propose use of orthogonal arrays (OAs) to reduce the number of combinations to be tested. OAs are developed to estimate the effects of the variables by minimizing the number of combinations to be examined. They have been in use for quite a long time in the field of experimental design. In MTS, the variables are assigned to different columns of an OA. Based on S/N ratios obtained from different variable combinations,

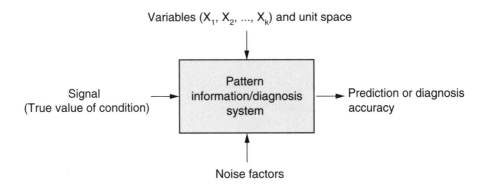

Figure 7.1 Pattern information or diagnosis system used in MTS.

important variables are identified. The future diagnosis is carried out only with these important variables.

7.2.1 Computation of Mahalanobis Distance

In MTS, the Mahalanobis distance (MD), which is a squared distance (also denoted as D^2), is calculated by using the following equation.

$$\text{MD} = D^2 = (1/k)\, Z_i\, C^{-1}\, Z_i^{\,T} \tag{7.1}$$

where Z_i = standardized vector obtained by standardized values of X_i ($i = 1 \ldots k$)

   $Z_i = (X_i - m_i)/s_i$

   X_i = value of ith characteristic

   m_i = mean of ith characteristic

   s_i = s.d. of ith characteristic

   k = number of characteristics/variables

   T = transpose of the vector

   C = correlation matrix

Since multivariate analysis involves matrix algebra, a quick review of matrix algebra required for the purpose of understanding MTS is provided in Appendix C.

7.3 Stages in MTS

The basic stages in MTS can be summarized as follows:

Stage I: Construction of a measurement scale

- Select a Mahalanobis space with suitable variables and observations that are as uniform as possible.

- Use the Mahalanobis space as a base or reference point of the scale.

Stage II: Validation of the measurement scale

- Identify the conditions outside the Mahalanobis space.

- Compute the Mahalanobis distances of these conditions and check whether they match with decision maker's judgment.

- Calculate S/N ratios to determine accuracy of the scale.

Stage III: Identify the useful variables (developing stage)

- Find out the useful set of variables using OAs and S/N ratios.

Stage IV: Future diagnosis with useful variables

- Monitor the conditions using the scale, which is developed with the help of the useful set of variables. Based on the values of Mahalanobis distances, appropriate corrective actions can be taken.

7.3.1 Orthogonal Arrays in MTS

As we know, the orthogonal arrays are used in robust engineering or the design of experiments to estimate the effects of several factors and required interactions by minimizing the number of experiments. In MTS, OAs are used to test various combinations of variables for better predictions. Such tests will help identify a useful set of variables that can be used for future diagnosis. In MTS we have to make sure that prediction accuracy with the useful set will be at least at the same level as with all the variables. To test different combinations with OAs, the variables are assigned to the different columns of the array. Here there are only two levels for the variables, presence or absence (on or off) of variable in a combination. Usually, "1" represents presence level and "2" represents absence level. For the purpose of illustration, let us consider the following example.

Let us suppose that we have four variables, X_1, X_2, X_3, and X_4. Consider the following two combinations (assume that they are part of OA).

1st Combination : 1-1-1-1

The combination with X_1, X_2, X_3, and X_4 is run and MS is constructed with these variables by using a 4×4 correlation matrix. The MDs corresponding to the abnormals are estimated using this correlation matrix.

2nd combination: 1-2-2-1

The combination with X_1 and X_4 is run and MS is constructed with these variables by using a 2×2 correlation matrix. The MDs corresponding to the abnormals are estimated using this correlation matrix.

For all combinations of the array, MDs corresponding to the abnormal conditions are computed. Only abnormals are used, because it is required to ensure the accuracy of the measurement scale for known abnormals.

7.3.2 Signal to Noise Ratio—A Measure of Prediction Accuracy

In the context of MTS, signal to noise (S/N) ratio is used as a measure of prediction accuracy. As mentioned before, the accuracy of prediction with useful variables should be at least equal to that with all variables. Use of S/N ratios will ensure a high level of prediction with useful variables. S/N ratios are computed for all combinations of OA based on MDs outside a reference group. With these MDs, S/N ratios are obtained. Using S/N ratios as the response, average effects of variables are computed at Level 1 (presence) and Level 2 (absence). Based on these effects, the utility of variables can be determined. As we know, S/N ratio captures the magnitude of real effects (i.e., signals) after making some adjustment for uncontrollable variation (i.e., noise). Therefore, it is desirable to have high S/N ratios.

Types of S/N Ratios in MTS

In MTS applications, typically the following types of S/N ratios are used:

- Larger-the-better type
- Nominal-the-best type
- Dynamic type

When the true levels of abnormals are not known, larger-the-better type S/N ratios are used if all the observations outside reference group are abnormals. This is because the MDs for abnormals should be higher. If the observations outside the reference group are a mixture of normals and abnormals then nominal-the-best type S/N ratios are used. When the levels of abnormals are known, dynamic S/N ratios are used.

Equations for S/N Ratios

Larger-the-Better Type

The procedure for calculating S/N ratios corresponding to a run of an OA is as follows:

Let there be t abnormal conditions. Let $D_1^2, D_2^2, \ldots, D_t^2$ be MDs corresponding to the abnormal situations. The S/N ratio (for larger-the-better criterion) corresponding to qth run of OA is given by:

$$\text{S/N ratio} = \eta_q = -10\text{Log}_{10}\left[(1/t)\sum_{i=1}^{t}(1/D_i^2)\right] \tag{7.2}$$

Nominal-the-Best Type

The procedure for calculating S/N ratios corresponding to a run of an OA is as follows:

Let there be t abnormal conditions. Let $D_1^2, D_2^2, \ldots, D_t^2$ be MDs corresponding to the abnormal situations. The S/N ratio (nominal-the-better type) corresponding to q^{th} run of OA is calculated as follows:

$$T = \text{Sum of all } D_i\text{'s} = \sum_{i=1}^{t} D_i$$

$$S_m = \text{Sum of square due to mean} = T^2 / t$$

$$V_e = \text{Mean square error} = \text{variance} = \sum_{i=1}^{t} \frac{(D_i - \overline{D})^2}{(t-1)}$$

Where $\bar{D}$ is average of D_i's

$$\text{S/N} = \eta_q = 10 \log_{10} \left[\frac{\frac{1}{t}\left(S_m - V_e\right)}{V_e} \right] \tag{7.3}$$

Dynamic Type

Examples of this type are weather forecasting systems and rainfall prediction. The procedure for calculating S/N ratios corresponding to a run of an OA is as follows:

Let there be t abnormal conditions. Let $D_1^2, D_2^2, \ldots, D_t^2$ be MDs corresponding to the abnormal conditions. Let $M_1, M_2, \ldots, M_t$ be true levels of severity (rainfall values in the rainfall prediction system example).

$$S_T = \text{Total sum of squares} = \sum_{i=1}^{t} D_i^2,$$

$$r = \text{Sum of squares due to input signal} = \sum_{i=1}^{t} M_i^2,$$

$$S_\beta = \text{Sum of squares due to slope} = (1/r)\left[\sum_{i=1}^{t} M_i D_i\right]^2,$$

$$S_e = \text{Error sum of squares} = S_T - S_\beta,$$

$$V_e = \text{Error variance} = S_e / (t-1)$$

The S/N ratio corresponding q^{th} run of OA is given by

$$\text{S/N ratio} = \eta_q = 10 \log_{10} \{(1/r) \, [S_\beta - V_e] / V_e\} \tag{7.4}$$

7.4 Example

The different stages in MTS analysis are explained with the following example.

Let us consider a case of four variables, X_1, X_2, X_3, and X_4. In a clinical situation, X_1 could be the age of the subject. X_2 could represent lab values of the subject's blood or acidity (pH) levels of blood tests. X_3 could represent potassium level in mEq/L units, and X_4 could represent another value of clinical test. The raw data for "healthy group" with 15 observations and "abnormals" with 10 observations are given in Tables 7.1 and 7.2, respectively.

Table 7.1 Healthy group data.

S.No	X_1	X_2	X_3	X_4
1	59	7	4.2	0.7
2	51	7	4.4	0.98
3	53	6.7	4.2	0.83
4	52	6.6	4.3	0.9
5	52	6.7	3.9	0.97
6	56	7.2	4	0.93
7	51	7.1	4	0.88
8	50	7.5	4.3	0.71
9	41	6.9	4.3	0.81
10	48	7	4.2	0.93
11	49	7.1	4	0.88
12	41	6.9	4.2	0.92
13	41	7.3	4.4	0.76
14	36	7.2	4	0.86
15	34	7.4	4.4	0.92

Table 7.2 Abnormal data.

S.No	X_1	X_2	X_3	X_4
1	30	8	4	0.59
2	46	7	3.3	0.48
3	22	7.2	3.8	0.52
4	31	7	3.8	0.57
5	33	6.7	3.4	0.51
6	38	7.1	3.8	0.61
7	34	8	3.7	0.62
8	42	6.7	3.2	0.54
9	30	7.4	3.9	0.34
10	28	7.3	3.6	0.53

The above data are standardized with means and standard deviations of the healthy group. Then a correlation matrix is constructed by evaluating correlations between the variables. The correlation coefficient (ρ) between two variables X and Y is given by the following equation:

$$\rho = \frac{Cov(X,Y)}{V(X)V(Y)} \tag{7.5}$$

where Cov (X, Y) = covariance between X and Y and

$$\text{cov}(X, Y) = \frac{1}{n-1} \sum_{i=1}^{n} \left(Xi - \bar{X} \right) \left(Yi - \bar{Y} \right)$$

$V(X)$ = variance of X and $V(Y)$ = variance of Y

Using Equation 7.5, correlation coefficients are calculated. They are represented in correlation matrix C, which is given in Table 7.3.

Table 7.3 Correlation matrix.

	X_1	X_2	X_3	X_4
X_1	1.000	−0.368	−0.289	−0.088
X_2	−0.368	1.000	0.194	−0.339
X_3	−0.289	0.194	1.000	−0.262
X_4	−0.088	−0.339	−0.262	1.000

The inverse matrix is obtained for this correlation matrix using the procedure outlined in Appendix III. The inverse matrix is given in Table 7.4.

Table 7.4 Inverse matrix.

	X_1	X_2	X_3	X_4
X_1	1.357	0.564	0.390	0.413
X_2	0.564	1.380	0.033	0.526
X_3	0.390	0.033	1.200	0.360
X_4	0.413	0.526	0.360	1.309

After the inverse matrix is obtained, the Mahalanobis distances (MDs) for observations in healthy group and for abnormals are calculated using Equation 7.1. Table 7.5 summarizes MDs for observations in the healthy group and abnormals.

Table 7.5 MDs for healthy group and abnormals.

S.No	Healthy	Abnormal
1	1.4016	7.3791
2	1.5880	19.4915
3	0.6447	15.7426
4	0.9995	11.3034
5	1.0397	23.0483
6	1.2154	7.2853
7	0.3880	9.7237
8	1.3582	22.7003
9	0.7886	17.7513
10	0.1772	15.7460
11	0.3589	
12	0.4335	
13	0.7547	
14	1.4309	
15	1.4210	

From Figure 7.2, it is clear that by using the MTS scale there is a good separation between normals and abnormals. Based on this validation process, we can safely say that the scale is good.

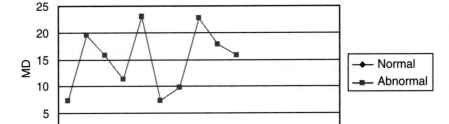

Normals versus abnormals

Figure 7.2   Separation between normals and abnormals.

The next stage is the optimization or screening stage. In this stage, a suitable orthogonal array is used to test different combinations of the variables. Since there are four variables, an $L_8(2^7)$ array (which can accommodate up to seven variables) is selected for optimization. The four variables are assigned to the first four columns of the array. For all combinations, reference (healthy) group or Mahalanobis space is obtained with variables at Level 1 (Level 1: presence; Level 2: absence) and the abnormals' MDs are obtained with information in respective reference groups. The larger-the-better type S/N ratios are calculated based on these MDs using Equation 7.2. Larger-the-better type S/N ratio is selected because we did not know true levels of severity of the abnormal conditions. For all combinations of OA, we select the observations outside the healthy group (abnormals in this case) for computing S/N ratios because we are interested in predicting the accuracy of the scale based on the observations that are not part of the reference group, which is actually used as the base of the measurement scale. In other words, S/N ratios also determine the suitability and applicability of the reference group for the chosen scale.

The following steps describe the computation of MDs and S/N ratios for the second combination of OA (look ahead to Table 7.9). In this combination the variables X_1, X_2, and X_3 are at Level 1, and the Mahalanobis space is developed using these three variables. The correlation matrix corresponding to X_1 and X_2 and X_3 is as shown in Table 7.6.

Table 7.6 Correlation matrix of X_1, X_2 and X_3.

	X_1	X_2	X_3
X_1	1.000	−0.368	−0.289
X_2	−0.368	1.000	0.194
X_3	−0.289	0.194	1.000

Table 7.7 shows the inverse matrix of the above correlation matrix.

Table 7.7 Inverse matrix of correlation matrix in Table 7.6.

	X_1	X_2	X_3
X_1	1.227	0.398	0.277
X_2	0.398	1.168	−0.111
X_3	0.277	−0.111	1.101

After we obtain the inverse matrix, we calculate the Mahalanobis distances for observations in healthy group and for abnormals using Equation 7.1. The MDs are shown in Table 7.8.

Table 7.8 MDs for healthy group and abnormals (based on X_1, X_2 and X_3).

S.No	Healthy	Abnormal
1	0.9638	6.6093
2	0.7904	10.3607
3	0.6591	8.1008
4	1.3294	5.0761
5	1.3197	12.2693
6	1.1434	3.1735
7	0.5127	9.7975
8	1.5498	14.0314
9	0.6577	4.2252
10	0.0123	9.0461
11	0.4784	
12	0.5688	
13	0.7691	
14	1.7420	
15	1.5038	

Based on the abnormal MDs, larger-the-better S/N ratios are calculated using Equation 7.2, which is given here again.

$$\text{S/N ratio} = -10\text{Log}_{10}\left[(1/t)\sum_{i=1}^{t}(1/D_i^2)\right]$$

Here $t = 10$. After substituting abnormal MD values (D^2 values), we have S/N ratio = 8.28 dB units.

In a similar way S/N ratios for other combinations are obtained. Table 7.9 summarizes the results of various combinations.

Table 7.9 Optimization with $L_8(2^7)$ array.

Run	X1 1	X2 2	X3 3	X4 4	5	6	7	Abnormal MDS 1	2	3	4	5	6	7	8	9	10	S/N Ratio
1	1	1	1	1	1	1	1	7.38	19.49	15.74	11.30	23.05	7.29	9.72	22.70	17.75	15.75	11.04
2	1	1	1	2	2	2	2	6.61	10.36	8.10	5.08	12.27	3.17	9.80	14.03	4.23	9.05	8.28
3	1	2	2	1	1	2	2	8.59	9.90	15.26	9.03	11.05	5.51	6.17	7.53	22.40	11.94	9.63
4	1	2	2	2	2	1	1	5.79	0.05	12.24	5.15	3.98	1.72	3.45	0.59	5.79	7.17	−3.89
5	2	1	2	1	2	1	2	8.91	11.25	8.10	6.66	12.36	4.59	8.25	10.67	18.29	7.41	9.29
6	2	1	2	2	1	2	1	13.78	0.02	0.38	0.02	1.73	0.05	13.78	1.73	1.94	1.01	−10.32
7	2	2	1	1	2	2	1	6.96	31.81	13.75	11.13	25.90	9.29	10.98	31.97	23.81	18.16	11.53
8	2	2	1	2	1	1	2	1.23	27.70	5.27	5.27	21.80	5.27	8.35	34.30	2.90	12.13	6.90

From the S/N ratios, average responses are computed at Level 1 (presence) and Level 2 (absence) of the variables. Figure 7.3 shows average response curves. From this figure, it is clear that except for X_j all variables are important in separating normals and abnormals because these variables have higher average S/N ratios when they are on the system (at Level 1).

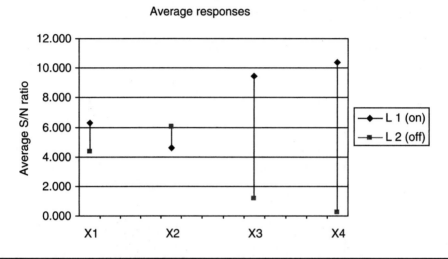

Figure 7.3   Average response curves.

With X_1, X_3, and X_j a conformation run was conducted. It is found that separation is good with these useful variables. In fact, separation after optimization is better than the initial separation. The results of confirmation are given in Table 7.10 and Figure 7.4. We can conclude that these variables are sufficient for future diagnosis.

Table 7.10   MDs from confirmation run.

S.No	Healthy	Abnormal
1	1.8431	8.8017
2	1.9700	24.0530
3	0.2352	18.4000
4	0.5695	12.3652
5	1.1897	24.1142
6	0.7906	8.7156
7	0.4203	11.4534
8	1.0899	25.5928
9	0.4587	21.9678
10	0.2257	19.7634
11	0.4230	
12	0.3716	
13	0.9863	
14	1.9050	
15	1.5213	

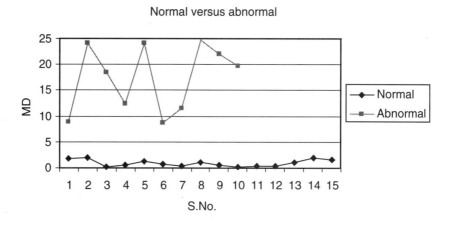

Figure 7.4 Separation between normals and abnormals (confirmation run).

7.5 Gram-Schmidt's Orthogonalization Process—MTGS method

In Mahalanobis-Taguchi strategy (MTS) typically, the MDs are used to measure the degree of abnormality. While measuring the degree of abnormality, higher distance means higher degree of severity. In some cases, such as stock market predictions, higher distance could also mean extremely good situations if the normal space is constructed using companies with average performance. Both poor companies and good companies will have higher distances, and it's extremely important to distinguish these abnormal situations. To distinguish between good abnormals and bad abnormals, we use Gram-Schmidt's orthogonalization process. Further, using Gram-Schmidt's process, we can also calculate MDs without having to invert the correlation matrix. Pattern analysis through Gram-Schmidt's process is referred to as Mahalanobis-Taguchi Gram-Schmidt's (MTGS) method.

The Gram-Schmidt's process can simply be stated as a process where original variables are converted to orthogonal and independent variables (Figure 7.5). In MTGS method, we perform Gram-Schmidt's process on standardized variables $Z_1, Z_2, \ldots, Z_k$. Using the signs of Gram-Schmidt's variables we can determine the direction of abnormals.

Figure 7.5 Gram-Schmidt's orthogonalization process.

7.5.1 Gram-Schmidt's Orthogonalization Process

If $Z_1, Z_2, \ldots, Z_k$ are standardized variables, then the Gram-Schmidt's variables are obtained sequentially by setting:

$$U_1 = Z_1$$
$$U_2 = Z_2 - ((Z'_2 U_1)/ (U'_1 U_1))U_1$$

$\quad\quad\quad\quad \cdot$

$\quad\quad\quad\quad \cdot \quad\quad\quad\quad\quad\quad\quad\quad\quad\quad\quad\quad\quad\quad\quad\quad\quad$ (7.6)

$\quad\quad\quad\quad \cdot$

$$U_k = Z_k - ((Z'_k U_1) / (U'_1 U_1))U_1 - \ldots - ((Z'_k U_{k-1})/ (U'_{k-1} U_{k-1}))U_{k-1}$$

Where ' denotes transpose of a vector. Since it operates with standardized vectors, the mean of Gram-Schmidt's variables is zero. If $s_1, s_2, \ldots, s_k$ are standard deviations (s.d.s) of $U_1, U_2, \ldots, U_k$ respectively, then Mahalanobis distance (MD) corresponding to jth observation of the sample can be obtained by Equation 7.6.

$$MD_j = (1/k) \ [(u_{1j}^2/s_1^2) + (u_{2j}^2/s_2^2) + \ldots + (u_{kj}^2/s_k^2)] \quad\quad\quad (7.7)$$

After obtaining MDs, the other stages of pattern analysis (MTGS method) are carried out in a similar way as in the inverse correlation matrix method.

7.5.2 Determining Direction of Abnormals

The procedure to determine the direction of abnormals is described for the two-variable case. The same logic can be extended if we have more than two variables. In the case of two variables, the Mahalanobis space usually has an elliptical shape for the original variables. Since the ellipses remain ellipses after the orthogonal transformation, the elliptical shapes are used in Figures 7.6, 7.7, 7.8, and 7.9. In all these figures, T is the threshold, which is a cut-off point between normals and abnormals. If U_1 and U_2 are Gram-Schmidt's orthogonal vectors corresponding to the two variables, then we have four possible cases.

Case 1: Both U_1 and U_2—Higher-the-Better Type

If the elements of U_1 and U_2 corresponding to an abnormal condition are positive and MD is higher than T, then the abnormal condition can be classified as "good" abnormality; otherwise it is a "bad" abnormality. This situation is shown in Figure 7.6.

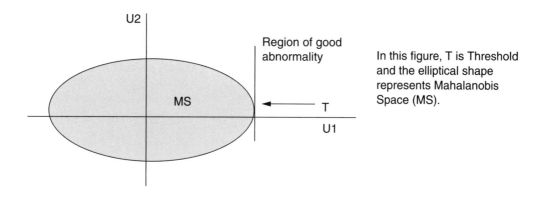

Figure 7.6 Both U_1 and U_2—higher-the-better type.

Case 2: U_1—Smaller-the-Better Type, and U_2—Higher-the-Better Type

If the element of U_1 is negative and that of U_2 is positive and MD is higher than T, the corresponding abnormal condition can be classified as "good" abnormality; otherwise it is a "bad" abnormality. This situation is shown in Figure 7.7.

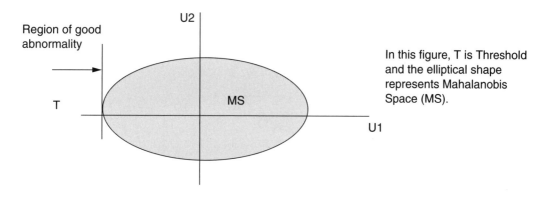

Figure 7.7 U_1—smaller-the-better type, and U_2—higher-the-better type.

Case 3: U_1—Larger-the-Better Type, and U_2—Smaller-the-Better Type

If the element of U_1 is positive and that of U_2 is negative and MD is higher than T, the corresponding abnormal condition can be classified as "good" abnormality; otherwise it is a "bad" abnormality. This situation is shown in Figure 7.8.

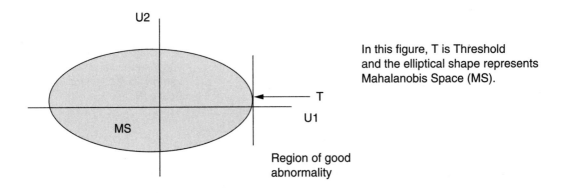

In this figure, T is Threshold and the elliptical shape represents Mahalanobis Space (MS).

Figure 7.8 U_1—larger-the-better type, and U_2—Smaller-the-better type.

Case 4: Both U_1 and U_2 Are Smaller-the-Better Type

If the elements of U_1 and U_2 corresponding to an abnormal condition are negative and MD is higher than T, the abnormal condition can be classified as "good" abnormality; otherwise it is a "bad" abnormality. This situation is shown in Figure 7.9.

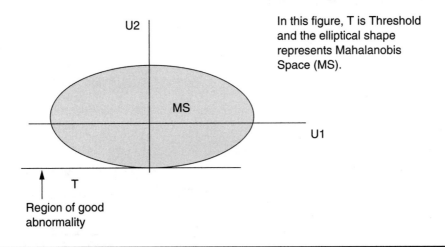

In this figure, T is Threshold and the elliptical shape represents Mahalanobis Space (MS).

Figure 7.9 Both U_1 and U_2 are smaller-the-better type.

For a detailed discussion on MTGS method and its advances, readers are encouraged to refer to the MTS book by Taguchi and Jugulum (2002).

7.6 Real-World Implications

Many companies are now using MTS method in various applications. Here we present summaries of some successful case studies. Detailed descriptions of three case studies are presented in Chapter 8.

7.6.1 Auto Marketing Case Study

The MTS method was used to predict customer behavior in five car segments based on 55 variables. The data on these variables, collected from a customer survey, represent personal views, purchase reasons, and demographics. Using MTS analysis, the number of variables in each segment was reduced to about 20 to design suitable marketing strategies.

7.6.2 Auto Transmission Inspection System Case Study

MTS technique was applied in "end of line" test of automatic transmission. The existing practice was to make decisions based on the individual characteristics. After a series of discussions, it was decided to consider 392 variables. These variables are selected from a list of about 900 variables. The selected 392 variables represent processes performed before transmission assembly. After validating the scale, a screening process is carried out to obtain a useful set of variables. Through S/N ratio analysis, it is found that only 147 variables are important. A confirmation run with the important variables indicates that they are sufficient for making accurate predictions and that results are highly promising.

7.6.3 Fire Alarm Sensor System

MTS was applied to identify actual "fire" conditions using a fire alarm's sensor system. This study was conducted by the Electrical Communication University of Japan with the help of the Ministry of International Trade and Industries, Japan. The performance (in terms of false alarms) after application of MTS was found to be much better than with the existing system. The study also helped engineers reduce the number of sensors from ten to four.

7.6.4 Liver Disease Diagnosis Case Study

The MTS method was used to construct a measurement scale based on 17 variables that cause problems related to the liver. A Japanese liver disease expert, Dr. Kanetaka, took the lead and conducted this work. It was concluded that the MTS scale provided better predictions. Using the MTS method, the number of variables was reduced to eight and the scale with these variables was found to be better than the scale that used all the variables.

7.7 Advances in MTS

A significant amount of research is done to advance MTS so that it can take care of many situations encountered in pattern-recognition problems. This section briefly discusses those situations. For detailed discussions on these topics, readers are advised to refer to the MTS book by Taguchi and Jugulum (2002).

7.7.1 Multicollinearity Problems

Multicollinearity problems arise out of strong correlations. When there are strong correlations, the determinant of correlation matrix tends to become zero, making the matrix singular. In such cases, the inverse matrix will be inaccurate or cannot be computed. As a result, scaled MDs will also be inaccurate or cannot be computed. Such problems can be avoided if we use the adjoint matrix method. Even the MTGS approach can take care of such situations to some extent. The MTGS method is also useful for small sample sizes.

7.7.2 Cases with Small Correlations

When there are incidences of small correlations, the β-adjustment method is used to take care of such situations. After computing βs, the elements of the correlation matrix are adjusted by multiplying them by β. This adjusted matrix is used to carry out MTS analysis.

7.7.3 Multiple Mahalanobis Distance Method

When we are dealing with large data sets with several numbers of variables, the selection of suitable subsets is very important for pattern analysis. Here we use a new metric called multiple Mahalanobis distance (MMD) for computing S/N ratios to select suitable subsets. MMDs are obtained from Mahalanobis distances. This method is useful in complex situations, illustratively including voice recognition or TV picture recognition. In these cases, the number of variables runs into the order of several thousands. Using the MMD method reduces the problem complexity and helps researchers make effective decisions in complex situations.

7.7.4 Cases with Zero Standard Deviations

Use of Gram-Schmidt's method (or MTGS method) is also useful where the reference group consists of the variables with small or even zero standard deviation or variance. This type of situation (that is, the situation where variables have zero standard deviations) is frequently seen in pattern-recognition problems.

In the most extreme cases, where if variables have zero standard deviations then their correlations with other variables cannot be obtained. Because of this, calculation of Mahalanobis distances is not possible, although variables with zero standard deviations represent very important patterns. Because the information associated with these variables is also important, they cannot be ignored in the analysis.

7.7.5 MTS for Root Cause Analysis

MTS method can also be very useful in root cause analysis. Here the role of MTS is to identify the variables contributing to a particular abnormal condition. OAs are typically used to identify variables causing abnormality. This type of analysis is quite useful in multivariate process control applications.

8

MTS Case Studies

The number of MTS case studies is increasing significantly. So far, there are about 100 published case studies in top companies around the globe. They include Nissan, Fuji, Xerox, Yamaha, Nikon, Ford, and Delphi and several medical fields. This chapter presents MTS case studies from the United States, Japan, and Europe.

8.1 Case Study 1: Exhaust Sensor Output Characterization Using the Mahalanobis Taguchi Strategy

This case study was carried out by Stephanie C. Surface and James W. Oliver II of Delphi, Flint, MI. The authors are thanked for presenting this case study in the 2000 robust engineering symposium.

8.1.1 Summary

Delphi Automotive Systems is a leading supplier of automotive emissions control systems. A key component in the system is the exhaust oxygen sensor, which functions as a discriminator of rich and lean exhaust environments for feedback to the engine control module (ECM). The oxygen sensor must consistently respond to air/fuel changes under a range of conditions and over the life of the vehicle. Test engineering conducts numerous measurements to characterize the sensor performance and ensure its output stability after vehicle and accelerated engine-aging exposure. Characterizing the sensor performance is mainly accomplished by analyzing the sensor output signal (0–1 volt) under a controlled set of engine and air/fuel conditions.

The Mahalanobis Taguchi Strategy (MTS) evaluation described here considers the change in exhaust sensor signal performance resulting from an accelerated engine test environment. This study confirmed the feasibility and improved discrimination of the multivariable MTS approach to detect and quantify even small changes in signal output response. Future evaluations will increase the sample size and the number of variables considered to verify the results. Implementation of this approach allows early detection of product performance shifts (enabling shortened testing), detailed evaluation of product design changes, and the potential to comprehend bias introduced by test conditions.

8.1.2 Introduction

As a major automotive emissions control systems supplier, Delphi Automotive Systems manufactures exhaust oxygen sensors for engine management feedback control. The stoichiometric switching sensor, located in the exhaust stream, reacts to rich and lean exhaust conditions. The sensor output signal (0–1 volt) must maintain a consistent response throughout its life to ensure robust operation and allow tight engine calibrations that minimize tailpipe emissions.

Test engineering at Delphi performs a variety of accelerated test schedules to realistically expose the sensor to representative vehicle conditions. Sensor performance measurements are conducted to monitor the sensor output characteristics throughout its life. Characterizing the sensor performance is often accomplished by recording and analyzing the sensor output voltage under a range of controlled exhaust conditions.

As emission control standards become more stringent and sensor technology improves to meet these demands, the testing community needs to improve its techniques to describe product performance accurately. The multivariable MTS evaluation presented here considers the change in the stoichiometric exhaust oxygen sensor signal performance resulting from an accelerated test environment.

8.1.3 Sensor Aging Responses

The exhaust oxygen sensor is expected to perform in a high-temperature environment with exposures to water, road salt and dirt, engine vibration, and exhaust-borne contaminants with minimal change in performance from the manufacturing line to the end of vehicle life, which can exceed 150,000 miles. However, decreasing development cycles do not permit the accumulation of extensive vehicle mileage, so accelerated durability cycles have been developed in the test laboratory. These test schedules simulate the thermal, chemical, environmental, and mechanical demands that would be experienced on the vehicle.

A new sensor and an aged sensor will respond differently to these exposures based on product design combinations that include the electrodes, coatings, and package design selections. Test engineering evaluates these design combinations by exposing the product to various accelerated durability tests and reporting the sensor response. Figure 8.1 shows sensor output responses after exposure to a few of these durability tests.

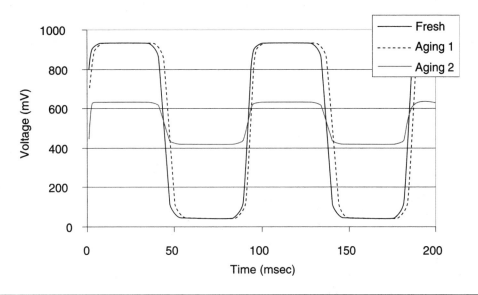

Figure 8.1   Sensor output for different sensors after various aging tests.

8.1.4 Sensor Performance Testing

Various methods exist to evaluate sensor performance including electrical checks, flow bench tests using single or blended gases, and engine dynamometers. Engine dynamometers create a realistic exhaust gas stream typical of a vehicle, and with proper engine control, they can create a wide variety of stable engine running conditions.

One of the engine dynamometer performance tests is an open-loop perturbation test in which the test sensor reacts to alternating rich and lean air/fuel mixtures about stoichiometry. These air/fuel ratio perturbations can be conducted at different frequencies and amplitudes and under different exhaust gas temperatures. From the simple output waveform, the measured signal is analyzed to derive more than 100 characteristics. The most descriptive characteristics were chosen for this preliminary evaluation. Figure 8.2 shows a schematic of the system considered. The data used to support this analysis were already available from previous traditional studies.

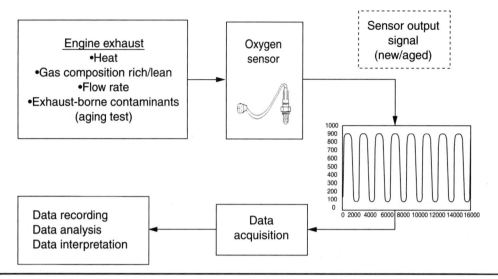

Figure 8.2   System, subsystems, and components considered.

8.1.5 Experiment

Traditional methods of sensor performance analyses consider key characteristics of interest to customers and ensure that product specifications are met. Product development teams, however, want to understand not just time to failure, but also the initiation and rate of signal degradation. Sensor output characteristics must indicate this response change over time.

The goals of this evaluation were to determine whether discrimination among aged test samples could be achieved, whether the analysis could comprehend both product and test setup variations, and whether it would provide a tool capable of detecting early sensor signal change. The MTS method used here generates a numerical comparison of a reference group to an alternate group to detect levels of abnormality. The method also identifies the key factors associated with these differences.

Definition of Groups

This evaluation was based on sensors with differing levels of aging. Twenty-six oxygen sensors were chosen as the reference (normal) group. These sensors had no aging and were of the same product design with similar fresh performance. These sensors were divided into two groups with similar test conditions.

Next, the abnormal population was selected. A total of nine sensors were selected based on end-of-test post-aging performance. The sensors had completed the full exposure of a highly accelerated engine-aging environment. Six sensors showed excellent post-test performance with little to no signal degradation ("aged"). Three abnormal sensors selected showed noticeable degradation, although they were still switching and functional ("degraded"). Representative voltage signals are shown in Figure 8.3. The "fresh" belonged to the reference group, while the "aged" and "degraded" were abnormal.

Definition of Characteristics

As discussed, the open-loop engine-based performance test generates an exhaust stream to which the test sensors respond. Traditional sensor output characteristics that are often specified include the maximum voltage, minimum voltage, voltage amplitude, response time in the lean-to-rich direction and response time in the rich-to-lean direction. These parameters, denoted in Figure 8.4, were included in the evaluation. One test-related parameter indicating the location of the test sensor (nest position) was also included, as multiple sensors are tested simultaneously. Considering the reference group sample size of 26, only nine additional characteristics were selected for a total of 15 (referred to as factors A through O). The other characteristics, although not defined here, comprise a best attempt at variables that "describe" the waveform.

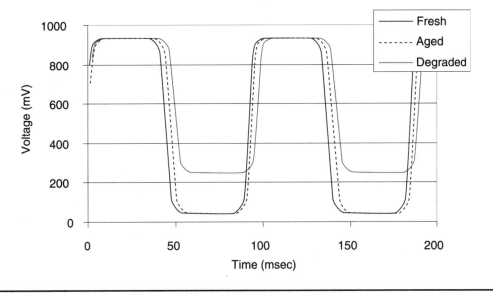

Figure 8.3   Sensor output voltage traces before and after aging.

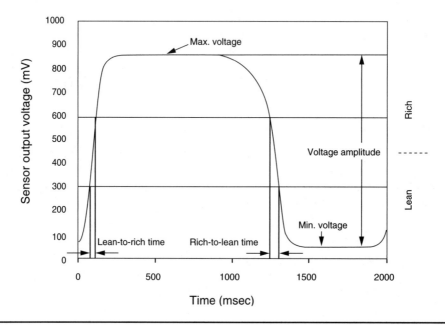

Figure 8.4   Sensor output parameters during the engine perturbation test.

Mahalanobis Distance Calculations

The purpose of the MTS evaluation is to detect signal behavior outside the reference group. Existing data for the 15 characteristics of interest were organized for the 26 reference (nonaged) sensors. The data were normalized for this group (Table 8.1) by considering the mean and standard deviation of this population for each variable of interest.

Table 8.1   Reference group output data normalization.

		Reference data						Normalized data			
	Variable 1 X_1	Variable 2 X_2	Variable 3 X_3	... ...	Variable 15 X_{15}			Variable 1 Z_1	Variable 2 Z_2	Variable 3 Z_3 ...	Variable 15 Z_{15}
1							1				
2							2				
3							3				
4						→	4				
5							5				
6							6				
7						→	7				
8							8				
:							:				
:							:				
:							:				
26							26				
Mean	$\overline{X}_1$	$\overline{X}_2$	$\overline{X}_3$	...	$\overline{X}_{15}$		Mean	0.0	0.0	0.0 ...	0.0
St Dev	σ_1	σ_2	σ_3	...	σ_{15}		St Dev	1.0	1.0	1.0 ...	1.0

(Sample number)

Upon review of the correlation matrix (Table 8.2), it is clear that correlation between parameters exists. For this reason, the application of the Mahalanobis Taguchi system approach makes sense because no one characteristic can describe the output fully.

Table 8.2 Correlation matrix results for the reference group.

Factor name		Normal group correlation matrix - R														
		A	B	C	Vmin	Vmax	Vampl	LRTime	RLTime	I	J	K	L	M	Position	O
		1	2	3	4	5	6	7	8	9	10	11	12	13	14	15
A	1	1.000	0.956	0.679	0.696	0.710	-0.096	0.116	0.732	0.933	0.772	-0.478	-0.043	0.597	0.388	0.005
B	2	0.956	1.000	0.636	0.542	0.631	0.042	0.135	0.611	0.897	0.597	-0.304	-0.056	0.618	0.389	-0.046
C	3	0.679	0.636	1.000	0.553	0.305	-0.480	-0.123	0.456	0.659	0.599	-0.572	-0.326	0.074	0.218	0.144
Vmin	4	0.696	0.542	0.553	1.000	0.815	-0.446	-0.208	0.439	0.812	0.968	-0.538	-0.364	0.048	0.236	0.231
Vmax	5	0.710	0.631	0.305	0.815	1.000	0.155	-0.156	0.393	0.850	0.796	-0.112	-0.295	0.241	0.414	0.244
Vampl	6	-0.096	0.042	-0.480	-0.446	0.155	1.000	0.119	-0.150	-0.075	-0.422	0.743	0.167	0.286	0.230	-0.026
LRTime	7	0.116	0.135	-0.123	-0.208	-0.156	0.119	1.000	0.174	-0.090	-0.052	-0.366	0.899	0.719	0.281	-0.948
RLTime	8	0.732	0.611	0.456	0.439	0.393	-0.150	0.174	1.000	0.544	0.597	-0.581	0.213	0.587	0.281	-0.005
I	9	0.933	0.897	0.659	0.812	0.850	-0.075	-0.090	0.544	1.000	0.826	-0.337	-0.304	0.358	0.353	0.167
J	10	0.772	0.597	0.599	0.968	0.796	-0.422	-0.052	0.597	0.826	1.000	-0.660	-0.206	0.200	0.291	0.119
K	11	-0.478	-0.304	-0.572	-0.538	-0.112	0.743	-0.366	-0.581	-0.337	-0.660	1.000	-0.251	-0.282	-0.093	0.326
L	12	-0.043	-0.056	-0.326	-0.364	-0.295	0.167	0.899	0.213	-0.304	-0.206	-0.251	1.000	0.717	0.241	-0.822
M	13	0.597	0.618	0.074	0.048	0.241	0.286	0.719	0.587	0.358	0.200	-0.282	0.717	1.000	0.453	-0.561
Position	14	0.388	0.389	0.218	0.236	0.414	0.230	0.281	0.281	0.353	0.291	-0.093	0.241	0.453	1.000	-0.225
O	15	0.005	-0.046	0.144	0.231	0.244	-0.026	-0.948	-0.005	0.167	0.119	0.326	-0.822	-0.561	-0.225	1.000

The inverse of the matrix is then computed and finally the Mahalanobis distance (Equation 8.1), denoted by MD, is found. This completes the calculations for the normal group. All reference samples had MD distances of less than 2 (Table 8.3).

$$MD = \left(\frac{1}{k}\right) Z R^{-1} Z^T$$

8.1

where: k is the number of characteristics

Z is the (1×15) normalized data vector

R is the (15×15) correlation matrix and

Z^T is the transposed vector (15×1)

The MD for the abnormal samples is then calculated. Again the data are normalized, but now the mean and standard deviations of the reference group are considered. The previously solved inverse correlation matrix of the reference group is also used. The resultant MDs of the abnormal samples are summarized in Table 8.3.

Table 8.3 Mahalanobis Distance Values (MD) for the reference & abnormal groups.

Sample #	S/N	0 hours Normal Group MD	Aged Abnormal Group MD
1	24720	0.9	14.1
2	24716	1.2	15.7
3	24730	0.8	9.6
4	24719	0.6	14.3
5	24728	1.4	15.1
6	24723	1.6	5.3
7	22963	0.8	79,651.8
8	23013	1.5	86,771.7
9	23073	1.1	84,128.8
10	24673	1.4	
11	24700	0.8	
12	24694	0.9	
13	24696	1.1	
14	24701	1.2	
15	24697	1.1	
16	24633	0.6	
17	24634	1.0	
18	24635	1.1	
19	24636	1.0	
20	24637	0.6	
21	24593	1.1	
22	24595	0.5	
23	24598	0.7	
24	24599	1.2	
25	24602	1.0	
26	24603	0.7	

Discussion

As is evident in the MD of the abnormal samples, tremendous discrimination between fresh and degraded performance was accomplished (Figure 8.5). Additionally, complete discrimination of the aged samples to the fresh samples was seen. While the calculated MD value is nondirectional and does not indicate "goodness" or "badness," it does indicate difference from normal. A consistent signal (low MD over time) is one goal for sensor output.

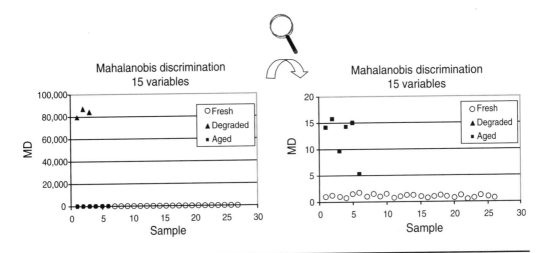

Figure 8.5 Separation between normals and abnormals.

Importantly, this performance separation is not apparent in the traditional one-variable-at-a-time approach. For this type of aging test, typical performance metrics that will change are V_{min} and RL_{Time}. As shown in Figure 8.6, this independent variable consideration would merely allow detection of the degraded sensors with no clear discrimination of the aged sensors.

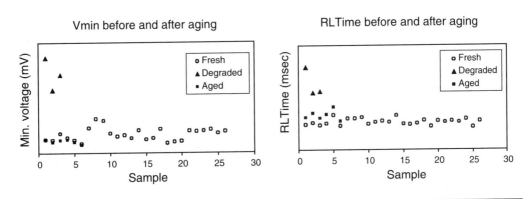

Figure 8.6 Separation not evident with traditional single variable approach.

Selection of Useful Variables—Optimization with L_{16} Orthogonal Array

To reduce data processing complexity, it is desirable to consider fewer characteristics and eliminate those not contributing to product discrimination. An L_{16} orthogonal array was used for this purpose (Table 8.4).

All 15 characteristics were considered at two levels. Level 1 used the variable to calculate the Mahalanobis distance, and Level 2 did not use the variable to calculate the MD. Reconsideration of both the reference group and abnormal group MD was made for each run. The experiment design and results are shown in Table 8.4.

Table 8.4 Calculated MDs for abnormal group within L_{16} orthogonal array.

L16	Factor Name															MD for 9 abnormal samples								
Run Number	A	B	C	D	E	F	G	H	I	J	K	L	M	N	O	1	2	3	4	5	6	7	8	9
1	1	1	1	1	1	1	1	1	1	1	1	1	1	1	1	14.1	15.7	9.6	14.3	15.1	5.3	79,651.8	86,771.7	84,128.8
2	1	1	1	1	1	1	1	2	2	2	2	2	2	2	2	1.6	2.2	1.5	2.2	6.5	1.0	9,722.0	11,988.6	11,349.3
3	1	1	1	2	2	2	2	1	1	1	1	2	2	2	2	2.9	5.2	1.8	3.3	8.0	1.1	25,731.9	32,363.5	30,961.9
4	1	1	1	2	2	2	2	2	2	2	2	1	1	1	1	2.4	2.8	1.6	3.0	9.5	1.5	6,300.9	7,283.8	7,102.0
5	1	2	2	1	1	2	2	1	1	2	2	1	1	2	2	2.5	2.8	1.0	2.9	7.3	2.6	25,535.4	28,754.8	27,635.1
6	1	2	2	1	1	2	2	2	2	1	1	2	2	1	1	4.0	3.0	3.3	2.0	5.1	1.5	1,560.3	1,538.7	1,526.0
7	1	2	2	2	2	1	1	1	1	2	2	2	2	1	1	1.8	2.5	1.2	2.3	6.1	1.1	9,156.7	10,742.5	10,330.4
8	1	2	2	2	2	1	1	2	2	1	1	1	1	2	2	1.6	1.8	1.3	1.1	5.4	3.1	11,568.6	13,508.6	12,824.1
9	2	1	2	1	2	1	2	1	2	1	2	1	2	1	2	2.0	3.3	1.5	3.1	5.6	1.7	151.6	30.2	49.2
10	2	1	2	1	2	1	2	2	1	2	1	2	1	2	1	6.4	1.9	2.3	4.8	9.5	3.1	279.1	37.0	57.8
11	2	1	2	2	1	2	1	1	2	1	2	2	1	2	1	3.4	3.8	1.6	3.4	6.9	1.9	348.6	25.7	35.4
12	2	1	2	2	1	2	1	2	1	2	1	1	2	1	2	7.4	1.7	2.6	4.7	7.3	1.7	287.0	33.4	47.5
13	2	2	1	1	2	2	1	1	2	2	1	1	2	2	1	4.0	4.9	2.0	3.9	10.5	2.6	379.9	44.9	59.5
14	2	2	1	1	2	2	1	2	1	1	2	2	1	1	2	0.9	1.1	0.8	0.6	4.9	1.7	74.1	12.3	25.3
15	2	2	1	2	1	1	2	1	2	2	1	2	1	1	2	1.2	3.0	1.0	2.3	7.9	2.4	161.1	35.1	53.1
16	2	2	1	2	1	1	2	2	1	1	2	1	2	2	1	0.5	2.3	0.8	0.7	7.8	2.2	131.4	35.3	49.3

From these runs, signal to noise ratios and mean responses were calculated for the main effects of each variable. As the goal was to improve separation, larger MDs were preferred and the larger-the-better S/N ratio equation (8.2) was used. Response charts and tables are shown in Figure 8.7 and Table 8.5.

$$\eta = -10 \log \left[1/n \sum_{i=1}^{n} \left(1/y_i^2 \right) \right]$$

(8.2)

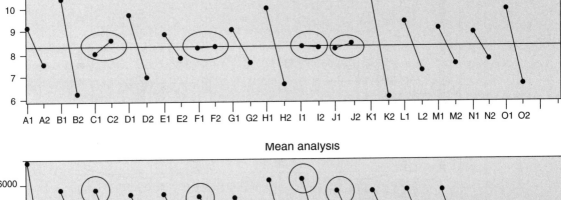

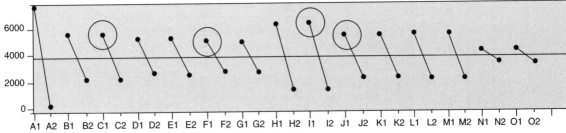

Figure 8.7 Signal to noise and means response charts.

Table 8.5 Signal-to-noise and means response tables.

Traditional metrics for performance characterization.

S/N Response Table

Factor Name	A	B	C	Vmin D	Vmax E	Vampl F	LRTime G	RLTime H	I	J	K	L	Position M	Position N	Position O
Level 1	9.2	10.4	8.0	9.7	8.9	8.3	9.0	10.0	8.4	8.2	10.6	9.4	9.1	8.9	9.9
Level 2	7.5	6.2	8.6	7.0	7.8	8.4	7.6	6.7	8.3	8.5	6.1	7.3	7.6	7.7	6.7
Delta	1.7	4.2	0.6	2.7	1.1	0.1	1.4	3.3	0.1	0.3	4.5	2.1	1.5	1.2	3.2
Rank	7	2	12	5	11	15	9	3	14	13	1	6	8	10	4

Means Response Table

Factor Name	A	B	C	Vmin D	Vmax E	Vampl F	LRTime G	RLTime H	I	J	K	L	Position M	Position N	Position O
Level 1	7,614	5,486	5,481	5,161	5,161	4,903	4,907	6,297	6,292	5,324	5,331	5,452	5,450	4,267	4,275
Level 2	36	2,165	2,170	2,490	2,489	2,748	2,743	1,354	1,358	2,327	2,319	2,198	2,200	3,383	3,376
Delta	7,578	3,321	3,311	2,671	2,672	2,155	2,164	4,943	4,934	2,997	3,012	3,254	3,250	884	899
Rank	1	4	5	11	10	13	12	2	3	9	8	6	7	15	14

Variables *C, F, I,* and *J* are shown to have little contribution to signal to noise and could be considered for elimination. This would reduce the MD calculation to 11 characteristics. All variables however contributed positively to the mean.

Confirmation

A confirmation run with 11 variables (eliminating the low S/N contributors) showed reduced discrimination. However, these variables all contribute significantly to the mean (Figure 8.7) and therefore cannot be eliminated. This conclusion is somewhat indicated within the results of the L_{16} OA (Table 8.4). Run 1, which considered all the variables, had by far the largest calculated MD compared to any other run, each of which considered only seven variables. Therefore, all of the 15 variables initially selected should be used to maximize discrimination.

Discussion

Although the optimization evaluation may seem disappointing as no variables can be eliminated, it is not an unlikely conclusion, as there are more than 100 variables output in an effort to characterize the waveform. This initial evaluation only considers 15 "best guess" candidates and, more than likely, other important variables are still to be identified. The MTS method does, however, confirm the value of combining the influence of many variables to interpret a change in response as compared to considering one variable or even a few variables at a time.

The "traditional" metrics, factors *D* and *H,* which are used to detect signal degradation, are ranked high but not the highest in terms of contribution (Table 8.5). The influence of factor *N,* the nest position during the test, is seen to have low influence on variability and low contribution to the mean, as is desired.

8.1.6 Conclusions

The feasibility of using the MTS multivariable approach has been demonstrated. The combination of 15 variables from the sensor output waveform allowed much improved discrimination compared to the traditional one-variable-at-a-time approach. The method also identified some alternate variables that contributed more to separation than the traditional "favorites."

MTS allows separation of even very subtle differences due to aging, allowing detailed feedback on product performance. If continued studies support these preliminary findings, the excellent discrimination will allow product optimization based on significantly shorter tests. Full-length test exposures could then be confined to the product confirmation and validation stages. Robust engineering evaluations for sensor product optimization are ongoing. By applying MTS to characterize sensor performance, the MD can confirm improvements in aging response over time (Figure 8.8).

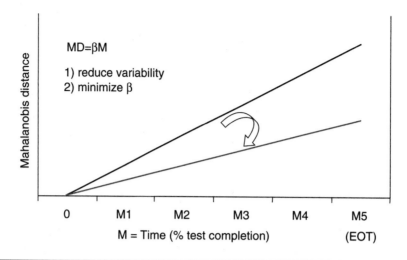

Figure 8.8 Used in conjunction with product optimization, MD can confirm improvements in aging response over time.

8.1.7 Implications of Study

Many ideas have evolved as a result of this study. The first key finding is related to detecting small changes in signal output through MTS. With this detection method, shortened tests (to save time and money) should suffice to help us understand aging trends and optimize designs. Further, rather than supplying our product engineers with more than 100 data variables related to a waveform, the Mahalanobis distance could help them make decisions during product development evaluations.

This study used existing data with no new experimental tests needed. The study points out the potential of its application, as no new test procedures are required with the exception of additional data calculations, demonstrating the power of appropriate data analysis.

8.2 Case Study 2: Health Check for a Recipe of Oil-in-Water Emulsion by MTS

This case study is carried out at Fuji Photo Film Co., Kanagawa, Japan, by Yoshio Ishii, Jun Okamoto, Yasuaki Deguchi, and Akira Ikeda. Thanks are due to them for presenting this work in the 2002 robust engineering symposium.

8.2.1 Summary

The purpose of this study is to predict the "health" of oil-in-water emulsion by MTS. Oil-in-water emulsion contains oil-soluble organic compounds as oil droplets dispersed in water. The oil droplets of "unhealthy" emulsion easily cause coalescence or recrystallization, which deteriorates the original function of the compounds. Therefore, even if one wanted to create a "healthy" emulsion, it has been difficult to predict the "health" of the emulsion. The company found that MTS makes it possible to distinguish between recipes that hardly cause coalescence or recrystallization and recipes that easily cause such problems (Figure 8.9). Furthermore, when MD is large, item selection enables detection of specific property variables that cause a large MD, leading to quick adoption of an improved recipe.

8.2.2 Introduction

Color negative films and other photosensitive materials are composed of very thin photosensitive layers, and a variety of compounds are incorporated into these photosensitive layers. These compounds play an important role in terms of performances of photosensitive materials.

In photosensitive layers, gelatin is used as a binder, and water-soluble compounds can be directly added as an aqueous solution. However, oil-soluble organic compounds are dissolved in a solvent and emulsified using surfactant. Then compounds are added in the state of "oil droplets" (so-called oil-in-water emulsion) to photosensitive layers.

Whether or not the oil-soluble compounds can display their function adequately in a photosensitive material depends greatly on the properties of "oil droplets." For example, recrystallization of compounds in "oil droplets" or an increase in particle diameter due to coalescence of "oil droplets" itself may deteriorate the original function of compounds.

In order to design "oil droplets" that will not cause recrystallization or coalescence, it is necessary to optimize the quantity of various compounds such as dye-forming couplers, solvents, and surfactants. "Oil droplets" are designed by taking into consideration many factors like solubility of compounds. For example, when many types of compounds are mixed, they may act as mutual solvents, and besides, generally these kinds of factors must be determined empirically using past data.

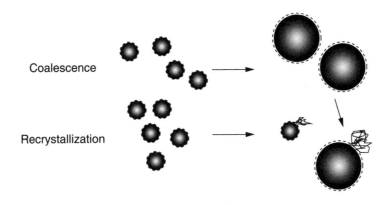

Figure 8.9   Recipes causing coalescence and recrystallization.

A Mahalanobis space was created according to the "healthy" emulsion recipes (with the manufacturing records), and the Mahalanobis distance of the emulsion recipe that was to be newly made was calculated in order to predict the "health" of the new recipe.

8.2.3 Use of the MTS Method

What Are "Healthy" and "Unhealthy" Recipes?

The "healthy" recipe is that of the emulsion made in the past, which hardly caused the problem of recrystallization or coalescence. Conversely, the "unhealthy" recipe caused such problems.

Creation of Mahalanobis Space (Reference Group) and Computation of MDs

Quite a large number of recipes for emulsions made in the past were collected to create Mahalanobis space.

Data in the past recipes were used as the property items. For more detail, the various kinds of compounds such as solvents, surfactants, and other additives included in "healthy" emulsions are used as property items, and respective dosages as property values.

Additives that have not been used before were treated as the nearest property items in consideration of their physical properties (including hydrophilic/hydrophobic properties and solubility).

A Mahalanobis space of "healthy" emulsion was created using that data. Based on this Mahalanobis space, the Mahalanobis distance was calculated with respect to the emulsion in which coalescence occurred in the past accelerating test that was intended to cause coalescence easily as well as the emulsion in which coalescence did not occur.

As shown in Figure 8.10, the rate of coalescence in the accelerating test is low when the MD is 5 or less, and the rate of coalescence is higher when the MD exceeds 5. Since there exists the threshold at approximately 5, MD can be used as prediction of the emulsion stability.

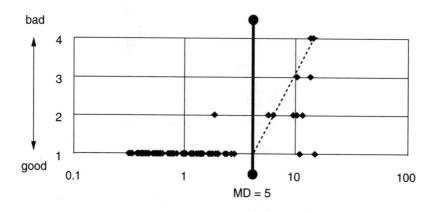

Figure 8.10 The rate of coalescence versus MD.

Therefore, accelerating tests can be simplified for recipes with MD of less than 5, resulting in reduced number of experiments. Meanwhile, recipes with MD exceeding 5 are to be examined in detail.

In this way, the MD indicates recipes that need careful attention prior to actual experiments, resulting in effective use of development resources (confirmation of the stability of recipes by experiments).

Detailed evaluation and confirmation of recipes with large MDs in early stages enables quick detection of problems, shortening the emulsion development period.

Assumption of the Cause of Abnormality by Item Selection

The "health" check described in this context can predict abnormal recipes. However, respective additives interact mutually in a recipe for oil-in-water emulsion, and analysis of abnormal recipes had depended many times on the experiences of recipe designers.

Therefore, an attempt was made to detect a specific additive, which caused an increase in the MD when its quantity was increased, using the method of item selection.

Specifically, the MD was calculated in the cases where the respective additives were used as the property items as well as the cases they were not used, and the property item without which the calculated MD becomes smaller was considered to be the cause of a large MD.

An example is shown in Figure 8.11. Each left point of the two long lines (enclosed with an ellipse) shows the MD with large value when the property item is used, and each right point shows the MD with small value when the property item is not used. Therefore, the items represented by a line with a downward slant to the right are considered to be the additives that make the MD larger. These results indicate that either the individual quantity of the additives surrounded by the ellipse or the synergetic effect of the two additives is the cause of a larger MD.

As already described, when the MD is large, a detailed experiment is preferred.

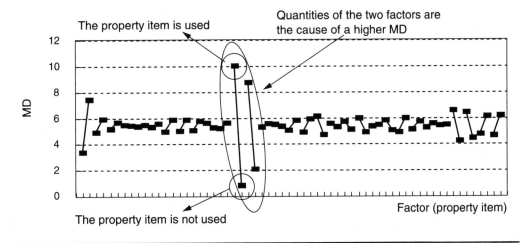

Figure 8.11 Estimation of the cause of abnormality by item selection.

However, you can make this experiment simpler and more efficient if you first adjust the quantity of the additives for the large MD by item selection to make the MD smaller.

The major purpose of item selection is the quick judgment of the abnormality (when quick judgment is necessary for online inspection, etc.) by quick MD calculations of various property items and the reduction of inspection items (reduction in cost). The purpose of item selection in this report is to detect the item (the kind of additives), which is the cause of abnormality by means of item selection, make an adjustment, and use the result in actual recipe design.

Application to Actual Recipe Design

Based on the result of examinations, an attempt was made to apply the result to the design of an actual recipe for emulsion. There were six kinds of emulsion, and the MDs of the respective kinds are shown in Table 8.6.

Table 8.6 The MD of the respective kinds.

Code No.	MD	Action	Result
A	0.8	A simple accelerating test was conducted	○
B	0.5		○
C	0.3		○
D	10.5	Priority was given to a detailed accelerating test	×
E	7.3		×
F	7.9		○

In recipes A–C, the calculated MD was small, so a simple accelerating test was conducted. As a result, it was confirmed that there was no problem.

In recipes D–F, priority was given to a detailed accelerating test in consideration of high MD value. Because abnormality was found in recipes D and E, corrective measures were taken.

Recipe F was evaluated in detail. It was found that neither coalescence nor recrystallization had occurred.

The "manufacture-proof emulsion" used in the Mahalanobis space refers to the oil-in-water emulsion that was actually made in the past, that does not cause coalescence or recrystallization, and that is "healthy" in terms of the manufacturing of photosensitive materials and characteristics of photosensitive materials.

Therefore, it is necessary to check recipe F with a large MD to see if there are any other problems (for example, problems concerning manufacture and characteristics of photosensitive materials), even if there is no problem of coalescence and recrystallization.

8.2.4 Conclusions

1. Mahalanobis space (reference group) was created by using the data in recipes for oil-in-water emulsion that were actually manufactured in the past. It is now possible to distinguish between recipes that hardly cause problems and recipes that easily cause problems without preparation and evaluation of actual oil-in-water emulsion.

2. Item selection enables detection of the specific property items that causes a large MD, resulting in an efficient preparation of an improved recipe.

3. Implementation of the MTS method for designing recipes for oil-in-water emulsion has contributed to the increase in efficiency in research and development. Specifically, recipes with a small MD are subjected only to a simple confirmation test, reducing the manpower for experiments. Priority is to be given to detailed evaluation of recipes with a large MD to identify and solve problems in early stages.

4. The MTS is very effective, as it enables the distinguishing between "healthy" and "unhealthy" recipes.

8.3 Case Study 3: Detector Switch Characterization Using the Mahalanobis Taguchi Strategy

This case study was performed at ITT Cannon Switch Products, Dole, France, by Sylvain Rochon. We would like to thank him for presenting in the 2002 robust engineering symposium.

8.3.1 Summary

ITT Industries is a leading supplier of detectors and tact switches. Characterizing the detector performance is mainly accomplished by specifying the functional parameters.

The Mahalanobis Taguchi Strategy (MTS) evaluation considers the performances resulting from automotive requirements. This study confirmed the feasibility and improved discrimination of the multivariable MTS approach in detecting and quantifying the specified parameters. To improve the results, future evaluations will increase the sample size and the number of variables considered. Implementation of this approach allows early detection of product performance (enabling shortened testing), detailed evaluation of product, and the potential to comprehend bias introduced by test conditions.

Based on the specified switch parameters, an MTS study has been carried out with both good parts and bad production parts in order to select and to quantify the useful parameters that would be used for specifying and for checking the products at the lowest cost.

8.3.2 Introduction

ITT Cannon Switch Products, a division of ITT Industries, has sites in the United States, Germany, Asia, and France. The site in Dole, France, employs approximately 500 people in both the switch and connector product lines. The Dole site uses several fully integrated technologies, including stamping, plating, molding, overmolding, and high volume automated assembly processing.

The primary switch product types manufactured at Dole are tact, key, coding, and rotary switches and smart card connectors designed for the communication, automotive, consumer, and industrial markets. The largest customers are Motorola, Nokia, Ericsson, Siemens, Alcatel, Schneider Electric, Sagem, and Valeo.

The KSM6 switch (Figure 8.12) was designed specifically to meet automotive market requirements to detect a portion of the ignition key in a high-end car model.

An engineering team was created to address the switch design and to improve its mechanical and electrical performances. The specification was defined with the customer according to the constraints given by the application. It was decided to use lots of parameters to characterize the product.

8.3.3 Background

The KSM6 is a detector switch with the following specified parameters (Figure 8.13):

- Force characteristics

- Travel characteristics

- Hysteresis performances between the On and Off curves

- Noise and bounces characteristics

8.3.4 Objectives

As far as the KSM6 switch is concerned, we selected quite a lot of specified parameters necessary to guarantee both quality and reliability of this product. Indeed, 19 parameters were chosen.

The objective was to reduce the number of the specified parameters and validate the characteristics based on 19 parameters.

8.3.5 Experiment

The measurements were conducted in the ITT lab in Dole by using the so-called F/D method (force/deflection electrical and mechanical measurements).

It dealt with a traction/compression machine that enables engineers to establish the evolution curves of the component force according to the travel applied by an actuator. A connection enables engineers to obtain in the same way the electric state of the product.

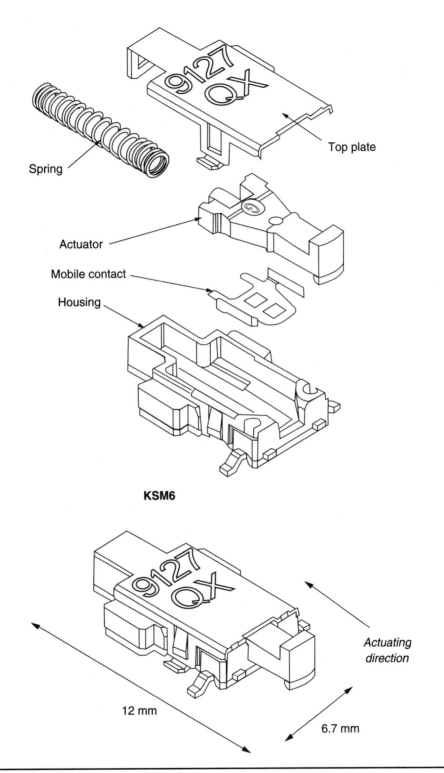

KSM6

Figure 8.12 3D and exploded assembly views of the KSM6 tact switch.

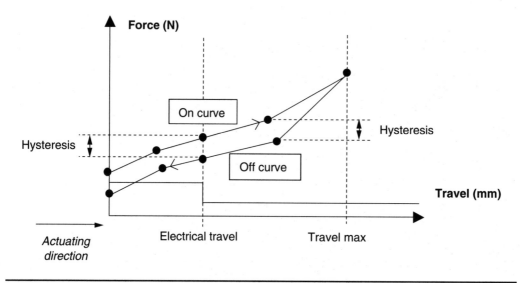

Figure 8.13 Typical F/D curve of the KSM6 switch.

This curve gives the points necessary to establish the mechanical and electrical characteristics of the product. These characteristics allow the validation of a product according to the specification.

Definition of Groups

The evaluation was based on switches coming from the assembly line. There were two types:

- Good switches

- Scrapped switches (rejected because of one or more parameters outside the specification)

Figure 8.14 shows parameters (characteristics) that define the condition of a switch.

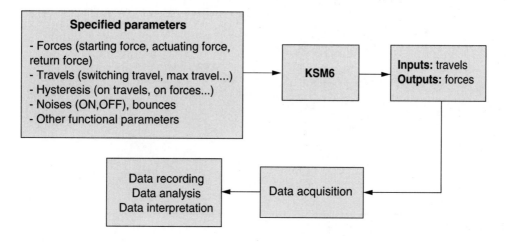

Figure 8.14 Parameters (characteristics) defining the condition of a switch.

Definition of Characteristics

The 19 specified parameters selected for the KSM6 switch are listed in Table 8.7.

The purpose of the MTS evaluation was to detect signal behavior outside the reference group. Existing data for the 19 characteristics of interest were organized for the 80 reference switches. The data were normalized for this group by considering the mean and standard deviation of this population of switches for each variable of interest.

The correlation matrix was then calculated as shown in Table 8.8. Upon review of the correlation matrix, it was clear that correlation between parameters exists. For this reason, the application of the multivariable MTS approach made sense because no one characteristic could describe the output fully.

Table 8.9 shows MDs for the normal group and abnormals.

Table 8.7 Specified switch parameters.

1	Contact preload (N)
2	Fa (N)
3	Electrical travel on (mm)
4	Electrical travel off (mm)
5	Mechanical travel (mm)
6	Electrical force on (N)
7	Electrical force off (N)
8	Return force (N)
9	Force (at 1.85 mm)
10	Return force (at 1.85 mm)
11	Delta preload force / return force (N)
12	Delta electrical force on / electrical force off (N)
13	Delta forces at 1.85 mm (N)
14	Noise beginning on curve
15	Noise beginning off curve
16	Noise total on curve
17	Noise total off curve
18	Contact resistance (mW)
19	Bounces (ms)

Table 8.8 Correlation matrix results for the reference group.

Factor Name		PRL 1	FA 2	CE ON 3	CE OFF 4	CM 5	FCE ON 6	FCE OFF 7	FR 8	FM ON 9	FM OFF 10	HYST1 11	HYST2 12	HYST3 13	NB OFF 14	NB ON 15	NT ON 16	NT OFF 17	RC 18	BOUN 19
PRL	1	1.000	0.812	0.511	0.477	-0.099	0.839	0.811	-0.281	0.814	0.797	0.716	0.510	0.587	-0.133	-0.130	-0.030	-0.025	-0.011	0.042
FA	2	0.812	1.000	0.770	0.734	-0.063	0.968	0.942	-0.733	0.983	0.961	0.869	0.569	0.753	-0.057	-0.236	-0.100	-0.096	0.012	-0.002
CE ON	3	0.511	0.770	1.000	0.961	0.072	0.807	0.831	-0.755	0.745	0.747	0.729	0.280	0.616	-0.042	-0.277	-0.009	-0.158	0.035	0.081
CE OFF	4	0.477	0.734	0.961	1.000	0.014	0.758	0.812	-0.736	0.719	0.715	0.711	0.210	0.577	-0.019	-0.231	0.025	-0.171	0.012	0.054
CM	5	-0.099	-0.063	0.072	0.014	1.000	-0.056	-0.030	-0.025	-0.143	-0.151	-0.001	-0.114	-0.204	0.006	0.179	0.112	0.007	0.041	-0.067
FCE ON	6	0.839	0.968	0.807	0.758	-0.056	1.000	0.937	-0.668	0.956	0.932	0.846	0.602	0.766	-0.072	-0.290	-0.083	-0.107	-0.017	0.056
FCE OFF	7	0.811	0.942	0.831	0.812	-0.030	0.937	1.000	-0.650	0.935	0.948	0.807	0.345	0.646	-0.102	-0.164	-0.025	-0.107	0.012	0.020
FR	8	-0.281	-0.733	-0.755	-0.736	-0.025	-0.668	-0.650	1.000	-0.705	-0.705	-0.792	-0.419	-0.577	-0.085	0.196	0.127	0.127	-0.105	0.044
FM ON	9	0.814	0.983	0.745	0.719	-0.143	0.956	0.935	-0.705	1.000	0.957	0.851	0.544	0.753	-0.054	-0.214	-0.091	-0.096	0.002	0.016
FM OFF	10	0.797	0.961	0.747	0.715	-0.151	0.932	0.948	-0.705	0.957	1.000	0.822	0.486	0.654	-0.100	-0.167	-0.074	-0.085	0.008	0.030
HYST1	11	0.716	0.869	0.729	0.711	-0.001	0.846	0.807	-0.792	0.851	0.822	1.000	0.549	0.674	0.009	-0.298	-0.066	-0.083	0.092	0.005
HYST2	12	0.510	0.569	0.280	0.210	-0.114	0.602	0.345	-0.419	0.544	0.486	0.549	1.000	0.689	0.004	-0.254	-0.192	-0.068	-0.038	0.017
HYST3	13	0.587	0.753	0.616	0.577	-0.204	0.766	0.646	-0.577	0.753	0.654	0.674	0.689	1.000	-0.026	-0.330	-0.187	-0.124	0.050	0.004
NB OFF	14	-0.133	-0.057	-0.042	-0.019	0.006	-0.072	-0.102	-0.085	-0.054	-0.100	0.009	0.004	-0.026	1.000	0.038	0.073	0.309	-0.080	-0.007
NB ON	15	-0.130	-0.236	-0.277	-0.231	0.179	-0.290	-0.164	0.196	-0.214	-0.167	-0.298	-0.254	-0.330	0.038	1.000	0.039	0.009	-0.028	-0.176
NT ON	16	-0.030	-0.100	-0.009	0.025	0.112	-0.083	-0.025	0.127	-0.091	-0.074	-0.066	-0.192	-0.187	0.073	0.039	1.000	-0.009	-0.122	0.050
NT OFF	17	-0.025	-0.096	-0.158	-0.171	0.007	-0.107	-0.107	0.127	-0.096	-0.085	-0.083	-0.068	-0.124	0.309	0.009	-0.009	1.000	-0.033	0.010
RC	18	-0.011	0.012	0.035	0.012	0.041	-0.017	0.012	-0.105	0.002	0.008	0.092	-0.038	0.050	-0.080	-0.028	-0.122	-0.033	1.000	-0.008
BOUN	19	0.042	-0.002	0.081	0.054	-0.067	0.056	0.020	0.044	0.016	0.030	0.005	0.017	0.004	-0.007	-0.176	0.050	0.010	-0.008	1.000

Table 8.9 Mahalanobis distance values for the reference group and abnormals.

Sample	Good parts	Rejected parts			
1	0.45588274	3.34905375	60	0.24485985	
2	1.11503408	2.40756945	61	0.45349242	
3	0.17740621	4.13031615	62	0.22177811	
4	0.67630344	2.44623681	63	0.29027765	
5	0.51367029	1.70684039	64	0.08698667	
6	0.91088082	3.62376137	65	0.15542392	
7	0.47617251	1.8801606	66	0.31067779	
8	0.48574861	2.74470151	67	0.09868037	
9	0.61893043	4.58774521	68	0.34478916	
10	1.27624221	2.46283229	69	1.23338162	
11	0.91560766		70	0.45290798	
12	0.73373554		71	0.29085425	
13	0.4391565		72	0.76586855	
14	0.37539039		73	0.3832427	
15	0.91071876		74	1.15630344	
16	0.29173633		75	0.70401821	
17	0.28862911		76	0.15559801	
18	0.40312754		77	0.29566716	
19	0.46821194		78	0.81947543	
20	0.29330727		79	0.35900551	
:			80	2.58171136	
:					

Discussion

As is evident in the MDs of the abnormals, a reasonable separation between good and bad switches was accomplished (Figure 8.15).

Optimization with L_{16} Orthogonal Array

To reduce data-processing complexity, it was desirable to consider fewer characteristics and eliminate those not contributing to product discrimination. Four out of 19 characteristics were selected as very important; these characteristics were used all of the time and were not considered for screening. The 15 other characteristics were assigned to an L_{16} array (Table 8.10).

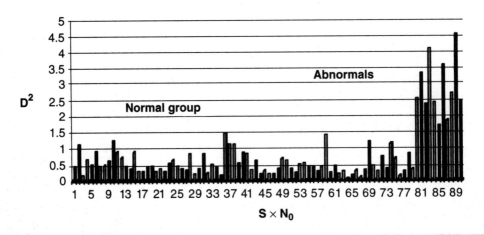

Figure 8.15 Mahalanobis distance for normal and abnormals.

Table 8.10 Calculated MDs for abnormal group within L_{16} orthogonal array.

L16		Factor Name															MD for 10 abnormal samples									
		A	B	C	D	E	F	G	H	I	J	K	L	M	N	O	1	2	3	4	5	6	7	8	9	10
R u n n u m b e r	1	1	1	1	1	1	1	1	1	1	1	1	1	1	1	1	3.349	2.408	4.13	2.446	1.707	3.624	1.88	2.745	4.588	2.463
	2	1	1	1	1	1	1	1	2	2	2	2	2	2	2	2	5.066	3.555	3.507	2.848	2.09	4.867	2.506	0.235	7.818	0.726
	3	1	1	1	2	2	2	2	1	1	1	1	2	2	2	2	4.615	1.247	1.826	3.466	1.209	2.64	2.28	2.403	7.784	0.805
	4	1	1	1	2	2	2	2	2	2	2	2	1	1	1	1	4.213	1.19	2.264	3.437	1.548	2.866	2.633	3.762	7.788	3.278
	5	1	2	2	1	1	2	2	1	1	2	2	1	1	2	2	5.198	1.873	6.523	3.057	1.443	1.094	1.203	0.918	7.835	0.56
	6	1	2	2	1	1	2	2	2	2	1	1	2	2	1	1	4.404	1.541	2.829	2.241	0.796	1.089	1.021	4.061	7.822	3.894
	7	1	2	2	2	2	1	1	1	1	2	2	2	2	1	1	4.492	2.8	1.141	2.645	2.029	3.73	1.035	2.965	7.799	3.23
	8	1	2	2	2	2	1	1	2	2	1	1	1	1	2	2	4.321	2.906	1.658	3.11	2.435	4.467	1.204	2.898	7.81	0.586
	9	2	1	2	1	2	1	2	1	2	1	2	1	2	1	2	4.842	3.027	4.105	3.384	1.983	1.426	2.37	2.825	7.81	3.474
	10	2	1	2	1	2	1	2	2	1	2	1	2	1	2	1	4.183	2.941	3.128	1.898	1.318	1.366	2.146	3.102	7.8	0.617
	11	2	1	2	2	1	2	1	1	2	1	2	2	1	2	1	5.135	0.668	1.337	2.097	1.548	5.294	2.334	1.094	7.804	0.911
	12	2	1	2	2	1	2	1	2	1	2	1	1	2	1	2	5.262	1.117	2.499	3.1	2.092	4.619	2.166	2.648	7.826	3.809
	13	2	2	1	1	2	2	1	1	2	2	1	1	2	2	1	4.878	1.251	4.353	2.739	1.657	4.367	2.037	2.648	7.826	0.552
	14	2	2	1	1	2	2	1	2	1	1	2	2	1	1	2	4.119	1.045	3.491	1.422	1.475	4.627	1.534	3.672	7.794	3.371
	15	2	2	1	2	1	1	2	1	2	2	1	2	1	1	2	4.621	2.465	1.894	1.644	1.415	2.481	1.483	4.436	7.794	3.705
	16	2	2	1	2	1	1	2	2	1	1	2	1	2	2	1	4.383	2.847	2.668	2.976	2.037	2.78	1.962	0.504	7.793	0.531

All these 15 characteristics were considered at two levels. Level 1 used the variable to calculate the Mahalanobis distance, and Level 2 did not use the variable to calculate the MD. Reconsideration of both the reference group and abnormal group MD was made for each run. The experiment design and results are shown in Table 8.10.

From these runs, signal to noise ratios and mean responses were calculated for the main effects of each variable. As the goal was to improve discrimination, larger MDs were preferred and the larger-the-better S/N ratio was used. The response charts are shown in Figure 8.16.

Variables *A, C, F, G, I, J,* and *O* were shown to have little contribution to S/N and could be eliminated. This reduced the MD calculation to 12 characteristics.

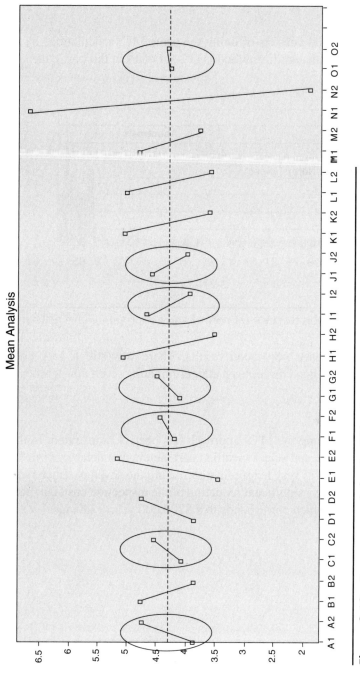

Figure 8.16 Response graph for the S/N ratio.

Confirmation

The confirmation method consists of doing the same MTS calculations by taking off the insignificant factors. With significant factors (12 out of 19 in this case), the separation is as shown in Figure 8.17.

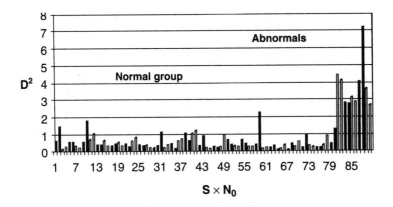

Figure 8.17 Mahalanobis distance for normal and abnormals (with significant factors).

The optimization gave very good results. There was still a very good separation between the bad and the good pieces even after eliminating seven nonsignificant parameters.

8.3.6 Conclusions

The feasibility of applying the MTS approach has been demonstrated. In this case, MTS was used to characterize and select specified parameters of a detector switch.

The MTS method was very helpful in eliminating the seven parameters from the specification and in realizing a significant reduction of the inspection costs. In this case, the cost was reduced by 37%, which corresponds to a $200,000 yearly savings.

Appendices

Appendix A

ISCNOx Hardware Response Graphs

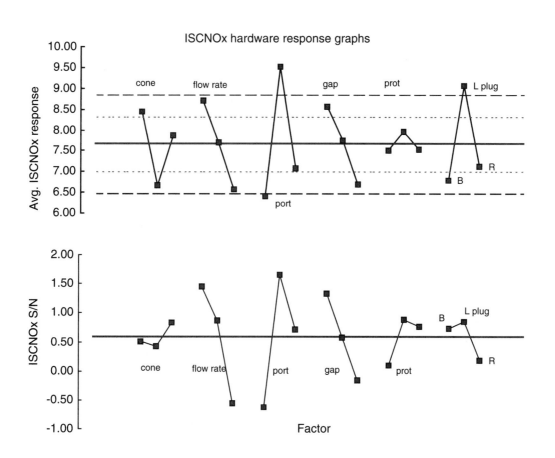

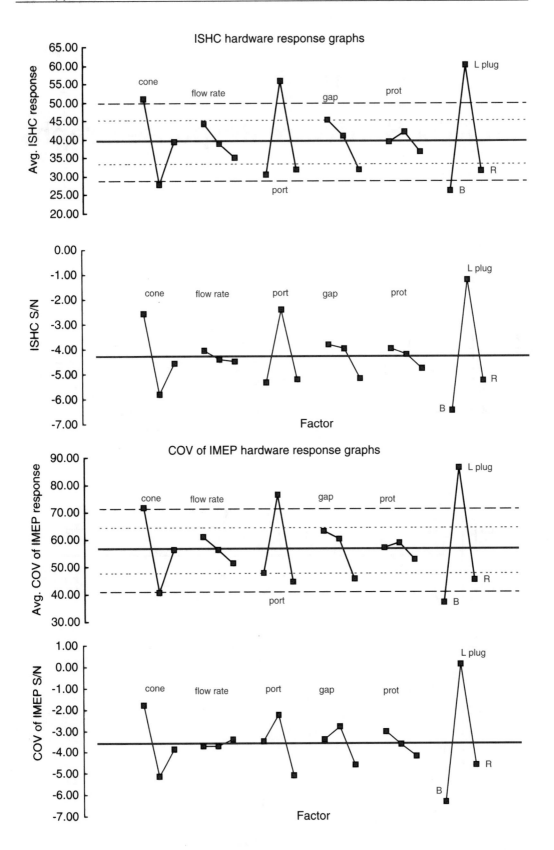

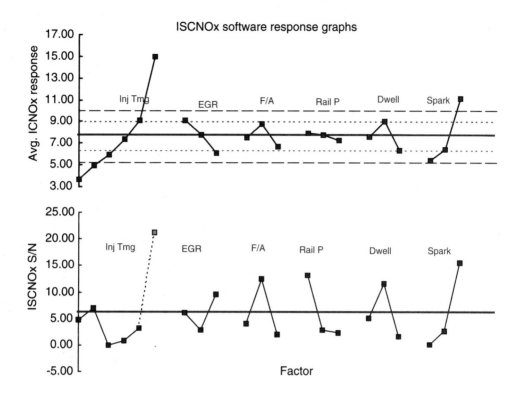

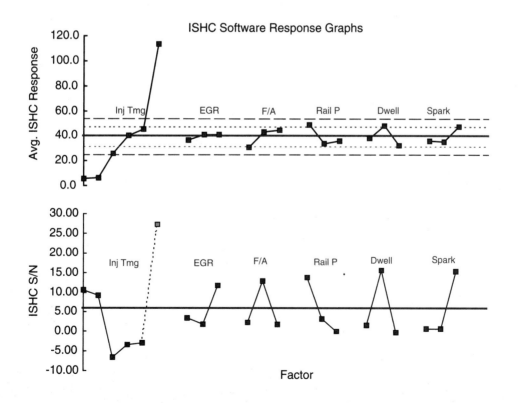

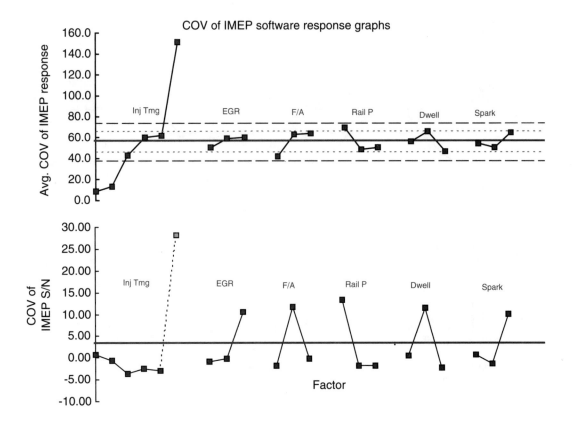

Appendix B

Signal to Noise (S/N) Ratio Equations

1. Nondynamic signal to noise ratios

   - Nominal-the-best

   - Smaller-the-better

   - Larger-the-better

   - Operating window

2. Dynamic signal to noise ratio

   - Simple case

   - More precise equation

Nondynamic Signal to Noise Ratios

Nominal-the-best

Type I:

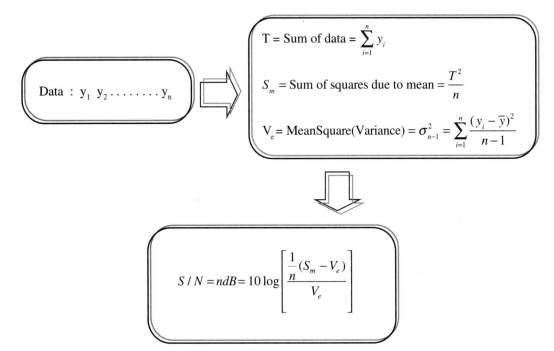

$$\text{Data} : y_1 \ y_2 \cdots\cdots y_n$$

$$T = \text{Sum of data} = \sum_{i=1}^{n} y_i$$

$$S_m = \text{Sum of squares due to mean} = \frac{T^2}{n}$$

$$V_e = \text{MeanSquare(Variance)} = \sigma_{n-1}^2 = \sum_{i=1}^{n} \frac{(y_i - \overline{y})^2}{n-1}$$

$$S/N = ndB = 10\log\left[\frac{\frac{1}{n}(S_m - V_e)}{V_e}\right]$$

Its short-cut equation is as follows:

$$S/N = \eta_{dB} = 10\log\left[\frac{\frac{1}{n}(S_m - V_e)}{V_e}\right] = 10\log\left[\frac{\frac{1}{n} - \left(\frac{T^2}{n} - \sigma_{n-1}^2\right)}{\sigma_{n-1}^2}\right]$$

$$= 10\log\left[\frac{\frac{T^2}{n^2}}{\sigma_{n-1}^2}\right]$$

$$= 10\log\left[\frac{\overline{y}^2}{\sigma_{n-1}^2}\right]$$

Note: 1) $1/n(Sm - V_e)$ is an unbiased estimate of m2, where m is the population mean.

2) V_e is an unbiased estimate of σ^2.

3) The higher the S/N becomes, the smaller the variability in terms of $\pm\%$ around the mean.

4) A gain of 3 dB is equivalent to halving the quality loss.

5) Sensitivity (Mean) is calculated by (a) or (b).

$$\text{(a) } S = 10\log\frac{1}{n}(S_m - V_e) \qquad\qquad \text{(b) } \bar{y} = \frac{\sum\limits_{i=1}^{n} y_i}{n}$$

Nominal-the-best

Type II:

$$S/N = \eta_{dB} = 10\log\left[\frac{1}{V_e}\right] = 10\log\left[\frac{1}{\sigma_{n-1}^2}\right]$$

Note: The higher the S/N becomes, the smaller the variability is, in terms of $\pm$ absolute units around the mean. Maximizing this S/N is equivalent to minimizing σ.

Smaller-the-Better

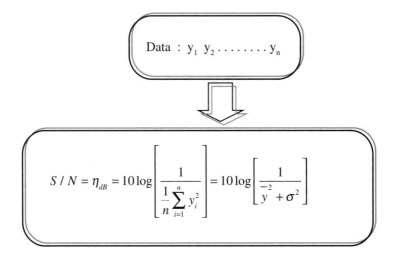

Note: Maximizing this S/N is to minimize the mean and σ.

Note: A gain of 3 dB is equivalent to halving the quality loss.

Larger-the-Better

$$S/N = \eta_{dB} = 10\log\left[\cfrac{1}{\cfrac{1}{n}\sum_{i=1}^{n}\cfrac{1}{y_i^2}}\right] = -10\log\left[\cfrac{1}{n}\sum_{i=1}^{n}\cfrac{1}{y_i^2}\right]$$

Data : $y_1\ y_2\ \ldots\ \ldots\ y_n$

Note: Maximizing this S/N is to maximize the mean and to minimize σ.

Note: A gain of 3 dB is equivalent to reducing the quality loss by half.

Operating Window

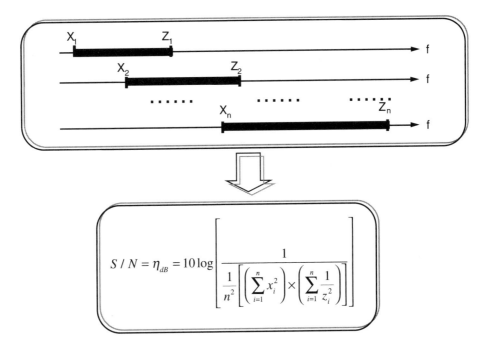

$$S/N = \eta_{dB} = 10\log\left[\cfrac{1}{\cfrac{1}{n^2}\left[\left(\displaystyle\sum_{i=1}^{n}x_i^2\right)\times\left(\displaystyle\sum_{i=1}^{n}\frac{1}{z_i^2}\right)\right]}\right]$$

Dynamic Signal to Noise Ratio (Simple Case)

Data set from outer array (n = 16)

	M_1	M_2	M_3	M4
N_1Q_1	Y_1	Y_2	Y_3	Y_4
N^1Q_2	Y_5	Y_6	Y_7	Y_8
N_2Q_1	Y_9	Y_{10}	Y_{11}	Y_{12}
N_2Q_2	Y_{13}	Y_{14}	Y_{15}	Y_{16}
Total	Y_1	Y_2	Y_3	Y_4

n = # of data = 16

$r = M_1^2 + M_2^2 + M_3^2 + M_4^2$

r_0 = # in data in M_i = 4

Y_i = Total sum of data from M_i

(continued)

(continued)

$$S_T = \sum_{i=1}^{n} y_i^2$$

$$S_\beta = \frac{1}{r \times r_0} [Y_1 M_1 + Y_2 M_2 + Y_3 M_3 + Y_4 M_4]^2$$

$$V_e = \frac{S_e}{n-1}$$

$$S_e = S_T - S_\beta$$

$$S/N = \eta_{dB} = 10\log \left[\frac{\dfrac{1}{r \times r_0}(S_\beta - V_e)}{V_e} \right]$$

Note: 1) $\dfrac{1}{r \times r_0}(S_\beta - V_e)$ is an unbiased estimate of β^2

2) V_e is an unbiased of Mean Square.

$$\beta = \sqrt{\frac{1}{r \times r_0}(S_\beta - V_e)} \cong \frac{1}{r \times r_0}(Y_1 M_1 + Y_2 M_2 + Y_3 M_3 + Y_4 M_4)$$

Appendix C
Related Topics of Matrix Theory

What Is a Matrix?

A matrix is an array of elements arranged in rows and columns. Matrix manipulations play a significant role in multivariate analysis or pattern analysis. If matrix A has m rows and n columns, then we say that matrix A is of size $m \times n$. An example of a 3×4 matrix is shown below.

$$A = \begin{bmatrix} a_{11} & a_{12} & a_{13} & a_{14} \\ a_{21} & a_{22} & a_{23} & a_{24} \\ a_{31} & a_{32} & a_{33} & a_{34} \end{bmatrix}$$

Transpose of a Matrix

If the rows and columns of a matrix A are interchanged, the resultant matrix is called transpose of matrix A and is denoted by A^T or A'. If A is of size $m \times n$ then A^T is of the size $n \times m$. The transpose of A is a 3×4 matrix and is as shown below.

$$A^T \text{ or } A' = \begin{bmatrix} a_{11} & a_{21} & a_{31} \\ a_{12} & a_{22} & a_{32} \\ a_{13} & a_{23} & a_{33} \\ a_{14} & a_{24} & a_{34} \end{bmatrix}$$

Square Matrix

If the number of rows and columns of a matrix are the same, that matrix is called a square matrix.

Determinant of a Matrix

The determinant is a characteristic number associated with a square matrix. The importance of the determinant can be realized when solving a system of linear equations using matrix algebra. The solution to the system of equations contains inverse matrix term, which is obtained by dividing the adjoint matrix by the determinant. If the determinant is zero, the solution does not exist.

Let us consider a 2 x 2 matrix:

$$A = \begin{bmatrix} a_{11} & a_{12} \\ a_{21} & a_{22} \end{bmatrix}$$

The determinant of this matrix is $a_{11}\,a_{22} - a_{12}\,a_{21}$.
Now let us consider a 3 x 3 matrix:

$$A = \begin{bmatrix} a_{11} & a_{12} & a_{13} \\ a_{21} & a_{22} & a_{23} \\ a_{31} & a_{32} & a_{33} \end{bmatrix}$$

The determinant of A can be calculated as:

$$\det. A = a_{11}A_{11} + a_{12}A_{12} + a_{13}A_{13}$$

Where, $A_{11} = (a_{22}a_{33} - a_{23}a_{32})$; $A_{12} = -(a_{21}a_{33} - a_{23}a_{31})$; $A_{13} = (a_{21}a_{32} - a_{22}a_{31})$ are called as cofactors of the elements a_{11}, a_{12}, and a_{13} of matrix A, respectively. The cofactors can be computed from submatrices obtained by deleting the rows and columns passing through the respective elements. Along a row or a column, the cofactors will have alternating plus and minus signs with the first cofactor having a positive sign.

The previous equation for the determinant is obtained by using the elements of the first row and their cofactors. The same value of determinant can be obtained by using other rows or any column of the matrix with corresponding cofactors. In general, the determinant of a n x n square matrix can be written as:

$$\det. A = a_{i1}A_{i1} + a_{i2}A_{i2} + \ldots + a_{in}A_{in} \text{ along any row i, where, i} = 1, 2, \ldots, n$$

or

$$\det. A = a_{1j}A_{1j} + a_{2j}A_{2j} + \ldots + a_{nj}A_{nj} \text{ along any column j, where, j} = 1, 2, \ldots, n$$

Cofactor

From the above discussion, it is clear that the cofactor of A_{ij} of an element a_{ij} is the factor remaining after the element a_{ij} is factored out. The method of computing the cofactors is explained above for a 3 x 3 matrix. Along a row or a column the cofactors will have alternating signs of positive and negative with the first cofactor having a positive sign.

Adjoint Matrix of a Square Matrix

The adjoint of a square matrix A is obtained by replacing each element of A with its own cofactor and transposing the result.

Let us again consider a 3 x 3 matrix as shown below:

$$A = \begin{bmatrix} a_{11} & a_{12} & a_{13} \\ a_{21} & a_{22} & a_{23} \\ a_{31} & a_{32} & a_{33} \end{bmatrix}$$

The cofactor matrix containing cofactors (A_{ij}'s) of the elements of the above matrix can be written as:

$$A = \begin{bmatrix} A_{11} & A_{12} & A_{13} \\ A_{21} & A_{22} & A_{23} \\ A_{31} & A_{32} & A_{33} \end{bmatrix}$$

The adjoint of the matrix A, which is obtained by transposing the cofactor matrix, can be written as:

$$A = \begin{bmatrix} A_{11} & A_{21} & A_{31} \\ A_{12} & A_{22} & A_{32} \\ A_{13} & A_{23} & A_{33} \end{bmatrix}$$

Inverse Matrix

The inverse of matrix A (denoted A^{-1}) can be obtained by dividing the elements of its adjoint by the determinant. It should be noted that $A A^{-1} = A^{-1} A = I$, where I is identity matrix with all on-diagonal elements as 1 and off-diagonal elements as 0.

Singular and Nonsingular Matrices

If the determinant of a square matrix is zero, it is called a singular matrix. Otherwise, the matrix is known as nonsingular.

Other Definitions

Chi-square (χ^2) distribution
The distribution of a non-negative random variable, skewed to the right. The distribution is specified by the degrees of freedom.

correlation coefficient
The measure of linear association between the variables $X1$ and $X2$. This value lies between -1 and $+1$.

correlation matrix
The matrix that gives correlation coefficients between the variables.

degrees of freedom
The number of independent parameters associated with an entity. These entities could be a matrix experiment, or a factor, or a sum of squares.

F-distribution
The distribution corresponding to F-random variable, which is a ratio of two χ^2 random variables. The distribution is specified by degrees of freedom of numerator and denominator.

normal distribution
The most commonly used distribution in statistics. This distribution is also known as Gaussian distribution. It is a bell-shaped curve and is symmetric about mean. The distribution is specified by two parameters, mean and standard deviation.

standardized distance
Distance of an observation from mean in terms of standard deviations.

standardized variable
Variable obtained after subtracting the mean from the original variable and dividing the subtracted quantity by standard deviation.

References

Anderson, T. W. 1984. *An introduction to multivariate statistical analysis* (2nd ed.). New York: John Wiley.

Brown, W. C. 1991. *Matrices and vector spaces.* New York: Marcel Dekker.

Djomani, D., P. Barthelet, and M. Holbrook. 1999. *Direct injection diesel injector optimization using robust engineering.* ASI Robust Engineering Symposium Proceedings.

Clausing, D. 1994. *Total quality development: A step-by-step guide to world-class concurrrent engineering.* New York: ASME Press.

Dasgupta, S. 1993. The evolution of the D^2-statistic of Mahalanobis. *Sankhya* 55: 442–59.

Ealey, L. A. 1994. *Quality by design: Taguchi Methods and US industry.* Dearborn, MI: ASI Press.

Gerla, M., and J. Tsai. 1995. Multicluster, mobile, multimedia radio network. *Wireless Networks* 1,3: 255–65.

Goldstein, S., and T. Ulrich. 2000. *Robust testing of electronic warfare (EW) systems.* ASI Robust Engineering Symposium Proceedings.

Hedges, T., and J. Schieffer. 2003. *Optimization of a discrete floating MOS gate driver.* Robust Engineering Symposium Proceedings.

Hirai, S., and M. Koga. 1990. *Robust design for transistors parameter design using simulation.* ASI Taguchi Methods Symposium Proceedings.

Hohn, F. E. 1967. *Elementary matrix algebra.* New York: Macmillan.

Ishii, Y., J. Okamoto, Y. Deguchi, and A. Ikeda. 2002. *Health check for a recipe of oil-in-water emulsion by Mahalanobis distance.* ASI Robust Engineering Symposium Proceedings.

Jaye, J. R. 1998. *Direct injection, spark ignition gasoline engine development using Taguchi Methods.* ASI Robust Engineering Symposium Proceedings.

Johnson, R. A., and D. W. Wichern. 1992. *Applied multivariate statistical analysis.* Upper Saddle River, NJ: Prentice Hall.

Jugulum, R., S. Taguchi, and K. Yang. 1999. New developments in multivariate diagnosis: A comparison between two methods. *Journal of Japanese Quality Engineering Society* 7, 5: 62–72.

Jugulum, R. 2000. *New dimensions in multivariate diagnosis to facilitate decision making process.* PhD Dissertation, Wayne State University.

Jugulum, R., and D. D. Frey. 2001. *Robustness through invention.* Japanese Quality Engineering Society, Annual Quality Meeting Proceedings.

Jugulum, R., G. Taguchi, S. Taguchi, J. O. Wilkins, D. M. Hawkins, B. Abraham, and A. M. Variyath. 2003. Discussion of a review and analysis of the Mahalanobis-Taguchi System by W. H. Woodall et al. *Technometrics* 45: 16–29.

Kamoshita, T. 1997. *Optimization of a multi-dimensional information system using Mahalanobis Distance.* ASI's Total Product Development Symposium Proceedings.

Kanetaka, T. 1988. Application of Mahalanobis distance, standardization and quality control. *Japanese Standards Association* 41, 5 and 6.

Katz, L. E., and M. S. Phadke. 1985. Macro-quality with micromoney. Bell Laboratory Record.

Lin, C. R., and M. Gerla. 1997. Adaptive clustering for mobile wireless network. *IEEE JSAC:* 1265–75.

Chih-Lin, et al. 1995. Optimum location area sizes in PCS networks. IEEE 45th Vehicular Technology Conference Proceedings.

Lu, N. H. 1998. Dynamic clustering for mobile wireless networks. *Invention Disclosure, ITT Industries.*

Lu, N. H. 2000. *Robust formation of mobile wireless networks.* ASI Robust Engineering Symposium Proceedings.

Lu, N. H. 1999. Dynamic self-forming techniques for mobile wireless networks. Twelfth Annual Taguchi Symposium Proceedings.

Mahalanobis, P. C. 1936. On the generalized distance in statistics. *Proceedings. National Institute of Science of India* 2: 49–55.

Montgomery, D. C. 1984. *Design and analysis of experiments.* New York: John Wiley.

Morrison, D. F. 1967. *Multivariate statistical methods.* New York: McGraw-Hill.

———. 1990. *Multivariate statistical methods* (3rd ed.). New York: McGraw-Hill.

Nair, V. N. 1993. Taguchi's parameter design: A panel discussion. *Technometrics,* 34, 2: 127–61.

Park, S. H. 1996. *Robust design and analysis for quality engineering.* New York: Chapman & Hall.

Phadke, M. S. 1989. *Quality engineering using robust design.* Upper Saddle River, NJ: Prentice Hall.

Phadke, M. S., and G. Taguchi. 1987. Selection of quality characteristics and S/N ratios for robust design. In conference *Record,* GLOBECOM 87 Meeting. IEEE Communication Society, Tokyo, 1002–1007.

Rochon, S. 2002. *Detector switch characterization using Mahalanobis Taguchi System.* ASI Robust Engineering Symposium Proceedings.

Surface, S., and J. Oliver II. 2000. *Exhaust sensor output characterization using MTS.* ASI Robust Engineering Symposium Proceedings.

Taguchi, G., and J. Kiekakuho. 1976–77. *Design of experiments,* Vols. I and II. Tokyo: Maruzen.

Taguchi, G., and M. S. Phadke. 1984. Quality engineering through design optimization. IEEE Global Telecommunications Conference Proceedings, 1105–1113.

Taguchi, G. 1986. *Introduction to quality engineering.* Tokyo: Asian Productivity Organization.

———. 1987. *System of experimental design,* Vols. 1 and 2. Dearborn, MI: ASI Press.

———. 1993. *Taguchi on robust technology development.* New York: ASME Press.

Taguchi, G., and S. Konishi. 1993. *Taguchi Methods: Design of experiments.* Dearborn, MI: ASI Press.

Taguchi, G. 1988. The development of quality engineering. *The ASI Journal,* 1, 1: 5–29.

———. 1994. Diagnosis and Signal-to-Noise Ratio. *Quality Engineering Forum* 2, 4 and 5.

———. 1994. Application of Mahalanobis distance for medical treatment. *Quality Engineering Forum* 2, 6.

————. 1994. *Taguchi Methods: Vol. 1 Research & Development.* Dearborn, MI: Japan Standard Association and ASI Press.

————. 1994. *Taguchi Methods: Vol. 2 On-Line Production.* Dearborn, MI: Japan Standard Association and ASI Press.

————. 1994. *Taguchi Methods: Vol. 4 Design of Experiments.* Dearborn, MI: Japan Standard Association and ASI Press.

————. 1996. The role of D.O.E. for robust engineering: A commentary. *Quality and Reliability Engineering International,* 12: 73–74.

Taguchi, G., S. Chowdhury, and S. Taguchi. 1999. *Robust engineering.* New York: McGraw Hill.

Taguchi, G., and R. Jugulum. 1999. Role of S/N ratios in Multivariate Diagnosis. *Journal of Japanese Quality Engineering Society* 7, 6: 63–69.

————. 2000. New trends in multivariate diagnosis. *Sankhya* B, 2: 233–48.

————. 2000. Taguchi methods for software testing. Principles of JUSE Software Quality Conference Proceedings.

Taguchi, G., and Y. Wu. 2000–2001. *Quality engineering as a strategy for research and development.* Unpublished but distributed work.

Taguchi, G., and R. Jugulum. 2002. *The Mahalanobis-Taguchi strategy: A pattern technology.* New York: John Wiley & Sons.

Teshima, S., T. Bando, and D. Jin. 1997. A research of defect detection using the Mahalanobis-Taguchi system method. *Journal of Quality Engineering Society* 5, 5: 169–80.

William, F. Y., and M. C. Creveling. 1995. *Engineering methods for robust product design.* Menlo Park, CA: Addison Wesley.

Woodall, W. H., R. Koudelik, K. L. Tsui, S. B. Kim, Z. G. Stoumbos, and C. P. Carvounis. 2003. A review and analysis of the Mahalanobis-Taguchi system. *Technometrics* 45: 1–15.

Wu, Y. 1996. *Pattern recognition using Mahalanobis distance.* ASI's Total Product Development Symposium Proceedings.

ASI Training Materials on Robust Engineering. Livonia, MI: ASI.

Index